Time and Experience

Time and Experience

Peter K. McInerney

TEMPLE UNIVERSITY PRESS
Philadelphia

Temple University Press, Philadelphia 19122
Copyright © 1991 by Temple University. All rights reserved
Published 1991
Printed in the United States of America

The paper used in this publication meets the minimum
requirements of American National Standard for Information
Sciences—Permanence of Paper for Printed Library Materials,
ANSI Z39.48-1984 ∞

Library of Congress Cataloging-in-Publication Data
McInerney, Peter K.
    Time and experience / Peter K. McInerney.
        p.   cm.
    Includes bibliographical references.
    ISBN 0-87722-752-7 (alk. paper)
    1. Time.   2. Experience.   I. Title.
    BD638.M38   1991
    115—dc20   90-32383
                                                     CIP

Contents

Acknowledgments

I am grateful to the National Endowment for the Humanities for a Fellowship in 1985–86, which allowed me to write most of this book. I thank Bryn Mawr College and Villanova University for allowing me to use their facilities and Oberlin College for the leave of absence. Part of Chapter 7 was previously published in *Descriptions* (Albany: SUNY Press, 1985) and part of Chapter 8 was previously published in *The Journal of Philosophy* 85, no. 11 (November 1988). I am grateful to the editors for permission to utilize this material.

I also want to thank Norman Care, Claude Evans, Robert Grimm, Daniel Merrill, Izchak Miller, and Charles Sherover for helpful comments on earlier drafts. I especially want to thank Jane Mac-Donald-McInerney for making my life easier while I worked on this book.

Time and Experience

Introduction

Ordinary experience seems both to take place in time and to concern things that happen in time. This seemingly simple fact is the starting point for the most profound set of philosophical issues concerning human conscious existence and our awareness of other entities. Time essentially includes some type of separation of temporal parts. To be aware of anything that happens in time, human consciousness must *unify into one experience* the appropriate temporal parts of what is experienced. How human consciousness is able to do this, what it means for the ontology of consciousness, and what it reveals about the ontological reality of time are the subjects of this investigation.

How time and conscious experience are related may be the deepest philosophical issue because it bears importantly upon most other ultimate questions. Diverse religious traditions have questioned whether conscious life really begins and ends in time and whether it really takes place in time at all. Discussions of free will and responsibility inevitably gravitate around whether and how consciousness is in time, as do puzzles about personal identity. Metaphysical and epistemological theories that are grounded in experience have to confront the problems concerning how the experience of temporally extended events and changes in these events are possible. The list could go on and on.

This book examines the relationship of time and conscious experience through three tightly interconnected issues: how we are able to be conscious of time and temporal entities, whether time exists independently of conscious experience, and whether the conscious experiencer exists in time in the same way that ordinary natural objects are thought to exist in time.

The basic problems of time-consciousness are how it is possible to perceive and to conceive temporal extension and temporal passage. We regularly perceive objects enduring through time, changing in various ways, and coming into and going out of existence. On the normal suppositions that conscious experience itself takes place in time and that perception can grasp only what is simultaneous with it, there are tremendous puzzles about the perception of anything (an enduring object, a process, or a sudden change) that extends over time. How are we able at any given time to perceive the temporal extension of these entities since this temporal extension stretches over more than the current moment? Formulated in another way, how can consciousness perceive in the present those portions of a temporally extended entity that do not happen in the present or that happen at a temporal location other than that of the operative perceiving?

Time-perception becomes even more perplexing when the perception of temporal passage is included. In ordinary experience we perceive not only temporally extended entities but also the presentness, pastness, and futurity of different portions of the extended entity and the passage of a portion from futurity to presentness to pastness. For example, in seeing a car's movement down the street, we see both where in its path the car is at present and the change in where it is at present. How we are able to perceive such changes in what is present is a major puzzle of time-perception.

The question of temporal realism is whether time and the temporal features of entities exist independently of conscious experience or whether their only being is *in* and *for* consciousness. Is time just projected onto things by consciousness or does it exist on its own? This question arises from several sources. Epistemological uncertainties about what we really know apply to knowledge of time and temporal entities; is there any justification for the commonsense notion that time is real and that conscious experience itself takes place in time? Theories of time-consciousness are another source; many accounts of time-perception construe time as only a structure of our minds through which we perceive entities. The apparent contradictions of time are a further source. It is commonly held that if time is indeed contradictory, then it must be mind-dependent because a contradictory entity can not exist on its own.

The question of the special temporality of consciousness is whether the conscious experiencer exists in time in the same way that ordinary natural objects are thought to exist in time. While there is much medical and neurophysiological evidence that consciousness is in some ways a natural entity, there are also many factors that raise the issue of a special temporal nature. Our ability to perceive temporal extension and temporal passage suggests that consciousness at any given time may reach across time to other temporal locations. Our personal identity with earlier and perhaps later portions of our lifetime suggests that a special unity may exist. If temporal realism is false, then of course consciousness cannot be in the standard type of time at all.

These issues of time-consciousness, temporal realism, and the special temporal nature of the experiencer are fundamentally interconnected. Specific positions on any one issue will presuppose or require specific positions on the other issues.

In Part III of this book I develop and defend a set of interconnected positions concerning the nature of time-consciousness, the reality of time, and the special temporal nature of human existence. I argue in Chapter 8 that a revised version of Edmund Husserl's three-feature theory of time-consciousness best explains our awareness of the temporal features both of the objects of consciousness and of the acts and activities of consciousness. Our experience of the passage of time and our experience of our own ongoing mental life can be plausibly explained only by such a theory.

Since my theory of time-consciousness portrays phases (temporal parts) of consciousness as existing in and enduring unchanged through periods of real time, it assumes that there is a real time. In Chapter 9 I present several arguments for the reality of time, including the demonstration that consciousness could not be the sole source of experienced time. After showing that none of the ontological arguments against the reality of time are successful, I consider which temporal features should be taken to be real and present evidence that consciousness has real temporal relations with real worldly entities.

Human mental life shares some temporal features with other real entities, but it also has special temporal features, some of which are incompatible with some of the standard temporal features. In Chapter 10 I explore the special temporal features that are necessary for time-consciousness, for the unity of consciousness, and for personal identity. I argue that any successful theory of time-consciousness must conceive consciousness to "reach across" from one temporal location to other temporal locations. A phase of consciousness cannot exist completely at a standard temporal location. Furthermore, the unity of consciousness at any given time and personal identity over time require that phases of our mental life be defined by earlier and later phases. The temporal existence of human mental life is special because of the ways in which any temporal part is internally related to other temporal parts.

In considering the issues of time-consciousness, temporal realism, and the special temporal nature of the experiencer, I follow common sense in endorsing the existence of first-person experience. Although we always *live from* a first-person perspective, we may *think about* mental states and processes in either first- or third-person terms. To think about mental states and processes in first-person terms is to attribute an "inside" to consciousness. This "inside" includes different ways of experiencing (mental acts), such as perceiving, remembering, and desiring, different "objects of experience" ("intentional objects"), and different processes in experience, such as reasoning, controlling our bodily action, and metaphorical thinking. There is a "what it is like" for each of these. Thus, there is "what it is like" to have a particular mental act, "what it is like" to be engaged in a particular type of experiential process, and "what one's world is like" or the world-as-it-appears in experience. It is from this "inside" or "first-person perspective" that we each in our own cases experience the world. Thus, it is from the first-person perspective that "stream of consciousness" descriptions are made, and it is to first-person mental life that such descriptions are adequate or not. In thinking about the psychology of some other organism, we can attribute to that other organism a first-person mental life.

To think about mental states and processes in third-person terms is to treat the mental as whatever mediates between the environmental input and the behavioral output of an organism. Simply put, the mental is to be known in the same way that any natural entity is known. Since the "inner workings" of other organisms cannot normally be directly observed, we theorize what must be going on inside the organism that produces all the behavioral output given all the environmental input. The current debate in cognitive science between semantic and syntactic models of brain-processing systems is such a difference between theories of what is going on inside the organism.[1] If we are allowed to appeal to our own first-person experience with its "what it is like," we might attribute such subjective factors to what is going on in other organisms. However, if we are restricted to *exclusively* third-person resources, we cannot appeal to our own first-person experience and so cannot attribute it to others. The contemporary notion that ordinary mental terms are theoretical terms in a commonsense psychological theory about human behavior is such an exclusively third-person theory.

The problems of time-consciousness are heavily dependent upon the first-person perspective. There is no special ontological problem about time-perception if one considers the mental exclusively in third-person terms. In third-person terms, there could be some mechanism in the head (or in a box) that "represents time" by having the same "manifold characteristics" as time. All that is needed is something that can register and store one-dimensional order and that can provide for appropriate output. A line or any other one-dimensional matrix that could be marked on and read from would be sufficient. For example, to "perceive" the temporal extension of something moving from position a to b to c, we would need a "detector" that can detect an identical thing at all the different spatial positions and mark the results along the line (that represents the series of temporal positions). T_1 occurrences could be registered to the left of t_2 occurrences on the axis; t_2 occurrences could be registered to the left of t_3 occurrences on the axis. To tell whether the thing moved and which way it moved would be just a matter of "reading off" (at any given time) from the data stored along the line.

To represent past, present, and future, a token-reflexive account of the present could be employed. The present would be whatever is simultaneous with some specified token or operation. Past and future would be defined in terms of being earlier or later than the present. To "perceive" the temporal passage of something moving from a to b to c would require "reading off" that it is "at present" at one location while at an earlier "present" it was at another location.

Of course, this is an incredibly simplified model. Assuming an exclusively third-person approach, there is a great deal of empirical work to be done in determining exactly what information-processing structures are operative in humans. It should be noted, however, that all of this same empirical work is still to be done if one takes first-person mental life to be emergent upon neurophysiological structures. My point is that there are no special *ontological* puzzles about time-perception if an exclusively third-person approach is taken.

The question of the reality of time is also heavily dependent upon the first-person perspective. The third-person approach to the mental assumes that the environmental input, the behavioral output, and the internal processing occur in time. While I suppose that it is possible for some naturalized epistemology to question the reality of time, it is extremely unlikely precisely because the "naturalizing" of the mental involves treating it as a processing system that operates in time.

The question of the special temporality of consciousness is to some extent transposable into exclusively third-person terms. While the original forms for this question assume that there is a first-person consciousness, a similar question might be raised about brain-processing systems. Do brain-processing systems exist in time in the same way that ordinary natural objects are thought to exist in time? It may be, as I indicate in Chapter 10, that *as systems* they require some special temporal features, though not all the special temporal features that personal consciousness requires.

Any attempt to portray first-person experience must rely upon people's descriptions of their own experience. While having an experience is distinct from observing and describing the experience, observing and describing our own experiences is the only access to first-person experience that is useful for knowledge of it. The only epistemological access to first-person experience is phenomenological, in the broad sense of the term. Phenomenology as a specific approach to philosophical issues championed by Husserl is a particular disciplined form of this approach to first-person experience. In working out my views on time-consciousness, temporal realism, and the temporal nature of the experiencer, I have explored in depth the views of the major phenomenological thinkers on these issues.

Part II consists of a series of studies of the views of Immanuel Kant, Edmund Husserl, Martin Heidegger, and Jean-Paul Sartre on time-consciousness, temporal realism, and the temporal nature of the experiencer. Relying on experiential data that was phenomenologically discerned, each of these philosophers developed ontological positions concerning time and human existence. Despite their disagreements over the nature of phenomenology and time-consciousness, they all conceived human existence to be outside ordinary time and they all developed some form of temporal idealism.

My examination of phenomenologically based theories starts with Kant because he was the first major philosopher to make these issues about time the central problems of metaphysics, theory of knowledge, and philosophy of mind. His ideas about the non-reality of time and about how a non-temporal consciousness can project time onto experienced entities are, at least in general outline, familiar to all contemporary philosophers. The widespread appreciation of Kant's theory, its intrinsic interest, and its influence on the later phenomenologists make Kant's theory a natural starting point.

Husserl's deep and difficult investigations of these issues about time have been very influential among continental philosophers, but they have been less appreciated among analytic philosophers. Chapter 5 explores the phenomenological basis of Husserl's theory and elucidates his important insights into the nature of time-consciousness, the meaning of realism, and the ego's relationship to time. This examination of Husserl prepares the way for the revised version of his theory of time-consciousness that I defend in Chapter 8.

Husserl's investigations strongly influenced both Heidegger and Sartre, although both rejected many of his positions concerning time-consciousness and the nature of the transcendental ego. Both Heidegger and Sartre emphasized that humans are agents who are practically engaged in the world and who define themselves by their ongoing projects. Both conceived time-consciousness to be essentially connected with humans moving themselves into the future through action. Both conceived time to exist most basically as the temporalizing activity of humans. Chapters 6 and 7 explicate the existential ontological theories of Heidegger and Sartre. Through my focus on the central issues concerning time, I try to make the philosophical merits of these difficult thinkers more accessible.

No adequate theory of how time and conscious experience are related can ignore the developments in the "sciences of the mind." Although phenomenology is the main approach of this study, I do not rely exclusively upon first-person resources. I attempt to take into account in my theories current psychological studies of time-perception and of introspective access and psychological-neuro-physiological studies of the dependence of mental processes on brain functions.

The book is divided into three main parts. Part I explains each of the major issues in some detail and considers the range of alternative answers that have been proposed. Part II is a series of studies of the views of major phenomenological thinkers on these issues. Part III argues for my own position on the issues of time-consciousness, temporal realism, and the special temporal nature of the experiencer. I try to incorporate the insights and avoid the defects of the thinkers explored in Part II. For those not interested in the history of these issues, Parts I and III could be read independently of the studies in Part II.

Part I
The Issues

1

Time-Consciousness and the Ontology of Time

People are conscious of time in many ways. We keep track of time with clocks, we estimate how long something will last, and we rush to get things done on time. We also recollect past experiences and may be nostalgic about them or anxious about some future event. Many philosophers have thought that one form of time-consciousness, time-perception, is basic in that all the other forms depend upon time-perception but it does not depend upon them. Whether or not this dependence thesis is true, the perception of the temporal features of external entities is the most important form of time-consciousness, and it raises all the basic questions of time-consciousness.

I will start this chapter with a discussion of the differences between time-perception and other forms of time-consciousness. After a brief consideration of the main issues for a theory of time-perception, I will argue that the perception of the past-present-future features of time requires that the perceiving itself have temporal characteristics.[1] I will then examine the range of theories of time-perception and discuss what each theory presupposes about the ontology of time.

1.1 Time-Perception

We regularly perceive things enduring through time, changing in various ways, and coming into and going out of existence. Time-perception is simply the perception of the temporal features of the objects of perception. It is the direct awareness of entities as "being in and through time," whether or not these temporal features are emphasized or focused upon. Since there are many different theories about the nature of perception, correspondingly different theories about the nature of time-perception could be distinguished. However, since I am concerned *only* with the time parameter of time-perception, I will distinguish theories of perception *only insofar as* they involve differences in the account of the awareness of temporal features.

Physical objects and processes are perceived to extend through time and to pass through time. As temporally extended, temporal parts (what I call "phases") of these entities are earlier and later than other phases. We regularly perceive many of these phases *together* in perceiving the temporal extension of entities. In addition, we regularly perceive *changes* in which of these phases are present. For example, in seeing a ball's movement through the air, we see both where in its path it is at present and where it was at a just previous present. Thus, time-perception includes some features that could be said to concern the past (and the future), as well as features that concern the present.

In time-perception the focus of consciousness is on the present. What is perceived as present or "now" is the center around which what is perceived is organized. The past and future features of what is perceived form a background or context that contributes to the meaning of the present feature. In a manner analogous to space-perception, the past and future features form a temporal *horizon* for the present feature. Those parts of the horizonal structure that are most distant from the focus of consciousness (the present) are the least clear and distinct.[2] The temporal focus-horizon notion can be illustrated by a case of hearing a bell ring three times in succession. While we are hearing the third ring, it (the ring) is the temporal focus, but we are aware of it as the third ring because we perceive it as preceded by the previous two rings, and we anticipate other rings to follow.

Time-perception is different from recollective memory in that recollective memory focuses upon the *past as past*. Instead of having past occurrences as the temporal background for present occurrences, recollective memory focuses on the previous experiencing or on what was previously experienced. Time-perception is similarly different from emotions, such as nostalgia or guilt, that focus upon past occurrences as past.[3] In the other direction, time-perception is different from explicit expectation of the future that focuses upon the *future as future*, and from the corresponding emotions.

My discussion of time-perception in this chapter focuses on the perception of the temporal features of *external* entities, because external perception (seeing, hearing, smelling, etc.) is what is commonly meant by the term "perception." As I indicated in the Introduction, there is also a reflective observing of our own experiences that might be called "internal perception." This internal perception, which is different from our non-reflective awareness of the variety of mental act in which we are engaged, grasps the temporal extension and the temporal passage of our own mental life. The same theories of time-perception are applicable to both external and internal perception.

Time-perception does not require any discrimination of conventional or natural units of measurement of time. We perceive the temporal extension and temporal passage of entities independently of whether we conceptualize these temporal features in terms of seconds, hours, days, "the time it takes to say a prayer," or anything else. Although there is a sense of the length of temporal extension that comes about from perceiving together two or more entities that occur concurrently (so that the temporal extension of one may be wholly contained within the temporal extension of another), this does not require the use of any type of clock or units of measurement.

Having distinguished time-perception from other forms of time-consciousness with which it might be confused, I can turn to the problems that confront any theory of time-perception. The two basic issues are how it is possible to perceive the temporal extension and the temporal passage of entities. Both of these issues should be addressed in any adequate theory of time-perception. It has been all too common that one of these issues is ignored when the other is examined. Older theories, such as those of Saint Augustine and William James, have focused on the perception of temporal extension, while contemporary analytic philosophers have focused on the perception of the present, but neglected the perception of the past and future.[4]

The perception of temporal extension is problematic because the *perceiving* is commonsensically understood to occur in time (this commonsense notion will be defended in section 1.2). Perceptual acts can be divided into phases that occur at different times. For us to perceive *at any given time* the temporal extension of entities, the perceptual act-phase at that time must *somehow grasp* phases of the perceived entities that do not occur at that time. How can a perceptual act-phase perceive those temporal parts of an entity that are not simultaneous with the perceptual act-phase? Formulated in past-present-future terms, how can consciousness perceive in the present those temporal parts of a temporally extended entity that do not happen in the present?

The perception of the temporal passage of entities is inherently more complex than the perception of temporal extension. In passing through time, a phase of an entity moves or changes from being future to being present to being past. To perceive an entity as moving through time, we have to grasp not only phases of the entity that are earlier (or later) than the current phase but also that those earlier phases were present and were perceived to be present. That the earlier phases were present but are no longer present (and that later phases are not present but will be present) is essential to the passage of time. That all of this is in some way *perceived* is what composes the perception of temporal passage. A mere succession of independent perceivings is not equivalent to the perceiving of temporal passage. We must somehow perceive the succession of perceptual act-phases along with the succession of worldly entities and the "transient presence" of both of these. Different theories of time-perception attempt to explain these phenomenological features through different structures of perception.

1.2 Time-Perception and the Temporality of the Perceiving

We ordinarily understand ourselves and our perceptual acts to occur in time. If there is only one "level" in consciousness (a two-level non-temporal consciousness will be discussed in section 2.4), then this commonsense notion is supported by the perception of temporal passage. That a consciousness that perceives the past-present-future features of experienced entities must itself have temporal characteristics is shown by the following argument.

First, in perception the present phase of entities is *focal* or *central* with respect to the past and future phases; the past and future phases are not the focus of awareness but rather a temporal *background* or *horizon* that contributes to the meaning of what is focal.

Second, the perception of the passage of entity-phases from being future to being present to being past includes some perceptual awareness of the entity-phase *as future*, some perceptual awareness of the entity-phase *as present*, and some perceptual awareness of the entity-phase *as past*.[5] This is depicted in Diagram 1.1 (*x* and *y* represent entity-phases).

Third, because of the temporal focus–temporal background feature of time-perception, the perception of the passage of entity-phases requires *distinct* act-phases: one perceptual act-phase that is aware of the entity-phase as present and another that is aware of the entity-phase as past (and perhaps one that is aware of the entity-phase as future). One perceptual act-phase cannot both have as temporal background and temporally focus upon the *identical* entity-phase. Focusing upon *x* and having *x* as background are incompatible intentional features that can be instantiated only in distinct act-phases.[6]

Fourth, in order to perceive the past-present-future features of worldly entities (and entity-phases), these distinct act-phases must be unified in a certain way.

Finally, the only way that these distinct act-phases can be unified so as to yield the perception of the past-present-future features of worldly entities is for them to compose one perceptual act that *changes* its temporal focus over time. The act-phases themselves must be temporally located and temporally ordered. If these act-phases were not temporally located and were unified in some non-temporal way, such as composing a non-temporal ordered series, this could not provide for the perception of a (temporal) succession of present moments. Any non-temporal unification of perceptual act-phases, each of which has a different phase of the world as focal, would yield multiple foci that are non-temporally ordered (see Diagram 1.2). We would perceive *together* (as non-temporally ordered) a multitude of present moments, each with its own background of past and future. There would be no temporal relations between the past-present-future of act-phase$_1$ and the past-present-future of act-phase$_2$ and no *identification* of future$_1$ with present$_2$ or of present$_1$

Diagram 1.1

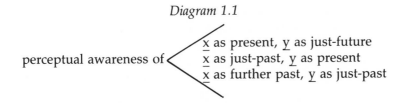

perceptual awareness of
$\underline{x}$ as present, $\underline{y}$ as just-future
$\underline{x}$ as just-past, $\underline{y}$ as present
$\underline{x}$ as further past, $\underline{y}$ as just-past

Diagram 1.2

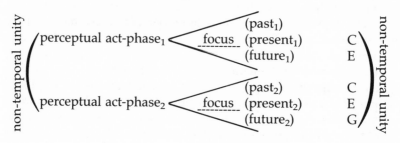

with past$_2$. Thus, it would be impossible to identify the identical entity-phase in the distinct temporal frameworks of each present moment. The note C at present$_1$ would not be identical with the note C at past$_2$. Even if an entity-phase could be identified across these frameworks, it could not be perceived to pass from being future to being present to being past because it would have to be perceived to be past without having *earlier* been perceived to be present.

Thus, there are always two temporal entities involved in ordinary time-consciousness: the temporal objects of awareness and the temporally characterized perceptual acts. The temporal features of acts of awareness are too frequently overlooked in theories of time-consciousness; presuppositions concerning these temporal features play important roles in the theories without being explicitly acknowledged, analyzed, and defended. In section 1.4 I will examine the presuppositions about the nature of time that are contained in each theory of time-perception.

1.3 Theories of Time-Perception

Theories of time-perception may include more than one level of consciousness. A "one-level" theory attempts to explain time-perception in terms of one (temporal) series of perceptual acts and phases of acts. A "two-level" theory attempts to explain time-perception in terms of two series of acts, one of which thinks of or intends the other one. Two-level theories have been introduced in order to explain how a non-temporal basic level of consciousness can be aware of temporal passage by thinking of a secondary level of consciousness that occurs in time. I will discuss such a two-level theory in section 2.4.

Only five different one-level theories of first-person time-perception seem to have been developed in the extensive history of philosophical thinking about these issues. I do not claim that no other theory could be developed. What I do claim is that these are the most influential theories, and that I have encountered no theory of time-perception that is not a recognizable variation on one of these theories. It should also be kept in mind that these are theories of time-*perception*. While they raise the same issues about portraying what is not present that arise for recollective memory, explicit expectation, and other forms of time-consciousness, the solution to these issues that each theory offers may not be generalizable to the other forms of time-consciousness.

1.3A   Theory 1: The Present Representation Theory

The most common theory of time-perception from Saint Augustine through the early Franz Brentano to contemporary cognitive psychologists and philosophers is the present representation theory.[7] Since there are different conceptions of the constituents of conscious awareness, there are variant versions of this theory. All of them embrace the central tenet that perception can be in direct contact *only* with entities that are simultaneous with it. In the past-present-future terms in which the theory is usually expressed, a present phase of perception can be in direct contact *only* with presently existing entities. Perception of just-past and just-future entities is possible only through presently existing representations of these past and future entities. These representations portray some entities as just-past and some entities as just-future. They must be able to depict this qualitative difference, as well as the difference of entities as past and entities as future from entities as present. Furthermore, the representations must be so ordered among themselves and so synthesized with the present perception of present entities that all the entities are experienced as serially ordered. Representations of distinct past entities must represent their temporal relation to each other, as well as their temporal relation to present and future entities. The present representation theory reduces all the issues concerning the perception of temporal extension to the one issue: what is the nature of that "representing character" of presently existing representations that allows them to perform all the above functions? (See Diagram A.1 in the Appendix for a spatial representation of this theory.)

Present representation accounts almost never address the issue of the perception of temporal passage. To do so makes the theory far more complicated. Present representations of past (or earlier) and future (or later) perceptual act-phases have to be introduced and related to the representations of past and future worldly entity-phases. Instead of the simple representation of an earlier phase of a worldly entity, there has to be a representation of the complex "worldly entity-phase as perceived by a perceptual act-phase," and this whole complex must be portrayed as earlier or past. (See Diagram A.2 in the Appendix.)

1.3B   Theory 2: Direct Awareness of Past and Future Entities by Present Acts

According to theory 2, perceptual acts (and act-phases) are in direct contact not only with entities that are simultaneous with the acts but also with earlier and (perhaps) later entities. In past-present-future terms, presently existing acts (and act-phases) are in direct contact not only with presently existing entities but also with past entities and perhaps with future entities. Present act-phases are able to transcend their temporal location in order to be aware of entities in other temporal locations (the spatial analogue of this is for a perceiving act that exists *here* to be directly aware of entities that are elsewhere). In a present act-phase there are three features that differ in character according to whether the feature is directly aware of a present entity (as in sensation) or directly aware of a past entity (as in immediate memory) or directly aware of a future entity (as in immediate anticipation). It is through the different characters of the features in a present act-phase that the differences in the temporal location of entities are experienced. (See Diagram A.3 in the Appendix.)

According to this theory, there should also be a direct awareness of some characteristic that provides for the serial ordering of entities. This characteristic could be either the position of an entity in absolute time, or the distance of an entity from the present, or the "earlier-later" relations of an entity with other entities. It should also be noted that this theory can be extended to cover the direct awareness of past and future acts of consciousness, since they can also be viewed as entities occurring at some time. Theory 2 differs from theory 3, however, in that it allows for direct awareness of past and future entities that is not mediated through past and future phases of acts.

Some advocates of this theory, such as Bertrand Russell,[8] limit the direct awareness to past (or earlier) entities. Troubled by the lesser degree of certainty of anticipation of future entities, they deny direct access to future entities, even just-future ones. Anticipation is then analyzed in terms of present representations of future entities, and these representations are thought to derive from projections into the future of patterns discerned in the past. Such theories are mixed theories incorporating features from both theory 1 and theory 2.

Theory 2 explains the perception of temporal extension by means of the direct contact of a present perceptual act-phase with earlier and later phases of worldly entities. This alone will not explain the perception of temporal passage. The most obvious way to incorporate an account of our perception of temporal passage within theory 2 is to include direct awareness of earlier and later act-phases too. If we are directly aware both of earlier act-phases *as perceiving* earlier phases of worldly entities and of later act-phases *as perceiving* later phases of worldly entities, an account of the perception of temporal passage could be given in these terms. Such an account makes theory 2 very similar to theory 3.

1.3C   Theory 3: Direct Awareness of Past and Future Act-Phases with Their Objects by Present Act-Phases

This theory is like theory 2 except that a present act-phase is in direct contact with past and future act-phases "through which it looks" to their objects. There is direct awareness only of past and future *perceivings* of entities, rather than of the entities alone. Our current awareness "looks right through" these earlier and later act-phases to their worldly objects. This accounts for the serial order, the temporal extension, and the temporal passage of perceived entities.

In one version of the theory of Husserl,[9] the major proponent of theory 3, all acts extend through time so that the present of an un-completed act must contain three features: (1) "now-consciousness," that is, the present feature of the act-phase that is concerned with only present entities, (2) retention, that is, the present feature of the act-phase that retains complete earlier phases of the act, and (3) protention, that is, the present feature of the act-phase that protends complete later phases of the act. (See Diagram A.4 in the Appendix.) In this account, each phase of an act refers to the earlier and later phases of the act; this provides for the unity of the act over time via "transverse intentionality" or cross reference. By "looking through" other act-phases to their intentional correlates, a present act-phase perceives earlier (and later) phases of worldly entities and the *serial order* of these phases. This explains the perception of temporal extension.

The perception of temporal passage is also explained by theory 3 in terms of an act-phase's "looking through" earlier (and later) act-phases to their intentional correlates. Retention is directly aware of the just-previous act-phase, portrays it as just-past, and "looks through" it to its intentional correlates. One feature of the retained act-phase, the "now-consciousness" feature, portrays its correlate as "now" or present. In both portraying an earlier now-consciousness feature *as just-past* and "looking through" it to its intentional correlate that is experienced as present for the now-consciousness feature, retention is able to experience a worldly entity-phase as *just having been perceived as present*. This experience along with its own now-consciousness feature's experience of a (later) worldly entity-phase as present is how a perceptual act-phase perceives temporal passage. In Chapter 8 I explore this theory in greater detail and defend it as the best account of time-consciousness.

1.3D   Theory 4: Direct Awareness of Past and Future Entities Through Past and Future Act-Phases

Theory 4 is similar to theory 3 except that the actuality of consciousness is not confined to the present. To unify consciousness, theory 3 employs present features of present act-phases that "reach across" to earlier and later act-phases; theory 4 allows earlier and later act-phases themselves to be active in contributing to our current perception.[10] Earlier and later act-phases are as actual or operative as present act-phases. In contributing to current perception with its focus on present entities, past act-phases are operative-as-past, present act-phases are operative-as-present, and future act-phases are operative-as-future. The temporal location of worldly entities is experienced by means of the different modes of being operative of act-phases. Theory 4 explicates the awareness of the temporal order of entities by means of the temporal order of act-phases. If one act-phase is more past than another act-phase yet both are operative, the object of the earlier act-phase is perceived as earlier than the object of the later act-phase. We can perceive a temporally extended occurrence, such as a series of notes (C–E–G), by means of the series of perceptual act-phases each of which focuses on the note that is simultaneous with it. Each of these perceptual act-phases also contributes to the perceiving that is centered at another time. When one note is present, the other notes are still perceived as a temporal context or horizon for it. (See Diagram A.5 in the Appendix.)

Theory 4 emphasizes the unity of past, present, and future phases of consciousness. These "parts" are intrinsically non-independent and merged into a temporally extended unity. The "parts" could not exist on their own independently of the other parts. This unity of the "temporal parts" of consciousness is reflected in the unity of the "temporal parts" of the objects of consciousness. Theory 4 claims that the entities that we ordinarily experience are unified temporally extended entities, not phases or individual appearances existing at different times that have to be assembled into an enduring object through understanding their serial order. We are directly aware of these unified temporally extended entities through a unified temporally extended awareness.

Theory 4 does not easily provide a full explanation of the perception of temporal passage. In contributing to the perception that is centered at a later time, an earlier perceptual act-phase is operative-as-past. Thus, its object (note C) is perceived as past in conjunction with note E as present. However, the pastness of note C does not obviously reveal its "having been present." To explain the perception of temporal passage adequately, some account would have to be given within theory 4 of how we perceive earlier phases as having just been present.

1.3E   Theory 5: The Ecstatic-Action Theory

The ecstatic-action theory of Martin Heidegger[11] and Jean-Paul Sartre[12] is similar to theory 4 in that the actuality of consciousness is not confined to the present. Past and future phases of acting consciousness actively contribute to our current perception (that is centered on the present), so that the awareness of past entities occurs by means of past act-phases and the awareness of future entities occurs by means of future act-phases. Any phase of consciousness is "outside of itself" or "ecstatic" in being defined by these other phases. Theory 5 also retains the notion from theory 4 that the awareness of the temporal order of entities depends upon the temporal order of act-phases.

What is novel in the ecstatic-action theory is the notion that ecstatic consciousness is intrinsically active in nature and is defined by the motivational and power features necessary for action. Perception is considered not to be an autonomous parameter of consciousness, but only an aspect abstracted from an acting consciousness. Our perceiving is essentially affected by our motivations, our powers to act, and our current and possible projects. Past, present, and future phases of perception are explicated in this theory as aspects of one unified extended action; their unity is that of the "temporal parts" of an action. The past phases of consciousness are the completed portions of an ongoing action. The future phases of consciousness are not just that which will be, but rather the goals of consciousness for itself (projects) that consciousness is bringing about by its acting. (See Diagram A.6 in the Appendix.)

Theory 5 also builds upon the claim in theory 4 that the objects of ordinary experience are unified, temporally extended entities. Theory 5 supplements this with the claim that these entities are always experienced in terms of their relevance to action. Entities are experienced as instrumental-things, that is, distinct enduring things with qualities that are related to each other in terms of their possible instrumental uses together in achieving some desired state of affairs (composed of instrumental-things) through action. The theory claims that we are aware of these temporally extended, action-relative entities through a temporally extended, acting consciousness.

Theory 5 considers consciousness to be essentially active. Ecstatic-acting consciousness is always changing itself in bringing about its future objectives (projects). In making its own future present, acting consciousness also provides for the transition in experienced entities from being future to being present to being past.[13] In changing itself, acting consciousness experiences temporal passage in the instrumental world because it experiences the instrumental world as having just been transformed by its action from one (present) condition to another (present) condition.

1.4   Theories of Time-Perception and Theories of Time

Any theory of time-perception presupposes an ontology of time. In one-level theories of time-perception, there are always temporal features of the mental acts that perceive the temporal extension and temporal passage of worldly entities. The specific ontology of time that is implicit in the conceptions of acts of awareness, of objects of awareness, and of their connections, strongly affects theories of time-consciousness. Any analysis of the ordinary perception of time includes some position on three interconnected issues:

(1) whether time has past-present-future features or only earlier-later features;
(2) what it is to be past, to be present, and to be future, that is, what is meant by these notions;
(3) what the elements of time are, that is, that which is serially arranged.

Concerning (1), most theories of time-perception have generalized the phenomenological fact that we ordinarily perceive worldly entities as having past-present-future features. They have assumed that perceptual acts are past-present-future too without analyzing this. Perceptual acts have been thought to have past, present, and future phases and to be constantly changing. In the twentieth century, particularly through the influence of relativity physics, there has been a strong movement toward conceiving real time to consist *only* of earlier and later temporal locations with no real temporal passage. Such a time is changeless. All entities occur at spatial-temporal locations that are (tenselessly) earlier or later than each other. I will call this type of time "earlier-later time."

Proponents of a real time that has only earlier-later features (B-series time) initially attempted to translate the concepts of past-present-future time into earlier-later concepts through token-reflexive analyses. Such complete translations of the meaning of past-present-future concepts into earlier-later concepts have proven to be impossible. Token-reflexive analyses of our ordinary past-present-future conceptions eliminate passage entirely, and are therefore eliminative reductions rather than straightforward translations.[14] Since past-present-future time is not definable in terms of earlier-later time, it is necessary to determine whether a theory of time-perception requires a past-present-future time, whether it is compatible with a time that is only earlier-later, and how it treats temporal passage.

Concerning (2), it is necessary to clarify the implicit differences in various theories between the conceptions of the "temporal modalities." Concerning the past, for example, is it assumed to be completely separate from the present or does it exert influence on the present? Is the present considered to be in transition toward the future or is the present a non-dynamic temporal location?

Concerning (3), some position concerning the elements or "parts" of time is necessary in either a past-present-future time or an earlier-later time. A time that passes requires some conception of what it is that passes and some determination of the "extension" of the present (what the present can contain). If parts of time are to be serially arranged, there has to be some conception of the elements that are earlier and later (or more past or more future) than each other.

In the remainder of this chapter I will consider the positions on the three issues that each theory of time-perception presupposes or requires.

1.4A   Theory 1

1. Present representation theories have usually presupposed a past-present-future time. In such theories the *origin* of present representations requires temporal passage. Presently existing representations of past entities have been thought to be derived from awareness (however this is analyzed) of entities that occurs when both the awareness and the entities are present. Since the representations are never simultaneous with the present awareness of the entities represented, the process of "giving rise" to the representations, which is considered to be a causal process, must operate *between* elements of time. In passing from being present to being just-past, the present awareness of entities gives rise to the presently existing representations of the entities *as just-past*. Similarly, these presently existing representations in passing to being past give rise to other presently existing representations of the entities *as further past*. The nature of passage from being present to being past is therefore an essential ingredient in the account of the connection of the (later) present representation of entities as past with the (earlier) present awareness of entities as present.

Representation theories have been conjoined with earlier-later (B-series) ontologies of time, but this conjunction produces two serious problems. (*a*) Because representations intrinsically refer to other temporal locations and portray what supposedly occurs at these temporal locations, their "representing character" conflicts with earlier-later time as it is ordinarily conceived. It is hard to see how an *any* analysis of their "representing character" representations could exist tenselessly *only at* a temporal location. By representing earlier times, representations seem to "exist across" temporal locations. (See section 10.1.) (*b*) In an earlier-later time there are problems about the origins of the representations. In the absense of real causal influences across temporal locations,[15] the existence at a later date of representations of earlier experiences is rather mysterious. Why is there such a "pre-established harmony" between later representations of earlier experiences and the earlier experiences?

2. In an earlier-later time, all temporal locations and their "occupants" exist tenselessly and so in the same way. Past, present, and future can be specified only with respect to some specific temporal location. The future is whatever is later than this location, and the past is whatever is earlier. For a representation theory with an earlier-later time, the present is the temporal location at which a perception-phase (with its representations) exists. The past is whatever is earlier than this perception-phase, and the future is whatever is later. Although it may *seem* to us humans that what is past, what is present, and what is future exist in different ways, in reality these all exist in the same way.

In a past-present-future time, present representation theories consider the present to be the primary and practically the only locus of existence. Past entities and future entities do not fully exist; this supposition is the major reason why present representations are necessary. First of all, only *present* conscious awareness counts; only present phases of perceptual acts can contribute to that of which we are aware. Since both past and future act-phases do not fully exist (at the present time), they cannot contribute to experience at all. Second, present conscious awareness has direct access only to presently existing entities. Since past and future entities do not fully exist, there is only indirect access to them through presently existing representations.

While neither type of entity exists in the full-fledged sense, past entities are usually thought to have a type of existence that does not apply to future entities. Since past entities have been present, they are able to have played a role in the generation of representations. Future entities do not participate in the generation of representations; representations of future entities are generally thought to be derived from complex projections into the future of patterns discerned in the past.

3. Both past-present-future and earlier-later representation theories have presupposed that time is composed of non-extended in-

stants in which no change can occur. The reason is the same in both cases. Such an instantaneous, changeless element ensures that all representations within that element are exactly simultaneous with each other. If any were earlier or later than others, the direct grasping of such successive representations in one act of awareness would threaten to introduce direct contact with past (or earlier) and future (or later) entities.

However, it might be possible for an ontology of time to divorce the changeless character from the instantaneous character. If so, representations in a changeless element would still be exactly simultaneous, though not necessarily instantaneous.

Within representation theories, *experienced* time may or may not be portrayed as composed of non-extended instants. The entire set of present representations represents the serial order of the parts of some stretch of time. Each element of that stretch of time must be represented as distinct from and serially related to the other elements. This is usually accomplished by having at least one representation for every element of time represented. To represent any stretch of time that was composed of non-extended instants would in this case require an infinite number of representations. If experienced time was composed of extended elements, only a finite number of representations would be necessary to represent a stretch of time.

1.4B   Theory 2

1. In theory 2 present act-phases "reach across" to other temporal locations. For this reason theory 2 is not consistant with an earlier-later (B-series) time as it is ordinarily conceived. This inconsistency does not concern temporal passage, but rather whether everything must exist tenselessly *at* a temporal location. (See point 2 below.) A proponent of an earlier-later time could abandon this requirement so as to allow present act-phases to be in direct contact with earlier and later entities, as Russell did.[16] However, further inconsistencies would arise if, in response to the difference in epistemic certainty between immediate memory and immediate anticipation, the future is claimed to be different ontologically from the past.

Concerning past-present-future time, theory 2 as presented involves the same direct contact with the future as with the past. This requires that there be a definite future to be contacted. To account for the difference in epistemic certainty between immediate memory and immediate anticipation, two alternative forms of this theory would eliminate this direct contact with a definite *singular* future. (*a*) The future might be a set of alternatives, only one of which becomes present. There could then be direct contact with a determinate future that nevertheless was not singular. The fallibility of anticipation would then be the result of anticipation's grasping of only one of the alternatives, rather than the whole set as a set. (*b*) Direct contact might be limited to the past, as in Russell's version of this theory.

In a past-present-future time, theory 2 includes both direct contact with entities as past, as present, and as future, and direct contact with some characteristic that provides for the serial ordering of entities. Theory 2 would seem then to require direct contact with the passing of entities. If being present includes the characteristic "being in transition to being past" and being future includes the characteristic "being in transition to being present" and being past includes the characteristic "being in transition to being further from the present," then it would seem that a direct awareness of entities as present or as future or as past would include some direct awareness of these forms of "being in transition." This conclusion, however, depends on two premises: (*a*) that being present, being future, and being past do essentially include these characteristics, and (*b*) that direct awareness is non-opaque with respect to essential characteristics.

2. As I noted in point 1, an earlier-later version of theory 2 would require a modification in the standard conceptions of earlier-later (B-series) time so that a perceptual act-phase at one time could be in direct contact with entities at earlier and perhaps later times. Such a perceptual act-phase would portray whatever is earlier to be past and whatever is later to be future.

The past-present-future version of theory 2, in contrast with theory 1, attributes a type of existence to past and future entities that allows them to be the objects of direct awareness. Whatever differences there are among pastness, presentness, and futurity, these are all alike in that they allow for entities that exist in their "modality" to be directly contacted by consciousness. Of course, in the mixed version where only the past is contacted, there is a major difference between futurity and pastness.

The differences of presentness from pastness and futurity, on the other hand, are at the basis of the claim that awareness operates through *only* present phases of acts. Present entities are thought to be actual or "operative" while past and future entities are not, so that all awareness of past and future entities must be by means of present phases of acts, not past and future act-phases. This notion is complicated, however, by the fact that the objects of awareness of these act-phases are past and future. Even though only present act-phases are operative, the "awareness relation" spans time. Hence, the act-phase is not exclusively within the present because it is not separable ontologically from its intentionality that stretches into the future and the past.

3. Concerning the elements of time, theory 2 presupposes a changeless present for the same reason that theory 1 does. They both ascribe an ontological primacy to present phases of consciousness (or perception-phases *at* a time). If successive act-phases were allowed into one present that was conceived as a unitary change, the unity of the earlier and later act-phases in one present consciousness would be problematic. Theory 2 would under these conditions become a version of theory 4. The changeless elements of time have traditionally been taken to be non-extended instants.

If time is composed of moments within which no change can occur, a perceptual act-phase would have to be aware of all the moments in order to be aware of an entire stretch of time. However, theory 2 does not require that a perceptual act-phase *individuate* each of the moments, only that it be aware of them in being aware of the stretch of time that they compose.

1.4C   Theory 3

Theory 3 has generally the same presuppositions and requirements as theory 2, so my discussion here will be very brief. In sections 5.5, 8.4, and 9.4, I explore the complexities of the relationship between the ontology of time and this theory of time-consciousness.

1. Theory 3 is also not consistent with an earlier-later time because the retentional and protentional features are intrinsically relational. Although they are actual at a time, they do not exist fully at a time.

Theory 3 has the same problems concerning direct contact with the future that theory 2 did. The same responses to these problems might be offered.

Although theory 3 provides a different account of the perception of the serial order of worldly entities, there is the same question whether it includes direct contact with a "being in transition" feature of entities.

2. Like theory 2, theory 3 allows past and future entities to be contacted but limits actuality to the present.

3. Theory 3 also presupposes elements of time within which no change can occur.

1.4D   Theory 4

1. Although it is naturally formulated in past-present-future terms, theory 4 does not require that time itself pass, but only that act-phases (or entire acts) contribute across temporal locations to experience. For this reason theory 4 is not consistent with earlier-later time as it is ordinarily conceived. Phases of perceptual acts do not just exist tenselessly at their temporal locations; they are operative also in the experience that is centered at other temporal locations. The perception that is centered at one time is partially constituted by act-phases that focus on another time.

In a past-present-future time theory 4 includes a passage of phases of consciousness. There is a transition of act-phases toward being more central in moving from being operative-as-future to being operative-as-present, and a transition of act-phases toward being less central in moving from being operative-as-present to being operative-as-past.

2. According to theory 4, actuality is not restricted to the present, in contrast with our commonsense conceptions. Pastness and futurity are such that at least one type of entity, conscious acts, can be operative though not present. Other types of entity are accorded an existence-as-past and an existence-as-future that allows them to be directly contacted by current perception. Present existence nevertheless has some distinction in this theory. Present act-phases and their objects are central to conscious awareness. Past and future act-phases and their objects are horizonal features of awareness that contribute to the meaning of what is central.

This theory does not provide any simple account of the lesser epistemic certainty of our perception of what is just-future. To account for the apparent fallibility of our perception of what is just-future, a complex theory of "being operative-as-future" would be necessary.

3. This theory does not presuppose any very specific position concerning the elements of time. While it does distinguish past from present from future, it emphasizes their unity in a temporally ex-

tended whole. Because of its denial of sharp separations between the "temporal parts" of entities, the theory favors a conception of the elements of time as merging into each other.

1.4E   Theory 5

1. As a theory not only of time-perception but of the temporality of acting consciousness in general, theory 5 is consistant only with a past-present-future time. Not only do phases of acting consciousness fail to exist tenselessly only at their temporal locations; they also essentially involve a process of bringing future phases into the present and displacing present phases into the past. Acting consciousness is itself a process of bringing its projected future into the present and displacing the present into the past. In sections 6.4 and 7.4 I explore the temporal idealism that Heidegger and Sartre conjoin with theory 5.

2. The major proponents of theory 5 have proposed differences between the temporal modalities of worldly entities and the temporal modalities of acting consciousness. What it is for a phase of acting consciousness to be future is different from what it is for a phase of the instrumental world to be future. These differences are explored in Chapters 6 and 7.

Concerning acting consciousness, theory 5 agrees with theory 4 in not restricting actuality to the present. Both past and future phases of acting consciousness are operative (as-past and as-future, respectively) in contributing to current perception and action. Although past, present, and future phases are all actual, theory 5 distinguishes sharply between the being of the past, which is fixed, unalterable, but still operative, and the being of the future, which is operative but possible. As I show in sections 6.5, 7.5, and 9.2, theory 5 has the same serious problems as theory 4 in accounting for the apparent fallibility of our perceptions of what is just-future.

3. Theory 5's position concerning the elements of time should relate these to action. Since the passage of experienced time depends upon acting to make projects present, the elements of time should be defined by the elements of action. Such an element of action would be the smallest division of an action that is still done (governed by an intention). Presumably, such an element would include change within it. As in theory 4, the elements of time merge into each other (like the parts of an action).

I will conclude this section by noting one general point that emerges from this survey. It seems to be necessary for time-perception that mental acts, phases of mental acts, or something else such as representations "reach across" from one temporal location to another. Only in this way could they grasp together the data at the multiple contiguous temporal locations that is included in time-perception. As I indicate in section 3.2 and defend in section 10.1, this reveals the special temporal nature of consciousness.

2

The Denial of Temporal Realism

Perception is commonsensically understood to involve the detection of events and states of affairs that exist independently of the consciousness that perceives them. In existing independently the perceived entities are understood to exist in a real time and a real space. Time, or perhaps the time parameter of entities, is itself commonsensically understood to exist independently of consciousness. Furthermore, consciousness is itself thought to be an entity that arises, passes away, and exists in real time. The *acceptance* of the reality of time, which is the position that I am calling "temporal realism," is an intrinsic part of commonsense notions.

Metaphysical realism asserts or accepts the independent existence of something. Since different types of entities exist in different ways, metaphysical realism is most easily described in terms of the "independent" component of "independent existence." To be metaphysically real the existence of an entity (other than human conscious life) must be non-dependent upon human conscious life. As not dependent upon human conscious life, real entities would exist whether or not human conscious life ever existed.

There are two main (overlapping) types of dependence that must not characterize the being or existence of a real entity. First, productive or causal dependence is the relationship in which human conscious life produces and sustains an entity that could not exist without this producing and sustaining. The paradigm case of such a dependent entity is an imaginary scene or object that exists only so long as it is imagined. Second, categorial dependence is the relation-

34

ship in which the categories that define the existence of an entity essentially refer to human conscious life. Just as traditional properties are categorially dependent upon substances, some entity may be what it is (such as a human intoxicant or hallucinogen) only in virtue of its categorial connection with human conscious life.

The metaphysical realism of commonsense conceptions portrays time, space, individual things, their properties, and their relations to exist "on their own" independently of consciousness. The reality of some of these features is more easily challenged than that of others. Most people believe that some of the commonsense relations between things (e.g., "x is more chic than y") are not metaphysically real, and the reality of secondary properties such as color and taste has been put seriously in question by natural scientific accounts of perceptual processes.

Despite the fact that time is among the most basic features of existence, the acceptance of the reality of time can be and has been challenged in many ways. Temporal realism is challenged by skeptics about reality in general and by metaphysical idealists. A more interesting position is that which denies the reality of time, while maintaining the reality of some other entities. The Kantian theory of the "thing-in-itself" is the prime example of such a doctrine that denies the reality of time without being totally idealist. A third position that in some ways denies the reality of time is the claim that some particular conception of time (for example, that time passes in an A-series fashion or that time is infinite in both directions) does not accurately depict reality. I will not consider this last view to deny the reality of time unless it is joined with the view that reality has no specifically temporal features of any sort.

In this chapter I will explore the motives for denying the reality of time, examine the range of non-realistic positions concerning time, survey the arguments against the reality of time, and discuss the two main ways in which temporal idealists try to explain our everyday experiences of time.

2.1   Motives for Denying the Reality of Time

The major motivation for denying the reality of time, though *not* the major justification for it, is the desire to defend the autonomy of the mental. The non-reality of time would be tremendously important because it would free conscious experience from any determinants based upon a metaphysically real time. The thought is that if there is an ontologically real time, human activities and conscious processes, including those that constitute the "world as experienced," must occur within it. As occurring within real time, human activities and conscious processes would be *subject to* laws and categories deriving from the real time that interfere with the complete autonomy of the mental. Three types of interference with the complete autonomy of the mental have been thought to be ruled out by denying the reality of time.

(1) The *beginning* and particularly the *end* of human existence cannot occur in real time if there is no such time. Those who fear death and lament the passage of time as consuming their finite lifetime would like to discover that time is "only a dream." The prospect of "eternal life" has been a major reason for denying the reality of time. The line of thought supporting this conclusion is the following. An individual experiencer cannot experience the cessation of his or her own conscious life. Through assuming the regular course of natural processes and relying upon the testimony of other people, we can think of ourselves as having been (or going to be) unconscious for some period of time, even forever. This is how we think of ourselves as finite. However, if there is no real time over and above individually experienced time, we can think of ourselves as going to die, but we cannot really die. If time is only a feature of individual consciousnesses, there is no way for that individual conscious life to end in time.

(2) Psychological determinism involving antecedent causation cannot occur if the basic mental processes do not occur in a real time. This was one of Kant's explicit reasons for construing time as only a structure of consciousness, and it has had a profound influence on the major "continental" philosophers of time. We think of everything, including ourselves, as taking place in time, and whatever takes place in time is subject to causal laws. However, if our deepest mental life does not really occur in a real time, we are not really subject to antecedent causation, and so may exercise free will.

(3) Non-psychological determinism in which conscious states and processes are dependent upon and caused by conditions and processes in other entities in real time, such as the functioning of a nervous system, cannot occur if there is no real time. People would like to be able to control their moods, their feelings of illness, their diminished or enhanced mental capacities, and their periods of energy, excitement, and tranquility. Medical and psychological data in-

dicate that such mental states and processes are heavily dependent upon the functioning of the nervous system, the body, and the environment, all of which are thought to be real entities in real time. If, however, such non-psychological states and processes did not occur in real time, the notion that they determine or even strongly influence our mental condition would be seriously weakened.

The question of the reality of time is more than an intellectual puzzle because of these connections with some of the deepest hopes of humankind. If it is only an illusion that conscious life takes place in a real time, we humans may be able to exercise the forms of control over ourselves that many religions and philosophies have claimed that we could.

In Chapters 9 and 10, I am going to argue that in certain respects human conscious life does occur in an ontologically real time and is subject to laws and categories governing entities in real time. For this reason human conscious life is not autonomous in the sense of either (1) or (3) above. Humans inevitably die, not because of something about human conscious life itself, but because of features of the neurophysiological and biological systems upon which conscious life is dependent. Although we can exercise some control over moods, energy levels, and such things, we are always in important ways dependent upon real factors.

I will also argue that in certain respects human conscious life does not occur in real time as standardly conceived. Consciousness is not subject to *all* the laws and categories that are thought to govern non-conscious entities. Although this raises the prospect of some type of autonomy from antecedent causation, I have not found that the special temporality of human being provides any specific support for free will.

2.2   Types of Non-realism Concerning Time

Since time is the focus of this book, I am particularly interested in those doctrines that deny the reality of time while maintaining that some entities are real. Such specifically time-oriented doctrines, deriving from Immanuel Kant and Gottfried Leibniz, have had a strong influence on continental philosophy in the twentieth century. However, since any denial of realism in general will also deny temporal realism, I will start from such denials of the acceptance of any independent existence.

There are two main forms of the denial of realism: skepticism and idealism. Skepticism itself encompasses two types of position concerning the notion of "metaphysical reality."

In the history of thought, most forms of skepticism have maintained that there is a "truth of the matter" but that it is inaccessible to us. Such skeptics have usually endorsed the notion of "metaphysical reality" or "independent existence," but have denied that we can know about its specific characteristics. One form of the denial of temporal realism is when time is included among these unknowable characteristics so that we cannot know whether metaphysical reality includes any temporal features at all.

Another position that has been called "skepticism" denies that the notion of "metaphysical reality" makes sense, so that the traditional realism-idealism debate is just confused. In the notion of "metaphysical reality," we are trying to represent existence that is in no way dependent upon or relative to consciousness, social practices, or cultural history. Such a thing is not thinkable, according to these skeptics, because any conception, even the conception of "independent existence as not dependent upon any conceptions," is our conception and so is relative to various changeable features about us. Such skeptics hold that we can never get outside our "conceptual system," "form of life," "set of language games," "regime of truth," or "historical-cultural world." Within a "historical-cultural world" (or any of the others) there is a conception of independent existence, such as the notion that silicate rock exists independently of people since silicate rock existed on the far side of Neptune before life arose on Earth. However, this conception is not the supposed "independent existence" of the metaphysicians, but rather a conception employing historically changeable notions of time, space, causal influence, properties of minerals, and so on.

This skeptical claim that there is no intelligible issue about realism and idealism in general would of course mean that there is no intelligible issue about the reality or ideality of time. If this issue is to be explored in this book, it is necessary to respond to this skeptical claim. My brief response will claim only that there is an intelligible issue. I will not attempt to sort out and to respond to all the issues that are raised in such skeptical positions.

I earlier presented what I take to be a perfectly intelligible notion of "independent existence." To be metaphysically real the existence of an entity must be non-dependent in two general ways on human conscious life. This "metaphysical conception" is not identical with our historical-cultural world's conception, but it is not a completely distinct notion either. Rather the "metaphysical conception" is something like a genus of which a historical-cultural world's conception is a species. As a more abstract conception, the "metaphysical conception" can take on many specific forms and can preserve its meaningfulness across historical-cultural worlds. We can identify in other historical-cultural worlds their specific forms of the notion "independent existence." Since the metaphysical notion of "independent existence" is partially distinct from our everyday (historical-cultural world's) notions of "independent existence," we can step back from features of the everyday notions and ask whether various basic parameters of the everyday notions, such as time and space, are themselves metaphysically real. Even though our everyday notions of "independent existence" and "real" may presuppose time, space, and other features, we can raise intelligible questions about the metaphysical reality of time, of space, or of other features.

According to idealism, the being of all entities is dependent upon consciousness. Different versions of idealism invoke different subjects of consciousness and different notions of dependence. The most extreme conception of the subject occurs in solipsism, where *my* consciousness is that upon which all other entities are dependent. Subjective or individual idealism holds that other consciousnesses with the same essential nature as mine exist and that all other entities exist for these consciousnesses. Social idealism considers all other entities to be dependent upon human societies that are not reducible to the sum of individual consciousnesses. For divine idealism, all entities exist for God's mind. In one version human consciousnesses are themselves dependent upon God's thought; in another, human consciousness is a component of the divine mind.

In all versions of idealism, the existence of other entities is either productively dependent, categorially dependent, or dependent in both ways upon the subject of consciousness. The specific differences are differences within these categories, for example, between the production of an imaginary object and the creation of a new idea.

The most controversial form of categorial dependence is "teleological directedness," where what might appear to be a self-sufficient entity is defined in its existence by its "being directed toward" something else. What something is at a given time, for example, an acorn, is dependent upon an apparently completely different state of affairs (an oak tree) toward which it is teleologically directed. For

Aristotle the "formal cause" of a substance coincides with its "final cause."[1] Georg Hegel expanded the scope of this notion by claiming that the universe is categorially dependent upon human conscious life in that the categories of nature have a teleological directedness toward the categories of human conscious life.[2] In considering the question of the reality of time, I am going to sidestep the question whether time is teleologically directed toward human conscious life. I am not going to consider this type of dependence for several reasons: teleological directedness is a questionable category of existence; it does not have the same profound implications for human life that the other types do; to support this type of teleological connection would require detailed claims about the specific features of real time that I am not prepared to make (see 9.4); none of the philosophers of time whom I examine have claimed that this dependence exists. In this work I will consider only the generally accepted notions of consciousness-dependence.

Time is dependent upon consciousness in all the versions of idealism, but there are significant differences between versions both with respect to the type of dependence and with respect to the implications for individual consciousnesses.

There are three main ways in which time has been thought to be dependent upon consciousness. First, time is a very encompassing *idea* that is thought by a non-temporal consciousness; it is something *of which* an ontologically non-temporal consciousness thinks. Time as idea is productively and categorially dependent upon consciousness, but consciousness is *not dependent* upon time. For example, God produces and sustains time by thinking of it, but it is possible that God not think of time.

Second, time is a framework or structure through which an ontologically non-temporal consciousness experiences or thinks. As in Kant's "Form of Intuition of Time" (abstracting from all reference to understanding and synthetic activity), time is a necessary structural feature of the intentional objects of consciousness. All objects of awareness (or of a particular type of awareness) have to "appear within the framework of time." However, consciousness is itself non-temporal in that its perceiving, sensing, thinking, and so on does not occur in time. Time does not characterize the "mental act" feature of consciousness.

Time as framework is categorially dependent upon consciousness. However, consciousness is also categorially dependent upon the framework of time in that consciousness (or a particular type of consciousness) cannot exist without experiencing "through" the framework of time. Since mental acts cannot exist without intentional objects and time is a necessary structural feature of intentional objects, the framework of time is necessary for the in other respects non-temporal existence of mental acts.

There is a variation on the notion of time as framework that emphasizes that time is productively dependent upon consciousness. According to this variation, consciousness is a non-temporal activity that generates the framework of time. The framework of time is not just a given structure, but is rather produced by the non-temporal activity of consciousness. However, this productive activity is not itself temporal; it does not stretch through time or have any other temporal features. The non-temporal activity is supposed to be a "logical process" similar to the way that conclusions "follow" non-temporally from premises. This perplexing notion of a logical process that is not a temporal process can be found in Kant's discussions of transcendental synthesis and of the choice of a moral self and in Hegel's notion of the dialectic of categories.

Third, time is *only* or *most basically* the temporal features of consciousness. In this notion of dependence, the mental act feature of consciousness and conscious activities do have temporal features. These temporal features of consciousness are how time exists; that is, time has no other independent existence. In a relational theory of time, time exists only as the temporal relations between entities. This type of dependence takes consciousness to be the basic entity, parts of which are temporally related to other parts. Instead of claiming that time exists as the temporal relations between portions of matter and energy, it claims that time exists as the temporal relations between portions of consciousness. Another way to explain this notion of dependence is to appeal to the idea that time exists only if change exists. Consciousness is then taken to be the entity that changes, so that the existence of time is dependent upon the changing that is characteristic of consciousness.

In principle this third type of dependence could apply to either a past-present-future time or an earlier-later time; that is, there could be either a past-present-future consciousness or an earlier-later consciousness. For the reasons that I will discuss in section 9.2, all proponents of this notion of dependence have made use of a past-present-future consciousness.

A past-present-future consciousness has to change or "pass" by its own resources. The passage of time cannot be a brute fact, but rather must be rooted in the essential nature of consciousness itself. Such a consciousness has been conceived to be an *activity* that changes itself. Heidegger and Sartre call such a consciousness a "temporalizing consciousness." Just as non-temporal activity may be thought to generate a framework of time, a temporalizing consciousness has been thought to generate something like a framework of time. I will explain in section 2.4 how such a produced framework of time has been employed to explain consciousness' experience of the temporal features of entities.

In different versions of idealism, time is dependent upon different subjects of consciousness; hence, the relation of individual consciousnesses to time is different. This is most apparent in the case of divine idealism, which is indistinguishable for an individual consciousness from realism unless God's mind is comprehensible to us. Even then, there are no practical differences between a real time and a God-dependent time unless the individual consciousness is itself a component of divinity. If time is dependent upon society or upon social conceptions that are not reducible to the sum of individuals or individual conceptions, time would also be partly independent of any individual consciousness, and so would be partly real with respect to that individual consciousness. The strong implications of temporal idealism discussed in section 2.1 would hold only if time is dependent upon individual consciousnesses (or to the extent that they are components of a greater subject).

Starting with Kant's pioneering work on the relation of time and consciousness, temporal idealism has usually been divorced from general idealism that has individual consciousness as the subject. The denial of the reality of time has been conjoined with the acceptance of something like the "thing in itself." Even though metaphysically real entities do have an impact on consciousness, time has been taken not to be a feature of such real entities. Rather, time is something that human consciousness contributes to experience. We perceive and understand events in terms of time, but time is solely dependent upon us (as individual consciousnesses or as forming a society).

Such versions of temporal idealism are in all but one respect the same as the temporal idealistic part of general idealisms. The one difference is that they have to give an account of how the non-temporal "impact" of real entities on consciousness is construed as temporal by consciousness. In section 2.4 I will examine the strategies for doing this.

2.3 Arguments Against the Reality of Time

In the preceeding section, I discussed the two types of skeptical position: that we have no way to know the characteristics of metaphysical reality, and that the notion "metaphysical reality" is meaningless. Both of these challenge realism concerning time. I discussed and rejected the attack on the meaningfulness of the notion of metaphysical reality. To survey skeptical challenges to knowledge of metaphysical reality in general would take me too far from the focus of this work. However, I will consider the major factors that cast doubt specifically on the reality of time, and I will consider the major types of ontological arguments against the reality of time.

One claim is that there is no reason to think that time is metaphysically real because a real time is unnecessary. All the experienced temporal features of entities can be explained without appealing to an independently real time. The strong version of this thesis claims that all the experienced temporal features of entities can be traced to the nature of consciousness (I will discuss the specific forms in section 2.4); experienced time is metaphysically dependent upon consciousness in one of the three ways discussed in section 2.2. Since experienced time is dependent upon consciousness, there is no reason to think that there is some other, metaphysically real time.

A second claim is that experienced time is in its very nature contradictory. Although this contradiction is located in different aspects of experienced time by Zeno, Kant, and John McTaggart, they agree that what is inherently contradictory cannot exist on its own. Humans can think contradictory thoughts, but an inherently contradictory entity cannot exist independently because it negates itself. Hence, experienced time must be dependent upon consciousness. McTaggart goes on to argue that no time, even one that is not experienced, could be non-contradictory because A-series change, which is the factor that generates the contradiction, is essential to time. The arguments of Kant and McTaggart will be explored in sections 4.4 and 9.3.

A third claim is that the being of time is identical with the being of acting consciousness. The categories that define the existence of time are identical with the categories that define the existence of human consciousness. This is determined by first abstracting the ontological nature of time from time as it is experienced and understood to be. The categories that define the existence of time are then compared with those of human consciousness and shown to be identical. From this identity of being, it is concluded that time is dependent upon consciousness in the third way from section 2.2. Time is and can be *only* the temporal features of consciousness. This ontological argument will be examined in sections 6.4, 7.4, and 9.3.

2.4　Temporal Idealism and the Experience of Time

One main problem that temporal idealists must face is how consciousness can be the source or basis of experienced time. Individuals regularly perceive objects enduring through time, changing in various ways, and coming into and going out of existence. These phenomenological facts have to be accounted for in any ontological theory of the relations between time and consciousness. With no independently real time to be detected and no independently real time within which consciousness occurs, how is it possible for individual consciousness to experience temporally extended entities and temporal passage? I will discuss these issues in terms of temporal idealism that accepts the independent non-temporal existence of natural entities, although the basic problem is the same for temporal idealism as part of general idealism.

In section 1.2 I argued that to perceive the past-present-future features of entities a consciousness must itself have temporal features. This argument proves that a one-level non-temporal consciousness could not perceive the temporal passage of entities. Thus, time cannot be dependent upon a one-level non-temporal consciousness either as an idea (type 1 dependence) or as a framework through which it experiences (type 2 dependence). This can be made evident by considering a diagram of a one-level non-temporal consciousness that perceives through a framework of time (Diagram 2.1). Suppose that this consciousness perceives a ball rolling from *a* to *b* to *c*. While there is no difficulty with perceiving the temporal extension of the ball's journey and in general with perceiving earlier-later features, the non-temporal consciousness cannot perceive the past-present-future features. The non-temporal consciousness can-

Diagram 2.1

non-temporal consciousness
t_1
t_2 ball at a
t_3 ball at b
t_4 ball at c
t_5

not perceive where in its path the ball is at present and the change in where it is at present. If one date in the framework was prominent over the others as "the present," it would have to be unalterably so. There could not be *changes* in which point was prominent since this would require that the perceiving consciousness change, which would make it temporal. Thus, a one-level non-temporal consciousness could not perceive the passage of time and the change in where the ball is at present.

To resolve this difficulty about the perception of temporal passage, a *two-level* non-temporal consciousness might be proposed. The most basic level of this two-level consciousness would be non-temporal and would experience through an earlier-later temporal framework. It would comprehend all of time (or of some era of time) as a series of dates that were related as earlier or later than each other. None of these dates would be "present" or have prominence over the others. The basic level of consciousness would *conceive* there to be a secondary level of consciousness existing *at* the earlier-later dates in the basic level's framework.[3] The secondary level of consciousness would not be *really* temporal but would be understood to be in an earlier-later time. The secondary level of consciousness would be composed of consciousness-phases each of which itself had a distinct time-framework with a prominent point that it regarded as present. (See Diagram 2.2.) Such a two-level consciousness might be able to perceive the temporal passage of entities. Each phase of the secondary level of consciousness would experience through its own framework; it would experience some entities as past vis-á-vis its present and some entities as future vis-á-vis its present. The basic level would be aware of all these phases of the secondary level of consciousness. If the basic level could "look through" the temporal frameworks of the phases of the secondary level of consciousness, a non-temporal consciousness might be able

Diagram 2.2

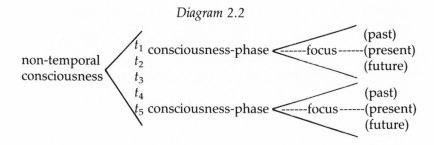

to experience past-present-future features in entities even though neither the consciousness nor any real entities had real temporal features.

There are several interesting features of such a two-level theory. The basic non-temporal level of consciousness could be interpreted either as an individual subject or as some type of "greater subject," according to different versions of idealism. There could be real non-temporal entities that are perceived within these frameworks; the basic non-temporal level of consciousness could interact with independently real, non-temporal entities to produce the sensory information included in perception. However, the secondary level of consciousness does not exist on its own, but rather is entirely dependent upon being thought by the basic level of consciousness. The secondary level is productively dependent upon the basic level. This dependence produces problems concerning the perception of real entities that I will explore in section 9.2.

An alternative way for temporal idealism to explain the perception of past-present-future features is by means of a temporalizing consciousness. As I explained in section 2.2, time might be *only* the temporal features of consciousness (type 3 dependence). A past-present-future temporalizing consciousness would itself intrinsically change or "pass," and since the consciousness is intentional, it would experience its intentional objects in past-present-future terms. A past-present-future temporalizing consciousness would produce a changing past-present-future temporal framework within which all other entities are perceived. The past-present-future temporalizing consciousness would be able to perceive temporal extension and temporal passage in the manner of an "ecstatic-acting" consciousness (see theory 5 in section 1.3E). Thus, real (non-temporal) entities might be able to be perceived in past-present-future terms by a temporalizing consciousness, even though there was no real time.

Both Heidegger and Sartre developed versions of temporal idealism in which a temporalizing consciousness was the source of all experienced temporal features, including the passage of time. The adequacy of their specific versions will be examined in Chapters 6 and 7, and the adequacy of any past-present-future temporalizing consciousness will be examined in section 9.2.

3
The Question of
a Special Temporality

First-person consciousness has always been considered to be something special. Whether as soul or mind or person, human consciousness has been conceived to be different from the non-conscious worldly entities of which it is aware. This difference should be reflected in the different ways that conscious and non-conscious entities are temporal. Although ontological theories have not always recognized the difference, human consciousness should have a special temporal (or even non-temporal) nature that is different from that of ordinary natural objects. In this chapter I will examine what a special temporal nature would be like, the types of reasons that have supported it, and some of the implications that have been drawn from it for how humans should live. In Chapter 10 I will defend my own position on these issues.

3.1 What Is a Special Temporality?

"Everything that is exists *in* time and *in* space. Time and space are containers, everything is located in them; every event occurs *at* some point in time and *at* some point in space."[1] Our commonsense ways of thinking about the existence of non-abstract entities portray them as existing in time and in space. Space and time are thought themselves to have various essential characteristics, and whatever

48

exists in space and in time inherits these characteristics. To exist in space and in time is to be determined by various categories that are specified by the essential natures of space and time.

A special temporality is a way of being temporal or "being through time" that does not conform to all the categories that are thought to be specified by the essential nature of time. An entity that exists in a special temporal way has at least some temporal characteristics that are different from those of ordinary entities existing in time. However, special temporality is not dependent upon a "container" conception of time or a conception of time as absolute. If time is nothing more than the temporal features of non-abstract entities, as in "relational" conceptions, some of these temporal features may still be special, that is, different from those of ordinary entities.

Since there are many temporal characteristics, it might be possible for an entity to share some but not all of them. This is more readily acceptable in a relational conception of time than in a conception of absolute time as a container. If we take the "container" conception of time seriously, an entity with any special temporal characteristics would not *exist in* this time or would not *exist completely in* this time. Existing partially within the container of absolute time has never been a popular conception both because it is somewhat puzzling how something could be partially within and partially without absolute time and because the notion of "another time" coexistent with the supposedly absolute time is troublesome.

I think that the tendency to think of time as a container is an important reason why major phenomenological theorists have denied that there is an ontologically real time. Thinking that if there is an ontologically real time human consciousness must occur within it and so must be subject to the laws and categories governing entities in real time, they have denied that there is such a real time, because they think that consciousness is not subject to the laws and categories governing natural entities. In Chapter 9 I will argue that, although human consciousness does have special temporal features, it also has some standard temporal features. Although this terminology may conjure up deceiving images, human consciousness could be said to exist partially within the ontologically real time of ordinary worldly entities and partially outside it.

Our commonsense understanding of time is basically Newtonian both with respect to the characteristics of time and with respect to time being distinct from the entities that occur in time. In the following sections I will be concerned only with the characteristics of a finite region of time. Since these characteristics are the same whether time is itself an entity or only the temporal features of other entities, I will not here take a position on this issue.

The temporal characteristics of ordinary worldly entities that are commonly taken to reveal the essential features of time itself are the following:

(1)   temporal location—that any non-conscious worldly entity exists at some definite location in one temporal coordinate system in which all other worldly entities exist;

(2)   temporal extension or duration—that any non-conscious worldly entity occupies some point or set of contiguous points of this temporal coordinate system (particularly if the temporal coordinate system is understood as a dense continuum of points);

(3)   length of duration—that there is a definite size to the temporal extension of an entity, that its size can be expressed as a multiple or fraction of any arbitrarily selected temporal extension;

(4)   temporal divisibility—that any non-conscious worldly entity's duration that occupies more than a single point can be divided into equally real temporal parts without any change in its non-temporal properties;

(5)   earlier-later relations—that the temporal parts of an entity are temporally related as earlier or later than each other, and that the temporal parts of any two entities are temporally related as earlier, later, or simultaneous with each other;

(6)   past-present-future features—that if there is a date at which a temporal part of an entity is present, there is an earlier date at which it is future and a later date at which it is past, and that it passes from being future to being present to being past.

With the exception of the temporal passage part of (6), which is excluded by B-series theorists, it is widely held that an entity that has any of these features will have all of them. This is not surprising since many of the features are not completely distinct from others. An entity that exists in a special temporal way is one that has at least one temporal feature that does not conform to the above specifications. If, for example, the temporal parts of an entity are internally temporally related to each other so that what exists at one temporal location is what it is only by means of its relations to the other temporal parts, these temporal parts would have special temporal features.

3.2   Time-Consciousness and the Special Temporality of Human Being

That humans experience temporally extended worldly entities and the passage of such entities through time is one major reason for ascribing a special temporal nature to human being. It appears that any one-level theory of time-perception will have to ascribe some special temporal features to the perceiving consciousness (a two-level non-temporal consciousness does not have either standard temporal features or special temporal features). Since the perceiving consciousness is itself in time, its perception at any given time will have to reach across time to other temporal locations. The plausibility of this claim can be seen by considering briefly how each of the theories of time-perception surveyed in Chapter 1 requires that consciousness have some special temporal features.

3.2A   Theory 1

The present representation model, in limiting consciousness' *direct contact* to present representations that exist simultaneously with the perceptual act-phase, initially seems to ascribe only standard temporal characteristics to consciousness. This is because most of the complexities of intentionality have been thrust over into the unanalyzed "representing character" of the present representations. However, as I will explore in more detail in section 10.1, these present representations do not just exist *at* their temporal location but rather intrinsically refer to other temporal locations and portray what supposedly occurred there. The representations "reach across" or transcend to other temporal locations. They would not exist as the entities that they are if they were completely separated off from these other temporal locations. Thus, they do not occupy temporal locations in the usual way but have a special form of temporal location. Since such representations are supposed to be consciousness-dependent, the consciousness that perceives time through them also has this special temporal feature.

3.2B   Theory 2

The direct awareness of past and future entities through present conscious act-phases ascribes the same special form of temporal location directly to consciousness, rather than to representations in consciousness. Since conscious awareness spans time in order directly to contact past occurrences, consciousness cannot be located in time in the standard way, and its temporal extension is of a special sort.

3.2C   Theory 3

The direct awareness of past and future act-phases with their objects through present conscious act-phases shares with theories 1 and 2 the same peculiarity of temporal location. Not only does a present act-phase "reach across" to other temporal locations, but it always contacts an earlier or later act-phase of the same consciousness. Thus, in addition to the special types of temporal location and temporal extension of the present act-phase, there is a further special temporal feature of the entire consciousness, its non-divisibility. An extended portion of consciousness can be such that it does not include direct contact with any date earlier or later than itself. The temporal location, duration, and length of duration of this extended consciousness considered as a whole would then be of the standard variety. What would be non-standard would be its non-divisibility into temporal parts. Since each phase of this extended consciousness is intrinsically in direct contact with other phases, phases cannot be completely separated off from each other without losing some of their properties.

3.2D   Theory 4

The direct awareness of past and future entities through past and future act-phases requires that act-phases that are earlier and later than a present act-phase contribute to that of which it is aware, specifically, that they provide the temporal context or background for the intentional correlate of the present act-phase. Since earlier and later act-phases can contribute to that of which we are aware at any given time, their existence and activity is not restricted to the time at which they are present. In this respect they have a non-standard temporal location and duration. Furthermore, the intrinsic unity of act-phases at different times denies standard forms of divisibility and prescribes special relations between the temporal parts.

3.2E   Theory 5

The ecstatic-action theory conceives consciousness to be essentially an agent. Acting consciousness' time-consciousness is complex. The most basic form is the awareness at any given time of our whole acting on the world, including the earlier and later phases. Since acting affects the facts of the world and is guided both by a "world-view" and by particular observations, the experience of temporally extended acting includes the interested perception of temporally extended worldly entities. It is because acting is "outside of itself" by unifying past and future phases of acting with the present that we experience the temporal features of worldly entities. Earlier and later phases of acting contribute to our awareness at any given time of the temporal extension and passage of worldly entities (instrumental-things). The existence and activity of phases of acting is not limited, therefore, to the time at which they are present. In this respect they have a non-standard temporal location and duration. Furthermore, the phases of acting have a special type of unity in that they are mutually dependent. Any phase would not be a phase of the specific action of which it is a phase unless it was connected to the other phases. This intrinsic unity of phases of action at different times denies the standard forms of divisibility and requires that special relations exist between the temporal parts of an action.

3.3   The Denial of Temporal Realism and the Special Temporality of Human Being

The mere refusal to accept the reality of time does not lead naturally to any claims about the special temporal nature of humans, nor do the traditional forms of temporal idealism. If time is dependent upon a *non-temporal* consciousness either as an idea or as a framework of experience, the non-temporal consciousness obviously does not have the standard temporal features, but it does not have special temporal features either. Only if time is categorially dependent upon consciousness in the third way (see section 2.2) is there an intrinsic connection between temporal idealism and a human special temporal nature.

A temporalizing consciousness is inherently active, and its activity is supposed to be the basic way in which past-present-future time exists. If time exists most basically as the temporal features of a temporalizing consciousness, those temporal features will have to be special ones. A temporalizing consciousness would not exist in time in the way that ordinary worldly entities are thought to exist in time. All the "temporal parts" of a temporalizing consciousness would have an intrinsic unity such that each phase was defined by all of the others (Heidegger calls this the "ecstatic character" or "being outside of itself" of temporalizing activity). Although a temporalizing consciousness defines temporal locations, a phase of temporalizing consciousness does not exist completely at a temporal location because of its "outside of itself" character. There are other special temporal features of a temporalizing consciousness that will be discussed in sections 6.3 and 7.3.

Some thinkers have claimed that experienced time is not real time. Experienced time may be dependent upon consciousness whether there is or is not another ontologically real time. Such a position is not temporal idealism proper, but it does assert the ideality of experienced time. If experienced time is taken to have the standard temporal features[2] and experienced time can be shown to be dependent upon consciousness, then an independent argument for the special temporality of consciousness could be made. Such an argument could take either of the following forms.

One is that experienced time is essentially contradictory so that the consciousness that experiences this time cannot itself exist in such a time. Assuming that the consciousness that experiences the contradictory time is temporal, its temporal features must be special ones.

Both Kant and McTaggart argue that experienced time is contradictory, although they locate the contradiction in different aspects of experienced time. Since McTaggart claims that the *essence* of time is contradictory (the validity of this argument is assessed in section 9.3), he concludes that the consciousness that experiences A-series (past-present-future) time must itself exist non-temporally. However, Kant never argues that any possible type of time need be contradictory (see section 4.4). Hence, it might be possible to develop an argument along Kantian lines from the contradictory character of experienced time to the *special* temporal existence of human being, even though Kant himself does not do this.

Another argument is that the connection of experienced moments into a temporally ordered series exists only *for* the experiencer. Sartre claims that a phenomenological analysis of the experienced temporal features of things reveals that the *unity* of diverse momentary states into temporally extended instrumental-things is not an intrinsic feature of the states themselves. Since the states by themselves are not unified into a series, they are not by themselves moments of time. The unity of what become the moments of time is provided by consciousness that synthesizes the distinct states into a temporal order. The temporal relations between experienced entities (and phases of entities) are external relations that can exist only for an experiencer.

If experienced temporal relations can exist only as objects of consciousness, consciousness cannot exist in a time *of this sort*. Although this argument might in principle be used to defend the non-temporality of human being, Sartre employs it to defend the special temporal nature of human being. Relying upon additional theses about time-consciousness, he claims that acting consciousness can unify the diverse states in a temporal way only because of its own special temporal nature. The validity of Sartre's argument will be explored in section 7.4.

3.4 Further Arguments for the Special Temporality of Human Being

Several other arguments that are connected with but not reducible to the arguments of sections 3.2 and 3.3 have been offered.

One is that human being is at any given time defined by its future that it is to be. Human being is "ahead of itself." Both Heidegger and Sartre maintain that acting consciousness at any given time is defined by projects, that is, features of a future self that acting consciousness is in the process of making itself be. The having of projects is not reducible to principles, wants, or any psychological factors that exist solely in the present. If any phase of acting consciousness is what it is only through its (futural) relation with future phases, then human being would have special temporal features.

Another argument is that human being is at any given time defined by its past that it has been. Both Heidegger and Sartre maintain that acting consciousness at any given time is defined by its previous experience of and action in the world. The details of this are complicated and will be explored in Chapters 6 and 7. The relevant point here is that "being its past" is not reducible to memories, *effects* of previous living, or any psychological factors that exist solely in the present. If any phase of acting consciousness is what it is only through its relation with past phases, then human being would have special temporal features.

A third argument is that human being is at any given time defined by its finiteness or being-toward-death. Humans are essentially rather than contingently finite. While the exact relation of being-toward-death to being-ahead-of-itself requires interpretation, Heidegger clearly maintains that being-toward-death includes a particular way of being *at any given time*. Being temporally finite is considered to be a way of existing at any time that is different temporally from the ways of existing of worldly entities (being-ready-to-hand and being-present-at-hand), and it is not reducible to any biological or psychological factors that exist solely in the present. As such, it would involve special temporal features.

In section 10.3 I will examine in detail these and other arguments for the special temporality of human being.

3.5   Valuational Implications of a Special Temporality

The interest of many philosophers in the special temporality of human being depends in part upon its implications, particularly its valuational implications. If humans have a special way of "being through time," this will have implications for how we should regard and treat other people and how we should think about our own lives. There are three main types of valuational implication that the special temporal nature of human being might have.

First, the special temporal nature of human being might be a necessary condition for free will. Kant, Heidegger, and Sartre all claim that free will is possible only if human consciousness does not exist in the standard temporal way. If human consciousness does exist in Newtonian time, then the following argument against free will applies to it.

Motivational factors (such as wants, emotions, and beliefs) are distinct from and precede the forming of an intention to act. If these motivational factors cause the forming of a specific intention to act, determinism holds. If these motivational factors do not cause the forming of the intention, the intention would be divorced from one's previous character and self, which are composed of such motivational factors. Such a spontaneous intention would not provide any basis for responsibility because it would be unconnected to its possessor's character and self. Since free will requires responsibility, free will could not exist in the non-causal case either.

The features of a special temporality that are relevant to free will are temporal location, temporal divisibility, and the relations between temporal parts. Both Heidegger and Sartre attempt to account for free will in terms of special temporal features. I cannot here explicate their complex theories of freedom, but I will note that a special temporal nature might block the above argument either by denying that motivational factors are distinct from and precede the forming of intentions or by denying that causation is the only important relation that can connect an intention to a person's character and self.

That free will is not ruled out by, and may be explicable in terms of, consciousness' way of existing through time is itself an ontological thesis rather than a valuational one. However, the possibility of free will itself has many valuational implications when combined with community practices, social theory, and moral requirements.

Second, the temporal parts of a person's life should be regarded in certain ways in valuational matters because of the special temporality of human being. The special forms of temporal location, temporal divisibility, and relations between temporal parts dictate that the supposed moments of a person's life cannot legitimately be considered to be self-contained and autonomous existents. This affects the outcome of utility calculations concerning oneself and other people. In considering the balance of burdens and benefits to someone of a course of action, we have to consider how tightly connected are the various temporal parts of the person's life. The connection of the parts of a person's life should also affect the application of deontological principles by requiring that a longer span of a person's life be that to which they apply.

Third, the special temporality of human being establishes an obligation to be self-determining. Following a "live according to your essential nature" line of thinking, some existential ontologists have claimed that our special temporal nature requires that we explicitly choose our values and world-view. The existential prescription not to live unthinkingly from out of culturally accepted and habitual values and conceptions, but rather to reflect upon and to decide to which values and conceptions to commit ourselves, has been thought to be derivable from our special temporal nature. Any other way of living is "inauthentic" or "in bad faith" because it requires hiding our special temporal nature from ourselves.

For the existential prescription to be derivable from our special temporal nature, basic values and conceptions must be an intrinsic component of it. Thus, it is only acting consciousness theories based on the notion of a project that can make this sort of claim. Accounts of special temporality that construe time-consciousness as an interestless perception, such as Husserl's theory, do not incorporate basic values and world-view into our special temporal nature. Such theories do not consider the existential prescription to be an implication of human special temporality.

In section 10.4 I will discuss the implications that do follow from the special temporal nature of human being.

Part II
Phenomenological Positions

The philosophy of time has a long history.[1] Many diverse metaphysical doctrines of time have been developed. The philosophers whom I discuss in the next four chapters were all conversant with this history and were attempting to improve on the earlier theories. Kant's thinking, for example, was influenced by the Leibniz-Clarke debate concerning the nature of space and time.

In surveying the major phenomenological thinkers about time and consciousness, I focus on the theories themselves and say little about historical influences. Although I do indicate how the later figures were influenced by the earlier figures, I could not explore historical influences in detail without sacrificing attention to the theories themselves.

In each chapter I first clarify the author's views on the phenomenological basis for his theory, and then discuss the theory of time-consciousness, the temporal nature of the experiencer, and temporal idealism.

4

Kant's Theory of Time-Consciousness and Time

Immanuel Kant was the progenitor of the tradition that made time and time-consciousness central issues of metaphysics, theory of knowledge, and philosophy of mind. Kant was not a phenomenologist in the technical sense in that he did not follow the specific procedures codified by Husserl for phenomenological investigation (transcendental phenomenological reduction, description of noetic acts and noematic correlates, eidetic variation). Nevertheless, his first-person approach to the investigation of consciousness, meaning, and knowledge was in many respects similar to phenomenology and was very influential for it. The deep influence of Kant's thought concerning the syntheses underlying consciousness, how objects and objectivity are thought, and how there can be consciousness of temporally extended occurrences, is obvious in the work of Husserl and Heidegger.

Kant was a phenomenologist in the broader sense of the term in that descriptions of first-person experience are the basic data for his studies of consciousness, meaning, and knowledge. His descriptions of first-person experience generally de-emphasize the mental act feature. He does distinguish the mental faculties of intuition, imagination, understanding, and reason, but he says little about the *experienced features* of the acts of perceiving, remembering, judging, etc. He focuses instead on the intentional objects of these acts. The intentional objects of perception, belief, and knowledge are analyzed into their many complex features: the intuitional data, the spatial and temporal frameworks of the data, the data conceptualized under sensory universals, the data referred to an object as its appearances, and the synthetic unity of appearances at different times wherein temporally extended objects and events are experienced. Our awareness of these complex features is what Kant's theory of consciousness and knowledge attempted to explain. Kant argued regressively from these features to the nature of knowing consciousness. Our minds must be structured and be active in certain ways if we are to be aware of all of the complex features of which we are aware.

The main distinction of features was between intuitional data and conceptually understood types. All perceptual experiences include intuitional data. Intuitional data are singular rather than general representations and relate immediately to their object.[1] They are *partially* indeterminate in that they do not classify themselves into types, but they do provide some basis for the development of types (concepts) through a process of reflection upon them.[2] Intuitional data are received and are experienced as received. Human intuition cannot create its own data but must rather be given its data through being affected by things.[3] Technical complications aside, intuitional data are just unconceptualized sense impressions, and Kant's claim is that there is such a feature included in perception and involved in claims (judgments) about the facts of the world.

In perception we also experience what we perceive in terms of types. The experiencing of anything as of a type requires the use of concepts. To have a concept is to understand a type. Concepts are general representations that refer to an object "mediatedly by means of a feature which several things may have in common."[4] Concepts are "predicates of possible judgments"[5] because "the only use which the understanding can make of these concepts is to judge by means of them."[6] The most basic use of a concept is the judgment in which we subsume an individual under a type. Intuitional data, which in a sense "refer" to their sources, are in perception understood to be of various types. Judgments of the form, "this is of type x," are necessary for all other judgments, such as those judgments in which an individual *of* a type is subsumed under another type and those purely conceptual judgments in which one type is predicated of another type.

The understanding and use of concepts requires mental activity. "Concepts are based on the spontaneity of thought, sensible intuitions on the receptivity of impressions."[7] Kant never fully clarifies the "functions" that underlie concepts, but the basic idea is fairly straightforward. We *bring together* and *grasp as similar* intuitional data in understanding a sensory concept. For example, the concept "red" is a matter of bringing together and grasping what is common to the class of red intuitional data. Sensory universals are the simplest type of concepts. All the concepts that we ordinarily use are predicated of objects in space and time, so that ordinary concepts require the concept of "object in space and time." The bringing together and grasping that is required for understanding this notion of "an object in general" (through the Categories, specifically, the Categories of Relation) is more complex. The activity of the mind that underlies the understanding of a multifaceted object in time will be explored in section 4.2B.

Kant's investigations of the relations of consciousness and time occur predominantly in works concerning the nature of knowledge and of *knowing* consciousness. Knowing consciousness is that which (*a*) makes claims about the essential features of the world, (*b*) makes claims about the specific facts of the world and about the specific laws governing these facts, (*c*) has evidence for these claims and acquires new evidence to support or to criticize them, and (*d*) revises its earlier claims, that is, makes new claims, based on its acquisition of evidence, that can differ from its earlier claims. Perception is an essential part of knowing consciousness in that perception is the basis for knowledge of specific facts and specific laws (empirical knowledge). In perception we make knowledge claims about the world, and what we perceive provides the basic evidence for empirical knowledge claims.

It is important to note that the claims of knowing consciousness themselves undergo change. There are changes in knowing consciousness with respect to what it claims about the specific temporal facts of the world. Kant's theory of time-consciousness has to incorporate this fact that knowing consciousness itself occurs in time because knowing consciousness changes its claims. Since Kant thinks that the ultimate subject of consciousness is non-temporal, a distinction has to be introduced between "ordinary knowing consciousness" (hereafter, OKC) and the "ultimate knowing consciousness" or "transcendental ego" (hereafter, TE). The transcendental ego does not exist in time and does not change its views about the world and the ordinary knowing consciousness within time.

4.1   Experienced Temporal Features

The experiential basis of Kant's theory of time-consciousness is in OKC's knowledge claims about the temporal features of the world. Each of us is an OKC who regularly makes such knowledge claims in perceiving and understanding the world. The world that is available to theoretical knowledge consists, according to Kant, of substances with properties in causal interaction with each other in space and time. OKC's knowledge claims that concern specific temporal facts of the world are of two kinds: claims about the before-after and simultaneity relations of states of substances (including claims that a state of one substance causes a particular state in another substance), and claims about the pastness, presentness, or futurity of states of substances.[8] These plus the essential features that are known *a priori* are the basic temporal characteristics of which humans are conscious and about which they may have knowledge. Kant does not examine the measurement of time. He discusses neither conventional units of time and time-measurement, such as days, months, or minutes, nor how we understand by means of time-measurement the changes of states of substances.

OKC makes claims both about the essential features of the time of the world and about specific temporal facts. If claims about the essential temporal features of the world (the essential features of the time of the world) are to be known, they have to be known *a priori* (not through sense perception). Claims about the specific temporal facts of the world, such as which specific state of a substance is present or which specific state precedes which other state, are known through sense perception (*a posteriori*).

4.1A   What Is Known *a Priori*: Essential Features

Although Kant is concerned in most cases with what is known *a priori*, concerning time itself his investigations focus primarily on what is known *a posteriori*. He is primarily concerned to analyze what we knowers must be like (which is known *a priori*) in order that we can know *a posteriori* about specific temporal facts. Yet there are some things that Kant claims that we know *a priori* about time itself.

1. "Time has only one dimension."
2. "Different times are not simultaneous but successive"

3. "Different times are but parts of one and the same time."
4. "The infinitude of time signifies nothing more than that every determinate magnitude of time is possible only through limitations of one single time that underlies it."[9]

Kant has very little to say about the essential features of time because there is no science (*Wissenschaft*, organized grounded knowledge) that concerns the essential features of time.[10] Kant's discussions of time in the Transcendental Aesthetic of the *Critique of Pure Reason* are just extensions of his discussions of space. For space there is a body of knowledge concerning its essential features, namely, Geometry. Kant is very concerned to justify our ability to know *a priori* this geometrical knowledge of the essential features of space. Since there is not a developed body of knowledge of essential features of time, there seems to be far less of an issue about *a priori* knowledge of time.[11] Whatever we know *a priori* about the essential features of time, we are able to know, according to Kant, *only because* time is *only* a structure of our consciousness. In the Transcendental Aesthetic, time is portrayed as only a form of intuition. Later this position is enriched by an account of how we OKCs are able to experience things in time.

4.1B   What Is Known *a Posteriori*: Specific Temporal Facts

We OKCs make claims about both (1) the earlier-later and simultaneity relations between specific states of substances, and (2) the pastness, presentness, or futurity of specific states of substances. Although both of these are known *a posteriori*, Kant never considers how claims about (2) can be confirmed or disconfirmed. He examines only how claims about (1) can be known on the basis of perceptual experience.

In perception we observe specific states of substances with an understanding of how what appears (a state) coheres with all other appearances (of states of the relevant substances) to comprise the substances. The goal of these claims is to coincide with the objective specific temporal facts of the world. The claims are true when they do coincide; false when they do not. As the argument of the Second and Third Analogies reveal, Kant is very concerned with *how we think of* earlier-later and simultaneity relations and how we can *justify* such knowledge claims. As the discussions in the First Antinomy, the Third Analogy, and the Synthesis of Reproduction of the A edition Transcendental Deduction reveal, Kant is also concerned with *how we think of* what is not present. However, he does not consider whether claims about pastness, presentness, and futurity can be objective or how they could be justified. Perhaps they cannot be known because they are features of time itself, rather than of things in time, and "time . . . cannot itself be perceived."[12] Alternatively, pastness, presentness, and futurity may not be features of objective time at all. Kant does claim that time "remains and does not change"[13] and that "time itself does not alter."[14]

In light of the above, Kant's account of the nature of a knowing consciousness that can come to know specific temporal facts must include the following features.

i.   How we OKCs can think of or represent simultaneity and earlier-later relations between states of substances. This is the basic Kantian version of the time-perception problem. Kant has to explain how we can perceive and think of the *temporal extension* of entities, and he formulates temporal extension primarily in terms of earlier-later time. Since substances are the basic entities of the objective world, how we OKCs can represent the temporal extension of substances is formulated in terms of representing the earlier-later order of their states.

ii. How we OKCs can think of or represent what is not present to or directly appearing to consciousness. This is the past-present-future form of the above problem of representing temporal extension. Kant does recognize that we OKCs experience the pastness, presentness, futurity of states of substances. However, he does not ever raise the question of how we OKCs are able to represent the *temporal passage* of entities.

iii. How we OKCs can represent or claim that specific temporal relations between specific states of substances are *objective*. The issue is how our representing of simultaneity and earlier-later relations (see *i*) can claim to conform to objective temporal facts.

iv. How we OKCs can confirm or justify these claims (iii) to the *objectivity* of state *a* being before, after, or simultaneous with state *b*.

v. How OKC's *making of claims* can at least appear to be in time so that the claims that are made can *change* as we gather more evidence (over time) in attempting to confirm them.

4.2   The Awareness of Experienced Temporal Features

At first it seems that there are two accounts in Kant's writings of how knowing consciousness represents specific temporal facts: a form of intuition account and a synthetic activity account. I will argue that these are not competing accounts, but rather the two levels in Kant's two-level theory of time-consciousness. In section 4.2A I will examine the form of intuition account from the Transcendental Aesthetic in order to show why it cannot be a complete account of time-consciousness. I will argue that Kant's claim that time is a form of intuition is his way of explaining how OKC can be or seem to be in time, even though time is ultimately not real. By intuiting ourselves through an earlier-later form of intuition, we OKCs seem to be in time. This then sets up the problems of time-consciousness to which Kant responds with the synthetic activity account from the Transcendental Logic. Section 4.2B discusses the synthetic activity account.

4.2A   Time as Form of Intuition

Time is not a discursive, or what is called a general concept, but a pure form of sensible intuition.[15]

We deny to time all claim to absolute reality; that is to say, we deny that it belongs to things absolutely, as their condition or property, independently of any reference to the form of our sensible intuition.[16]

Throughout the Transcendental Aesthetic, Kant considers time to be *only* a form of sensible intuition. Things-in-themselves are not temporal. Time exists only as a structure of awareness.[17] Time is an essential structure of human sensibility. Our reception of intuitional data requires a form or framework of time within which intuitional data appear.

Time as a form of intuition might be interpreted as an account of time-consciousness. To do so is to claim that the form of intuition is itself experienced as the earlier-later temporal relations among intuitional data. We have a basic intuitional grasp of temporal relations (see Diagram 4.1). Both the intuitional data and the temporal relations will undergo conceptualization, but the basic form of the perception of temporal extension and temporal order is intuitional.

That we have a basic intuitional grasp of the framework of time explains how we can know *a priori* the essential features of time. It is not necessary to investigate empirically any or all periods of time to know about their essential characteristics (see section 4.1A). In grasping the framework of time, we have access to the *temporal* features of all periods of time, since these are defined by the framework. The claim that we have an intuitional grasp of the framework of time that grounds our *a priori* knowledge of the essential features of time does run into difficulties concerning the infinitude of time. The form of intuition account requires that we intuitionally grasp an infinite temporal framework, one from which every possible date can be singled out (although this "singling out" requires further activity). This intuitional grasp of a completed infinity *by OKC* is later abandoned in the resolution to the First Antinomy.

As a form of intuition, time is a structure that is essential to our (receptive) sensibility. There have been two major interpretations of the "reception" of intuitional data, corresponding to inner representation and direct realism theories of perception. According to the first interpretation, a thing-in-itself causally produces (in "affection") intuitional data, which are distinct entities within the mind.[18] On this view Kant denies representational realism because intuitional data do not accurately picture their causes, the things-in-themselves. According to the second interpretation, intuitional data are the direct appearing of things-in-themselves to the mind.[19] Intuitional data are not entities distinct from things-in-themselves that might either

Diagram 4.1

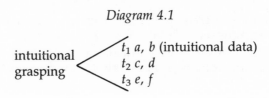

resemble or not resemble their causes. As the appearances of things-in-themselves to the mind, intuitional data distort only by limitation; that is, only certain features of the thing-in-itself can be manifested within the mind.

According to *both* interpretations, the framework of time is *only* a feature of the mind itself. The framework of time consists of temporal locations at which intuitional data could occur (however the occurrence is analyzed). These temporal locations form a framework by being related to each other as earlier-later. In occurring within this framework, intuitional data are experienced as themselves earlier, later, or simultaneous with other intuitional data. While pure concepts are necessary in order *to think* of the intuitional data as the appearances of states of substances, the consciousness of the *temporal* features of states of substances might be explained entirely in terms of the grasping of the intuitional framework of time.

This account of time-consciousness in terms of an intuitional framework explains how we represent simultaneity and earlier-later relations between states of substances *i*. To represent past, present, and future *ii*, the intuitional framework would have to be enriched by adding a central or focal temporal location. The temporal location that "stands out" is the present; whatever is earlier than this location is past, and whatever is later is future. However, as I explained in section 2.4, either a two-level non-temporal consciousness or a present that changed its temporal location would be necessary for the experience of temporal passage. Although Kant does not specifically explain the experience of temporal passage, it is clear that he would employ a two-level account (see *v* below).

The major deficiency of a form of intuition account of time-consciousness is that it is unable to represent the *objectivity* of experienced temporal features *iii*. The objectivity of these temporal features depends upon *understanding* that there is an objective standard in terms of which specific experienced temporal features are justified and verified. Experienced earlier-later relations reveal objective earlier-later relations in virtue of conforming to this objective standard. If experienced earlier-later relations are supposed to conform to the objective standard but fail to conform, they do not reveal an objective temporal order, although they purport to reveal such an order. Even to claim that our experienced temporal features are objective requires reference to such an objective standard. Thus, understanding concepts is necessary for a Kantian theory of knowledge of objective temporal facts, because understanding concepts is necessary in order even to think of states of substances being in objective temporal order (Kant himself argues this in the Second Analogy).

Since a form of intuition account of time-consciousness cannot explain how we can even think of our intuited temporal features as objective, it alone cannot explain *iv*, how we OKCs confirm or justify our claims about the objectivity of temporal features. Even the role that Kant does assign to intuition in confirming the objectivity of a represented temporal order is an entirely derivative one. In both the Second and Third Analogies of Experience,[20] Kant considers the order of the *perceivings* of sensory data to be indicative of the objective temporal order of what is perceived. If the perceiving of *a* precedes the perceiving of *b*, we know that *b* did not objectively precede *a*. However, since the temporal order of perceivings (intuitings) is not by itself a perceiving (intuiting) of temporal order, an account must still be given of how we represent the perceiving of *a* as preceding the perceiving of *b*. The account that Kant does give is a synthetic activity account, not the form of intuition account.

We OKCs can and do revise our claims about the objective temporal order of states of substances. Whereas we may initially have thought that the order was *a* then *c* then *b*, we may come to think that the order was *a* then *b* then *c*. Such revisions require that there be numerically distinct representations of the objective temporal order. These numerically distinct representations must succeed each other in time (or at least appear to succeed each other) if a later, improved representation is to replace an earlier, mistaken representation.

The form of intuition account could explain *v*, how the claims of OKC can at least appear to be in time so that they can change, by introducing two levels of consciousness, each with its own form of time. The transcendental ego (TE) would have its own temporal framework of intuition. States of OKC, each with its own temporal framework of intuition, would be located at the temporal locations of the TE's framework of time (see Diagram 4.2). Thus, states of OKC would appear to be in time and the claims of OKC could change. This two-level analysis could also attempt to explain the experience of temporal passage in terms of the later states of OKC having later temporal locations in their frameworks as present. These focal (present) temporal locations need not, however, make any claim to objectivity, and so there would be no necessity that they conform to an objective "moving present."

This two-level account brings out the actual role of the temporal

Diagram 4.2

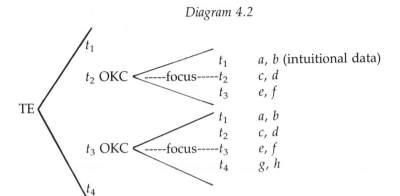

form of intuition in Kant's theory. Kant does have a two-level account of time-consciousness and time, but time as a form of intuition operates at only one of these levels. The non-temporal transcendental ego has a temporal form of intuition through which it experiences its mental life (that of OKC) to be in time. This is Kant's doctrine of inner sense.

Inner sense is the characteristic of the non-temporal transcendental ego in virtue of which the TE intuits the *ordinary knowing consciousness* as spread out through an earlier-later time.[21] In inner sense I as TE intuit myself as OKC, and since time is the form of inner sense, OKC exists (for the TE) as spread out through time. Considered without the contribution of understanding and imagination, there is nothing more to the OKC than the occurrence of intuitional data at different dates (that "I think" each of these intuitional data depends upon understanding). Thus, that intuitional data occur at different dates is the original and necessary (but not sufficient) condition of OKC being in time.

This account of inner sense makes sense of those passages, particularly in the Transcendental Aesthetic, where Kant claims that time is not originally a structure of outer intuition: "Time is nothing but the form of inner sense, that is, of the intuition of ourselves and our inner state. It cannot be a determination of outer appearances; it has to do neither with shape nor position, but with the relation of representations in our inner state."[22] Rather than portraying time and space as *equally* primordial forms of intuition so that there would be a spatial-temporal form of intuition, Kant portrays time as the form *only* of inner sense. Time applies to the spatial world and the appearances in the spatial world only *indirectly*, presumably because *each moment* of OKC's outer intuition has a spatial form.

> Time is the formal *a priori* condition of all appearances whatsoever. Space, as the pure form of all *outer* intuition, is so far limited; it serves as the *a priori* condition only of outer appearances. But since all representations, whether they have for their objects outer things or not, belong, in themselves, as determinations of the mind, to our inner state; and since this inner state stands under the formal condition of inner intuition, and so belongs to time, time is an *a priori* condition of all appearance whatsoever. It is the immediate condition of inner appearances (of our souls), and thereby the mediate condition of outer appearances.[23]

This priority of time indicates that there might be some unity of the OKC through time that *does not depend* upon the OKC's representation of outer entities. In section 4.2B I will consider such a "merely subjective unity."

Although all the moments of OKC exist in the TE's inner sense, this *alone* does not provide for a sufficient unity through time of OKC. First of all, without the activity of understanding and imagination, even the TE does not understand the temporal relations between moments of OKC with their intuitional data. The TE would have temporal relations "before the mind" in intuition but would not comprehend either the relations or the data related. The TE's understanding of temporal entities is dependent upon the same activities that unify OKC.

More importantly, *at the level* of ordinary knowing consciousness (OKC) there would be no unification through time of this data. While the TE, like God, has all moments of time *equally* before its mind, the experience of OKC is *centered at particular dates* because OKC is spread out in time. *At* time t_3 OKC has available only the intuitional data received at that time. *At* time t_3 OKC does not have "before the mind" the intuitional data that are received at times t_1, t_2, t_4, and so on (a form of intuition account of OKC's time-consciousness stipulates that it does have this other data "before the mind," as in Diagram 4.2, but does not explain how this occurs). In order that *at any given time* OKC can represent anything that extends through time, it must rely upon more than what is currently present in intuition. A phase of OKC must have some access to intuitional data from other times. If it is ever to know about things that extend through time, a phase of OKC *at any given time* must be able to represent occurrences at other times as being objective. A form of intuition account of OKC's time-consciousness is inadequate for this purpose. Kant employed a synthetic activity account to explain OKC's time-consciousness.

4.2B   The Synthetic Activity Accounts

Throughout the Transcendental Logic, Kant develops a complex theory of time-consciousness based on the synthetic activity of understanding and imagination. I will argue that Kant actually developed two supplementary theories, one that concerns OKC's understanding of an objective temporal order of states of substances and one that concerns OKC's awareness of a merely subjective succession of mental states. *Both* of these theories presuppose that OKC occurs in time. Synthetic activity to unify intuitional data is necessary because these data are spread out in time. Since Kant claims that time is not real (see section 4.4), the occurrence of intuitional data (and OKC) in time must be dependent upon some feature of consciousness. As I explained in section 4.2A, the TE's intuition of itself through the form of intuition of time produces the temporal separation. Synthetic activity joins together the temporally separated intuitional data.

Kant's two supplementary synthetic activity theories of OKC's time-consciousness depend upon many of the same synthetic activities. In order to build up to the theories of time-consciousness, I will start by explicating the synthetic activity included in the use of concepts. The synthetic activity underlying the use of those *pure* concepts (the Categories) through which we think of substances in objective time is the basis for one of Kant's theories of time-consciousness.

Kant views understanding as an active faculty that comprehends the meaning of concepts and uses concepts in judgments. In addition to the merely given intuitional data of experience, there is the organization of this data according to types. According to Kant, there are two fundamental types of concepts: empirical concepts that are based in intuitional data, and pure concepts that are not. Hence, there are two types of types that may apply to intuitional data.

The understanding of a concept is the comprehension of a type.

Concepts are always used in judgments, where either intuitional data or other concepts are comprehended according to types. Types are not given in intuition, so that the understanding has to "assemble" them by synthesizing activity. Thus, there is both an activity and the product of that activity included in understanding concepts. The activity is that of mentally putting together, with the aid of imagination, the constituents of the type: "By *synthesis*, in its most general sense, I understand the act of putting different representations together, and of grasping what is manifold in them in one [act of] knowledge."[24] The product of the activity is the grasped type. In a judgment there is a dual result: the grasping of the type and the comprehension of something as fitting under the type.

The application of these notions to sensory universals is fairly straightforward. The meaning of a sensory concept is directly tied to sensory (intuitional) data that are given and possibly given. To understand a sensory concept such as "red" is to grasp what this (red) datum has in common with that (red) datum and with many other actual and possible (red) data. The product of the activity is the comprehended commonness of the many instances or the comprehended class. At any time most of the instances or members of the class are not given in intuition so that mental activity is necessary to assemble them. Understanding, with imagination as a subordinate faculty, produces for itself and brings together the many instances of red and comprehends them as the same.

The three pure concepts of relation (substance-accident, cause-effect, reciprocal interaction) are more complicated than sensory universals because they have as instances *ordered series* of unspecified sensory data, rather than the qualitative content of the sensory data. This set of pure concepts constitutes the idea of an object of experience; to understand our sensory data in terms of these concepts is to understand these data *as* the appearances of objects.[25] It is by understanding data through these pure concepts that the subject-object split is thought. The way in which these pure concepts convert mere sensory data into appearances of objects is by imposing a complex order on the sensory data. Only those sensory data that have a particular complex spatial and temporal order are the appearances of one object.[26] This complex spatial and temporal order of appearances provides the objectivity of objects. Our claims about states of objects have to conform to this order to portray states of objects at all (*iii*).

These pure concepts alone do not specify *which specific* sensory data will be ordered in the ways that they require. They specify only an order to which *any* set of sensory data must conform to be the appearances of an enduring substance. This order itself is rather formal and schematic. Different types of objective substances may be different; a great deal of further experiential information would be required in order to determine which sets of appearances are allowable cases of water enduring through change and which sets of appearances are allowable cases of a tree enduring through change. Kant does not address these issues concerning concepts for empirical substances,[27] precisely because of their empirical element. He believes that transcendental philosophy can deal only with the formal elements.

A temporal order of actual and possible appearances is specified for every object or set of interacting objects by these pure concepts. It is through these temporal orders of appearances that substances are understood to endure through time, to interact causally with each other, and to change their states over time through the causal interactions. Experienced objective time is composed of these temporal relations of actually and possibly appearing states of substances.

Understanding concepts includes both synthetic activity and a synthesized result. The pure concepts of relation portray complex ordered series of unspecified sensory data. The main synthesis of these pure concepts is that of putting together *in order* the elements of the complex ordered series. At the level of OKC, the result of the synthetic activity is the comprehension (at every moment of OKC) of the complex ordered series, that is, the understanding of which appearances are earlier than, later than, and simultaneous with each other. Considered without any intuitional data, what is comprehended is just a formal pattern into which intuitional data would have to fit to be the appearances of an object (a substance in causal interaction with other substances). The many instances of this formal pattern, that is, the fact that there are many substances in the empirically encountered world that fit under this same formal pattern, depend upon the actual empirically received intuitional data.

There are two supplementary synthetic activity theories in Kant's writings. The first concerns OKC's understanding of the objective temporal order of states of substances. This theory relies upon the synthetic activity that I have just discussed, that of understanding objective events through the pure concepts of relation. The second concerns OKC's awareness of its own mental life as occurring in time. Kant himself emphasized the understanding-based theory because it provided for *a priori* knowledge of the physical world. He emphasized this theory to such an extent that most commentators have taken it to be his only theory of OKC's time-consciousness.[28] In light of Kant's emphasis on the understanding-based theory, I will devote the most attention to it. I will later explain the Awareness of Reproductive Activity theory, which provides for OKC's awareness of a merely subjective succession.

The understanding-based theory of time-consciousness explains our (OKC's) ability to know *a priori* the essential features of time in terms of our understanding of the complex spatial and temporal order of appearances that is prescribed by the pure concepts of relation. We OKCs do not have to investigate empirically any or all periods of time to know about their essential characteristics. Since temporal features are defined by the pure concepts, and we always think in terms of these concepts, we have available to our understanding that which defines the temporal features of all periods of time. The understanding-based theory does not have any trouble with the infinitude of time either in the forward or the backward direction. OKCs are able to think that temporally ordered series go on and on infinitely without having to have a completed infinite series given in intuition.

i. It is in terms of our understanding of the temporal order in the series of appearances that Kant's understanding-based account of time-consciousness explains how we OKCs think of or represent temporal relations between states of substances. The earlier-later relations and most of the simultaneity relations between states of substances are not intuitionally given; they are not fully present to consciousness. Yet they are experienced; conceptual representing brings before consciousness what is absent in the intuitional respect. These temporal relations are conceptually represented via our representing of the complex ordered series (with its temporal parameter) of appearances (see *ii*, below, for more detail on how this is done). Kant's most explicit discussion of this is in the Second Analogy of Experience, where he explores the connection between objective earlier-later relations and universal causality. He should also discuss earlier-later relations within one substance that is not causally changed by external forces, that is, the endurance through time of states of substances, in the First Analogy, but Kant's equivocation on the notion of substance (substance as matter versus substance as individual thing with properties) prevents him from doing so. The Third

Analogy treats (quickly and unsatisfactorily) simultaneity relations between states of substances.

ii. OKC does, at any given time, have intuitionally given sensory data present to it. These intuitions are the nucleus for representing the present. Whatever is understood to be simultaneous with these appearances is understood to be temporally in the present. Whatever is understood to be earlier or later than the states that are present is temporally past or future.

States that are past, future, or non-locally present are not fully present to consciousness; that is, they are not at the relevant time intuitionally given. It is these that have to be brought before consciousness by the synthetic activity of understanding and imagination.[29] In the 1781 version of the Transcendental Deduction, Kant provides his only detailed account of how this "bringing before consciousness" operates. As I will explain later, this detailed account actually involves a second synthetic activity theory of (subjective) time-consciousness. Since most commentators have interpreted this account as an instance only of the understanding-based theory, I will first explain that view.

Kant's detailed account of bringing before consciousness what is not currently given in intuition considers *only* past states that were previously intuited. Presumably this is because the synthetic unification of these into one experience is the minimum necessary for the building up of empirical knowledge and the refinement of empirical concepts for different substances.[30] Without this basic unification of what we have actually intuited over time, we could not develop our empirical understanding of the world.

The activity of bringing previously intuited past states before consciousness is described in terms of three syntheses: the synthesis of apprehension in intuition, the synthesis of reproduction in imagination, and the synthesis of recognition in a concept. Kant is quite clear that the first two are not separate activities at all,[31] and there is good reason to think that the third is not a distinct activity either.

Kant recognizes that the mere order of being intuited does not equal the intuition of order, because each set of data is intuitionally present for a different phase of OKC.

> For each representation, *in so far as it is contained in a single moment*, can never be anything but absolute unity. In order that unity of intuition may arise out of this manifold (as is required

in the representation of space) it must first be run through, and held together. This act I name the synthesis of apprehension.[32]

Since the intuited sensory data at different times are temporally dispersed, they must be brought together and held together. This "bringing and holding together" is portrayed as *reproducing at the later time* the sensory content that has just occurred.

> When I seek to draw a line in thought, or to think of the time from one noon to another, or even to represent to myself some particular number, obviously the various manifold representations that are involved must be apprehended by me in thought one after the other. But if I were always to drop out of thought the preceeding representations (the first parts of the line, the antecedent parts of the time period, or the units in the order represented), and did not reproduce them while advancing to those that follow, a complete representation would never be obtained: none of the above mentioned thoughts, not even the purest and most elementary representations of space and time could arise.[33]

Reproducing what has just occurred at a later time would produce the situation depicted in Diagram 4.3. It should be clear that the synthesis of apprehension is here accomplished by the synthesis of reproduction.[34]

However, mere reproducing in imagination will not portray the reproduced data as having occurred just previously. There is the question, common to all present representation theories of time-consciousness, how presently existing information can portray or refer to the past.

> If we were not conscious that what we think is the same as what we thought a moment before, all reproduction in the series of

Diagram 4.3

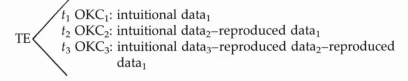

TE
t_1 OKC$_1$: intuitional data$_1$
t_2 OKC$_2$: intuitional data$_2$–reproduced data$_1$
t_3 OKC$_3$: intuitional data$_3$–reproduced data$_2$–reproduced data$_1$

representations would be useless. For it would in its present state be a new representation which would not in any way belong to the act whereby it was gradually generated.[35]

According to the understanding-based theory, Kant's solution to this question is provided by his account of the pure concepts of relation. There are two possible versions of this.

First, reproductive activity does its job automatically, producing the situation depicted in Diagram 4.3. At each date we then apply to the data (intuited and reproduced) the pure concepts of relation, which specify an objective temporal order of sensory data. The temporal order specified in the pure concepts is what portrays the reproduced data as having occurred previously and in a specific order. Not all the reproduced data fit under the temporal order specified by the pure concepts; such anomalous data are not referred to the past and are not considered to be appearances of objects. Our recognition of reproduced data as past is no different from our recognition of non-perceived appearances (non-intuited data) as past; the only difference is that reproduced data are already before the mind.

Second, reproductive activity is a special form of the synthetic activity of "putting together in order" the elements of the complex ordered series that is thought through the pure concepts of relation. According to this version, reproductive activity is guided by pure concepts; the pure concepts are rules for reproducing (as well as for other types of bringing an ordered series before the mind): "Their reproduction must, therefore, conform to a rule, in accordance with which a representation connects in imagination with some one representation in preference to another."[36] This rule-governed reproducing activity does not merely reproduce earlier sensory data; it reproduces these data *as joined* to other data in a complex ordered series generated by the rules. It is the place of the reproduced datum in this ordered series that marks it *as past* and that reveals whether it is earlier, or later, or simultaneous with *other* past data. Thus, reproduced sensory data are recognized as past in the same way that non-reproduced, non-perceived appearances are. Both are recognized as past through the temporal order of appearances that are specified by the pure concepts. Both are brought before the mind by the synthetic activity included in understanding concepts.

According to either version, the representation of the non-directly perceived (non-intuited) present, of the past, and of the future, is accomplished in the same general way. The other sides of perceived objects and other present states that are not in our perceptual field are brought before consciousness by imagination (with some differences from those reproduced) and understood to be simultaneous with directly perceived present appearances. These non-directly perceived appearances are portrayed as what *would be perceived* if we were differently located. The non-perceived past is understood in the same way, and the same applies to future states of objects except that these appearances can or could be perceived.

iii. OKC represents or claims that specific temporal relations are *objective* by means of the formal requirements on any complex of sensory data that is to be the set of appearances of an object. As I explained earlier, these formal requirements concerning spatial and temporal orders of appearances specify what it is to be states of objects in causal interaction with other objects. A set of sensory data that conforms to these requirements and that continues to conform to the requirements as new data are added to the set is a set of appearances of one object. The temporal order of these appearances is objective.[37]

It is noteworthy that the standard defining the objectivity of a conceived temporal order is a formal one. Objectivity is not a matter of *correspondence* of the conceived temporal order to a real temporal order. Yet there *is* a temporal order to the intuition of sensory data. Each state of OKC exists at a date, and each intuits its own sensory data. However, this temporal order of intuitings is *represented* in OKC only through understanding (see *ii*), and the standard for a correct objective temporal order is a formal one. The second synthetic activity theory, which is a supplement to the understanding-based theory, provides a way for OKC to represent its earlier intuitings without claiming that the intuitional data represent an objective temporal order.

iv. OKC confirms or justifies the objectivity of its claims concerning temporal relations through receiving and seeking out further appearances that should occur if its current understanding of states of substances is correct. Past and non-perceived present appearances cannot be sought out; claims about past and non-perceived present states can be confirmed only by the consistency (according to the formal requirements) of what is intuited with what should appear (now and later) if these past and present states did exist.[38] If an expanded set of sensory data turns out not to conform to the formal requirements, then the appearances are not the appearances of one object (or the set of interacting objects) that we thought. In this case the claimed temporal relations are not objective, and the appearances need to be reconceptualized. The formal requirements specify necessary but not sufficient observational conditions for objectivity. Further appearances can *disconfirm* putative objective temporal orders, but can never confirm them conclusively.

The process of assembling empirical confirmation for the objectivity of OKC's claims takes place over time. OKC must be able to "keep in mind" what it has previously experienced while it is adding new intuitional data. This "keeping in mind" of previous intuitional data has to be *distinct from* claims about the objective temporal order if these claims are to be able to be disconfirmed by the set of intuitional data. If at time t_2 previous sensory data (intuited at time t_1) were represented *only* by being thought through the pure concepts of relation, there could not be any disconfirmation. The data that were thought to precede present appearances would always accord with present claims about objective temporal order because these data would be "before the mind" only as an instance of the objective temporal order. Hence, confirming the objectivity of claims about objective temporal order requires that there be some independence of imagination from understanding. The second version of reproductive activity (see *ii*) that considers it to be just a special form of the synthetic activity of pure concepts cannot explain the process of empirical confirmation. The first version does give some independence to reproductive activity and so could give some account of the process of empirical confirmation. However, as I will explain shortly, there is a better explanation that involves a second theory of (subjective) time-consciousness.

v. As I have presented the understanding-based account, it presupposes that OKC is spread out in time. That OKC is (or appears to be) in time is the result of the transcendental ego's earlier-later form of intuition. The non-temporal transcendental ego experiences its own mental life (that of OKC) to occur in an earlier-later time. This explains how OKC can have at different times distinct intuitional data. That OKC *at each time* applies the pure concepts through which objective temporal order is thought to different sets of intuitional data (although there is a problem about how these sets are assembled) explains how OKC can revise its claims about the objective temporal order. A later, improved representation of the objective temporal order can succeed an earlier, mistaken representation because the representing occurs at different times.

The understanding-based theory of OKC's time-consciousness is able to explain most of the features concerning *a priori* and *a posteriori* knowledge of time that I discussed in section 4.1. The assembling of empirical confirmation for the objectivity of claims about temporal order (*iv*) presents the only problem. Kant emphasized this understanding-based theory because he was concerned with knowledge of the objective world. The understanding-based theory, however, limits the experienced unity through time of OKC. Phases of OKC are unified only with respect to representing the objective world. "Keeping anything in mind" is restricted to outward-directed claims about the objective temporal succession of states of substances. There is no account of the unity through time of feelings, emotions, and intentions. In all his discussions of practical reason, Kant recognizes that we are aware of ourselves as agents in time that act in time. Such practically acting agents require unity of consciousness through time. We are aware of what we have just felt, what our emotional experience has just been, and what we have been doing. The understanding-based theory *alone* does not allow this "subjective" unity.

There is a second synthetic activity theory in Kant's writings that supplements the understanding-based theory. This second theory, which is based in the reproductive activity of imagination, provides for "subjective unity," that is, the unity of OKC's experience through time without any claims about the outer world. The imagination-based theory, which I call the "Awareness of Reproductive Activity" theory, requires a different interpretation of the three syntheses that underlie time-consciousness.

Kant's only detailed account of how we "bring before consciousness" sensory data that are not given in intuition *at that time* involves the reproduction in the present of sensory data that were previously intuited. The understanding-based theory explains the reference of these reproduced data to the past by means of the ordered series of appearances specified by the pure concepts of relation (see the discussion of *ii*). The Awareness of Reproductive Activity theory explains the reference of reproduced data to the past by means of our faint awareness of the *activity of reproducing*. Reproduced data are marked *as reproduced*, that is, as having been brought into the present from an earlier (past) time at which they were intuited. That the reproduced data are produced by an activity that "picks up" earlier information and transfers it to a later time is how the reproduced data connect with the past. Our faint awareness of the reproduced data as the *result* of this activity is that through which the data refer to the past. Thus, *at any given time* OKC is aware of a temporally extended *experiencing*. It is aware of having previously been aware of certain data. Thus, in contrast with the understanding-based theory, OKC *can be* (though it usually is not) aware of having previously experienced certain data independently of understanding those data to be part of the objective temporal order of appearances of spatial objects.

Several passages express the Awareness of Reproductive Activity theory:

> If we were not conscious that what we think is the same as what we thought a moment before, all reproduction in the series of representations would be useless. For it would in its present state be a new representation which would not in any way belong to the act whereby it was gradually generated.[39]

> The word 'concept' might of itself suggest this remark. For this unitary consciousness is what combines the manifold, successively intuited, and thereby also reproduced, into one representation. This consciousness may often be only faint, so that we do not connect it with the act itself, that is, not in any direct manner with the *generation* of the representation, but only with the outcome [that which is thereby represented]. But notwithstanding these variations, such consciousness, however indistinct, must always be present; without it, concepts, and therewith knowledge of objects, are altogether impossible.[40]

Since Kant wanted to *identify* the unity of consciousness (synthetic unity of apperception) with *understanding* sensory data (through the Categories) as the appearances of external objects, he usually collapses the synthesis of imagination into the synthesis of pure conceptualization. However, even when Kant does subsume imagination under conceptualization, as in the above passage, he is *relying upon the awareness of reproductive activity to establish the reference of reproduced data to the past.* The reproduced data refer to the past because we recognize them as reproduced by an activity of consciousness, not because of their place in an abstract order. The Awareness of Reproductive Activity theory is invoked even if the reproductive activity is considered to be a part of conceptualization.[41]

Kant never explains the nature of this faint awareness of reproductive activity, whether or not it is part of the synthetic activity included in concepts. Concerning concepts, Kant recognizes that synthetic activity is an essential feature, but he does not emphasize that to be *aware of this activity* is something more than just to be aware of the result of the activity without recognizing it as a result.[42] Kant regularly appeals, in the notion of the unity of apperception, to the awareness of our thoughts as forming a unity through time. Perhaps because he thought that the unity of apperception was a fundamental and inexplicable requirement, Kant just assumes that we can be aware of synthetic activity and does not offer a theory of the cognitive faculties involved.

Kant never fully explored the Awareness of Reproductive Activity theory. In the revised 1787 edition of *The Critique of Pure Reason*, the detailed account of the three syntheses of time-consciousness was removed entirely. Kant still assumes that we are aware of our previous thoughts as past so that we can be aware of a merely subjective succession, but he does not develop this theory of OKC's time-consciousness. The later phenomenologists who were influenced by Kant's imagination-based theory had to rely upon limited texts, particularly the text concerning the three syntheses.

4.3   The Temporal Nature of the Experiencer

Both the imagination-based and the understanding-based theories of OKC's time-consciousness presuppose a split between the OKC that seems to occur within time and the non-temporal transcendental ego that has time as a framework of experience. This split is necessary in order that time can be *only* a structure of consciousness, even though we experience past-present-future features and *change* our claims about the world.

The non-temporal transcendental ego represents an earlier-later framework of time, within which states of OKC and intuitional data occur. The transcendental ego's representing of this form of intuition does not occur in time or have any temporal properties. The synthetic activities that are necessary for OKC's time-consciousness are also characteristics of the transcendental ego. The transcendental ego's activities of imagination and understanding produce its comprehension of OKC's existence through time. These synthetic activities must also be non-temporal, since there is no mind-independent time within which they could occur. That activities can be non-temporal is a difficult notion to understand, but it is central to Kant's thought both in theoretical and moral philosophy.

The notion of a non-temporal subject of consciousness is an essential factor in Kant's conception of the moral agent. Thinking that free will was necessary for moral responsibility, but that free will could not occur in time, Kant located the ultimate agent of morality outside of time.[43] Such an agent is active and somehow makes decisions about whether to be moral or not, but its activity is non-temporal and does not change.

> Now this acting subject would not, in its intelligible character, stand under any conditions of time; time is only a condition of appearance, not of things in themselves. In this subject no *action* would *begin* or *cease*, and it would not, therefore, have to conform to the law of determination of all that is alterable in time, namely, that everything *which happens* must have its cause in the *appearances* which precede it.[44]

There are notorious problems with Kant's conceptions of non-temporal freedom and non-temporal activity in his moral philosophy. My objective here is not either to clarify or to critique these conceptions. I want only to point out how central Kant's notion of a non-temporal transcendental ego, particularly a non-temporally active transcendental ego, is to his philosophical thought.

The transcendental ego's synthetic activities do not occur in time, but they do *concern* time. Synthetic activities could not occur without the form of intuition of an earlier-later time, which provides the initial separation of that which is to be synthesized. The reproductive activity of imagination operates *across* this earlier-later time by picking up information at an earlier date and reproducing it at a later time. The activity of understanding produces the transcendental ego's comprehension of the entire temporally extended and changing conscious life of OKC.

In contrast with the transcendental ego, OKC is essentially temporal, even though it exists only as represented by the transcendental ego. States of OKC occur at moments of time, but the moments of time and the states (at least *as* temporal) do not exist independently of their being represented. Since time as a form of intuition is continuous, there is a state of OKC at every moment of the appropriate period of this earlier-later time. However, the unity of these states with each other depends upon the synthetic activities of imagination and understanding. In light of the synthetic activities of understanding and imagination, how does OKC exist through time?

If understanding were the sole source of OKC's time-consciousness, which would be limited to claims about objective temporal order, there would be little unity through time to OKC. As I explained in section 4.2B, the understanding-based theory explains the representation of other times by means of the application *at each moment* of the Categories (and the empirical concepts developed in previous experience). According to this account each moment of OKC would be relatively separate. First of all, the occurrence in a later state of OKC of sensory data that was intuited in an earlier state would not be explained in terms of some activity that *stretches through time* from one state of OKC to another. It is not the earlier intuiting or some process connecting the earlier intuiting with the later state that explains the later (reproduced) data. The data is produced entirely by understanding (with its subordinate imagination). The (reproduced) data is produced in exactly the same way as non-perceived data, namely, by understanding what must have been earlier than the presently intuited appearances. Second, there would be no unity through time of "subjective" features such as intentions, feelings, and emotions.

The addition of the imagination-based theory of OKC's time-consciousness provides for a much greater unity of OKC through time. OKC's later states are dependent upon its earlier states for the representation of temporal extension. Only by maintaining (through reproductive activity) the sensory data intuited by the earlier state is OKC able to portray temporal extension at all. In being aware of the data *as reproduced* from its earlier states, OKC is aware of a temporally extended experiencing. Furthermore, since any type of conscious content can be reproduced, OKC can be aware of its own temporally extended intentions, feelings, and emotions. We can be aware of ourselves as agents engaged in temporally extended actions.

4.4   Temporal Idealism

Kant maintained that things-in-themselves were real, but that time was not. Although he never really presented an argument for the independent existence of things-in-themselves, he took them to be real because he conceived human intuition to be *receptive* in nature. In contrast to an originating intuition that would create its object, human intuition "is dependent upon the existence of the object, and is therefore possible only if the subject's faculty of representation is affected by that object."[45] Things-in-themselves were thought to be the source of intuitional data. According to either of the two major interpretations of affection (see section 4.2A), intuitional data "come from" something independent of the mind.

Time is *only* a framework of experience, not a feature of independently real things, according to Kant. He has two main arguments in support of this thesis. The first is the argument from the Transcendental Aesthetic that only if time is only a framework of our experience can we know *a priori* the essential features of time. The second is the argument in the First Antinomy that time is essentially contradictory. Since what is inherently contradictory cannot exist on its own, time cannot be real.

The argument from the possibility of *a priori* knowledge of the essential features of time is presented by Kant in support of time being only a framework of *intuition*. With certain modifications concerning the *synthetic* character of the propositions supposedly known *a priori*,[46] this same argument could be used to support the notion that time is only a combined *intuited and understood* framework for all experience. The features of the argument that are important for the realism or idealism of time do not depend on whether the earlier-later temporal framework is intuited or understood. At the level of the non-temporal transcendental ego, there are not many important differences between these alternatives.

Kant claims that we can and do know *apodictically* the essential features of time (see section 4.1). We know basic things about time that hold for all possible regions of time. Such knowledge has to be known *a priori* because empirical investigation could never justify such absolutely certain and fully general claims. In fact, empirical investigation itself always presupposes a spatial and temporal context within which it takes place. To obtain empirical information about a region of space or time, we have to know where to look, that is, from where the information is supposed to come.

The only possible way in which we could have such *a priori* knowledge of time and of space (Geometry), according to Kant, is if time and space are structures of our minds, not independently real existents. To know an independently real time and space we would have to have some type of access to it, but the only type of knowing access that we could have, through empirical observation, would not provide for "absolutely necessary and universally valid truths."[47] Since we do have *a priori* knowledge of time and space, time and space must be only mental frameworks whose structuring of any possible experience can be known.[48]

If this first argument were successful, it would establish *only* that the time about which we know *a priori* was not independently real. It would not establish that there was no real time. At most, assuming the truth of Kant's claims about the human mind's abilities to know, it would establish that we cannot know about any real time. However, Kant regularly draws the stronger conclusion that there could be no real time in addition to the time that is a structure of our minds.

> Time is therefore a purely subjective condition of our (human) intuition . . . and in itself, apart from the subject is nothing.[49]

> We deny to time all claim to absolute reality; that is to say, we deny that it belongs to things absolutely, as their condition or property, independently of any reference to the form of our sensible intuition.[50]

One reason why Kant draws this stronger conclusion is that if there were a real, absolute time (and space), there would be "two eternal and self-subsistent non-entities (space and time) which are there (yet without there being anthing real) only in order to contain in themselves all that is real."[51] Kant claims that such a real time and space would be limitations on God, which he rejects for religious reasons.[52] Another reason seems to be that if things-in-themselves were really temporal, we should be able to receive temporal relations between intuitional data, because the affecting would occur in a real time. The reception of temporal relations would contradict Kant's notion of an intuitional datum as a singular sensation.[53]

Kant's first argument for the ideality of time has been decisively refuted in the last two hundred years by the accumulating evidence that real time and space are not exactly the same as experienced time and space. This has shown that Kant's assumption that we actually know *a priori* about the essential features of time and space was wrong. The hypothetical claim (if we know *a priori*, then time is ideal) may still be disputed, but the antecedent has proven to be false.

Kant's second argument for the ideality of time *would*, if success-ful, *establish* that there was no real time. This argument from the First Antinomy claims that time is essentially contradictory because time is such that the world must be thought both to have a begin-ning and not to have a beginning in time. Since what is inherently contradictory cannot exist on its own, time cannot be real. However, we can have contradictory thoughts, so that time can exist as some-thing conceived or intuited by consciousness.

In the First Antinomy Kant attempts to prove that if time were real, then it could be proven both that the world necessarily has a beginning in time and that the world necessarily has no beginning in time. This Antinomy argument relies upon a past-present-future conception of time. The thesis argument assumes that time intrin-sically passes so that "if we assume that the world has no beginning in time, then up to every given moment an eternity has elapsed, and there has passed away in the world an infinite series of successive states of things."[54] The crucial notion is that an infinite series cannot be "run through" from its beginning to an end.[55] Assuming that the "present" continuously passes from earlier to later moments in time and thus from earlier to later states of the world, the "present" could never reach any specific date and any specific state of the world if an infinite time preceded the specific state or date. If there were no first state of the world, a "present" that passes from earlier to later dates could not arrive at any specific state unless it had already *passed through* an infinite number of states. According to Kant's definition of an infinite series, the "present" could not pass through an infinite number of states. Thus the world must be finite in time; it must have had a beginning.

The thesis argument could be formulated simply in terms of time without any specific reference to states of the world. It depends entirely upon a particular conception of infinity and certain features of a past-present-future time. One major problem with the argument is the past-present-future notion of a moving present. As I explain in section 9.4, many thinkers have challenged the intelligibility of a "changing present." However, if the passage of the present is intel-ligible but involves two temporal series (see section 9.4), Kant's thesis argument would be less convincing because the present would have passed through an infinite series of dates (t_1, t_2, t_3, . . . t_n) *in an infinite period of time* (T_1, T_2, T_3, . . . T_n).

The antithesis argument attempts to prove in a basically Leib-nizian way that the world has no beginning in time. Kant's argument is that if the world did begin in time, "there must have been a preceding time in which the world was not, i.e., an empty time."[56] Kant claims that since there is no way to distinguish one moment of such an empty time from another, we cannot meaningfully refer to one moment of such a time. If we cannot refer to any of its moments, we cannot refer to such an empty time at all. Kant concludes in a verificationist way that there cannot be such an empty time, so that the world must always have existed.

The main problem with the antithesis argument is the use of the verificationist claim that if we cannot know it or cannot refer to it, it cannot be. In the First Antinomy Kant claims to be proving that *if* time were real, contradictory claims about the world could be proven. The assumption for both the thesis and the antithesis argument is that time is real. Given Kant's notion of reality as "independent existence," reality is not subject to our ability to know it or to refer to it. Hence, there is no reason to conclude from the supposed unknowability of an empty time to its non-existence.

4.5   Problems

In explicating Kant's theory I have already noted most of the major problems. I will here just list these difficulties without repeating the earlier discussions.

1. Kant does not provide sufficient justification for the split between a non-temporal transcendental ego and an OKC that seems to itself to be in time, but is really only represented by the transcendental ego as being in time. Since our lived experience is at the level of OKC, it would be difficult to establish that we are ultimately non-temporal transcendental egos.

2. Kant does not devote enough attention to the imagination-based theory that provides for the awareness of unity of "subjective" consciousness through time. How this theory can coexist with and supplement the understanding-based theory is never explored. The relationship of the two structures of time-consciousness is of tremendous importance for a Kantian epistemology.

3. The understanding-based theory of time-consciousness presupposes that OKC understands the differences between different types of substances, such as between solids such as rocks and fluids such as water. The understanding of the differences between how these substances behave through time would presumably have to be

built up through empirical observation. However, Kant's account of how OKC represents objective time does not explain how this "building-up" process could take place.

4. Kant's theory does not adequately explain our awareness of temporal passage both in our own mental life and in worldly entities. His two-level theory relies upon the transcendental ego's unchanging awareness of *all* the states of OKC. This would produce an experience of multiple coexistent "presents," rather than an experience of a changing present (see section 9.2B).

5. There is a problem concerning OKC's experience of intuitional data as in time. If OKC exists only as represented by the transcendental ego, OKC cannot receive intuitional data through affection. Only the transcendental ego can receive such data. How then can this data be experienced *by OKC* as data that it can seek out (or not seek out) through further perceptual experiences?

6. Kant's two arguments for the ideality of time, the argument from *a priori* knowledge and the First Antinomy argument, both fail. There is therefore no reason to think that time is mind-dependent.

Kant formulated most of the basic issues about time and time-consciousness, but he was unable to resolve these issues satisfactorily because of his temporal idealism. As I will explain in the next chapter, Husserl's theory of time and time-consciousness, at least in its one-level version in which consciousness occurs in a real time, is able to avoid all these difficulties.

5

Husserl's Theory of
Time-Consciousness and Time

From the late 1890s to his death in 1938, Edmund Husserl refined and modified his phenomenological approach to philosophy. He changed many of his basic positions, including the primary way of entering into phenomenological research. In discussing Husserl's views on time-consciousness, the temporal nature of the experiencer, and temporal realism, I will emphasize the "Cartesian" approach to and method for phenomenology. Husserl advocated this approach and method until his last work, *The Crisis of European Sciences and Transcendental Phenomenology*, and even there, the self-constitution of the primal ego is recognized to be more fundamental than the intersubjective community of transcendental egos that constitute the "life world."[1]

Husserl's phenomenological method is a special type of reflection upon our being conscious. In reflection we observe our own first-order conscious life. All reflection upon consciousness reveals both a variety of conscious orientation (mental act) and that toward which consciousness is oriented (intended object). Ordinary (psychological) reflection assumes the truth of various claims both about the intended objects and about the experiencer. Phenomenological reflection suspends for itself any claims about independent reality. While bracketing for itself any claims about what might transcend the sphere of consciousness, phenomenological reflection investigates what is meant in consciousness and how it is meant. The initial procedure is just to observe without presuppositions and to describe what actually composes our conscious life, that is, what components and features of mental acts allow them to be conscious of all the components and features of the intended objects (as intended). Later, through the procedure of active eidetic variation, the essential natures of mental acts and intended objects are sought through considering possibilities as well as actualities.

The complexities of the intended objects serve as the "guiding thread."[2] For all the multifarious components and features of the intended objects, the phenomenologist seeks the components and features of the mental acts that provide for the awareness of this complexity. Husserl's technical term for this is "constitution." Aspects, components, relations, and activities of mental acts constitute what is meant; that is, they compose the consciousness of it. With some qualifications to be discussed later, Husserl considers temporal features to be the most basic constitutional features because all constituting presupposes them. The temporal parts of conscious life have to be unified if they are to constitute any type of intended object whatsoever.

The interpretation of Husserl's views that I will present draws upon most of his work that is now published and attempts to synthesize positions defended in different contexts.[3] The diversity of the texts and the different periods of their composition means that other interpretations might be viable.

5.1 Experienced Temporal Features

Husserl maintains that phenomenological reflection provides direct access both to the mental act "side" and to the intended object "side" of the "intentional relation." Since features and components of these "sides" are always coordinated with each other, in principle phenomenological investigation could "key on" either one. In practice the complexities of the intended objects always serve as the guiding thread because in ordinary life our attention is focused there; we are initially more sensitive to the differentiations in the intended object.

Picking up one of the traditional problems of time-consciousness, Husserl's investigations up until 1907 were concerned with the question how perception of temporally extended external objects is possible.[4] Husserl considered perception to be the basic form of awareness of the temporal features of external objects because it was the basic form of awareness of external objects in toto. Other forms of intending and knowing external objects all rely upon the basic data provided by perception. Furthermore, other types of mental acts that expressly concern external temporal features themselves presuppose perception. Recollective acts of past occurrences are analyzable as the remembering of the perceiving of the occurrence, and expectational acts of future occurrences are analyzable as the expectation of the perceiving of the occurrence.[5] While recollective and expectational acts do contribute to our overall comprehension of time and temporal objects, Husserl considered perception to include the awareness of all the basic temporal features of external things.

At least during this period, Husserl understood perception to be interestless in nature.[6] Although he considered perception to be very complex (for example, epistemologically in that what is self-given in a perceptual act is only a minute portion of what is meant, namely, the complete physical thing with its specific characteristics), perception proper was considered not to concern a thing's desirableness, usefulness, value, emotional character, or cultural importance.[7] Features such as these belong to higher levels of meaning that are *based upon* the doxic levels; the acts whereby these further characteristics are meant are *founded upon* doxic acts, the most basic of which are perceptual acts.

Given his focus upon the external objects of ordinary perception and his account of perception as interestless, the temporal features with which Husserl was concerned were those that are commonsensically attributed to things in time. Husserl attributes to perceived entities all the six standard features discussed in Chapter 3: temporal location, temporal extension (duration), length of duration, temporal divisibility, earlier-later relations, and past-present-future features. He considers perceived entities to pass from being present to being past, although he does not analyze what this involves in any detail. He does not consider any temporal features other than these ordinary ones.

Starting in 1907 Husserl's focus in his time-consciousness studies shifted to how we are aware of *inner* conscious entities, mental acts and the sensa that are a part of some types of mental acts. In addition to our perception of temporally extended and passing external objects, there is our awareness of our own psychological entities and mental operations as extended and passing in time. With this shift in focus, a two-level theory of time-consciousness was developed. The second level will be discussed in the next section.

The importance of this shift is that the account of the "inner objects" of time-consciousness seems to inherit from the "outer objects" its notion of the relevant temporal features. Inner conscious entities are not explicitly portrayed as having *special temporal features*, but rather are portrayed as having the same temporal features as physical objects in the commonsense conception. This is most obvious when Husserl considers our awareness of inner sensa, which are categorially just like attributes of perceptual objects. Even when he is considering our awareness of (inner) acts, however, these are not explicitly portrayed as having the special forms of temporal location, temporal extensions, and temporal divisibility that they might be thought to have.[8]

5.2   The Awareness of Experienced Temporal Features

Husserl consistently maintained that some levels of consciousness are dependent upon others and that the structure of inner time-consciousness is the most basic level of consciousness. The structure that provides for the awareness of the temporal features of mental acts unifies the phases of mental acts into *one* flow of consciousness. The unity of this flow of consciousness is necessary for all other features of consciousness, including the "intentional relation" between a mental act and its intended object. Husserl's complex analysis of intentionality presupposes the unity through time of the phases of a mental act.

Husserl postulates one structure to explain both external and internal time-consciousness. Whether or not he realizes this, this structure is a theory designed to explain certain data, rather than something that is found in phenomenological reflection. The three-feature structure and retentions of retentions are not given in reflective experience. They are ways of comprehending what is given, namely, the experienced temporal features of mental acts and intended objects (see section 5.1).

The problems of external time-consciousness have traditionally been posed in terms of perception. Starting with the commonsense notion that perception grasps what is simultaneous with it, the question is how it is possible to perceive temporally extended entities and their temporal passage. If each temporal part (phase) of a perceptual act *perceives only* what is simultaneous with it, there would be no perceiving of the whole sequence. A mere succession of independent perceivings is not sufficient; by themselves these are not equivalent to the perceiving of a succession. Rather, what is perceived in each independent perceiving (phase) must be *joined together in a temporal order* with what is perceived in each of the others, and what is joined together must be *perceived together* rather than just abstractly understood.

Our perceptual life is not neatly divided into separate perceptual acts. There is a continuous quality to this parameter as well as to other parameters of mental life. Husserl explicated this continuous quality in terms of the notion of horizons. Although we perceive through different sensory modalities, and at any given time we perceive a great deal of information with any one sensory modality, all this information is (ideally) organized into a wholistic structure. Some things are the focus of awareness, and others are part of the background that contributes to the meaning of what is focused upon. Perceptual acts can be isolated for analytic purposes, but they always essentially exist within a horizonal structure. In the following temporal analyses, I will discuss the successive phases of one perceptual act. It should be kept in mind that the same analysis applies between *any* successive phases of perceptual acts. Thus, the same retentional-protentional structure applies to the last phase of one act and the first phase of a succeeding act.

Abstracting from the differences between one-level and two-level accounts, Husserl's answer to the traditional problems is in his notion of the three features of any perceptual act. A perceptual act-phase (an instantaneous slice of a perceptual act) has one feature that retains earlier phases of the perceptual act, another feature that perceives whatever is present, and a third feature that protends later phases of the perceptual act (see Diagram A.4 in the Appendix). It is through retention's direct contact with earlier perceiving and (more problematically) protention's direct contact with later perceiving that perception *at any given instant* of temporally extended entities can occur.

Truly, however, it pertains to the essence of the intuition of time that in every point of its duration (which, reflectively, we are able to make into an object) it is consciousness of *what has just been* and not mere consciousness of the now-point of the objective thing appearing as having duration.[9]

Husserl contends that any perceptual act-phase *intuits* an object that has duration, that is, a temporally extended portion of the world. At any time, t_n, one feature of the perceptual act-phase perceives what is "now," that is, the object-phase that occurs at t_n. The retentional feature "reaches through time" to contact just-past phases that themselves have a now-consciousness feature that perceives an object-phase given as "now" (at t_{n-1}, t_{n-2}, etc.). Retention grasps the just-past phases as just-past and "looks through" them to their intended objects that are also grasped as just-past. Thus, retention's direct contact with the previous now-consciousness feature is also a direct contact with the object-phase perceived by this feature. Hence, to the presently perceived object-phase there is attached a continuum of just-past perceived object-phases that are experienced as just-past. This continuum of perceived object-phases stretching from the present moment backwards is the temporally extended object as perceived. In the example of the series of notes, we would hear the sequence C–E–G, even though precisely speaking the G alone was present, the E was just-past, and the C was further past.[10]

The notion of retention is the crucial feature in Husserl's solution to the traditional problem of time-consciousness.

> For only in *primary remembrance do we see what is past*; only in it is the past constituted, i.e., *not in a representative but in a presentative way*. The just-having-been, the before in contrast to the now, can be seen directly only in primary remembrance. It is the essence of primary remembrance to bring this new and unique moment to primary, direct intuition, just as it is the essence of the perception of the now to bring the now directly to intuition.[11]

Although retention is actual at one time, its intentional object is at an earlier time. Retention reaches to earlier moments in time and directly intuits earlier moments *as earlier*. As indicated in the above quotation, it is the direct givenness of the past as past. As the unmediated intuition of the past, retention has the same degree of epistemological certainty as any form of direct intuition. Husserl even goes so far as to claim that retention is absolutely certain,[12] probably because he sees no way in which its claims about the just previous phases of mental life might be corrected.

Retention is *of* a just-past act-phase. Since each act-phase itself has a retentional component, a continuum of retained act-phases results; the perceptual act-phase at t_n retains the perceptual act-phase at t_{n-1}, which retains the perceptual act-phase at t_{n-2}, and so on. Husserl notes that as a greater number of act-phases intervene between a retained act-phase and a retaining act-phase, the retained act-phase becomes less clear to retention and merges together with those surrounding it. Expressed in another way, as an act-phase becomes farther from the present, "the greater the blending and drawing together"[13] of it for present retention until it becomes completely imperceptible.[14]

Husserl has very little to say about protention. In several places he portrays it as like retention except that it concerns the just-future rather than the just-past.[15] As such it would directly intuit later phases of mental life as just-future. Presumably his thought is that we have a direct intuition of the continuation of our mental life into the just-future. However, Husserl also says that protention portrays the future emptily,[16] and that it portrays the future as indeterminate and open.[17]

Husserl's theory provides a particularly insightful account of how perceptual act-phases are unified into one perceptual act that perceives the temporal passage of worldly entities. Any perceptual act-phase is unified with earlier and later phases by means of their interlocking retentional-protentional structure. The later phases retain the earlier ones, and the earlier phases protend the later ones. The temporal passage of a worldly entity (or entity-phase) is perceived by means of the "look through" feature of retention and protention. Retention is directly aware of the just-previous mental life-phase, portrays it as just-past, and "looks through" this mental life-phase to its intentional correlates. The now-consciousness feature of a mental life-phase consists of all those components (of the simultaneous mental act-phases that compose a mental life-phase) that intend what is temporally focal or "now" as contrasted with the temporal background. In both portraying a previous now-consciousness feature *as just-past* and "looking through" it to its intentional correlate that is experienced as now for the now-consciousness feature, retention is able to experience a worldly entity-phase as just having been perceived as now. Similarly, protention can experience a worldly entity-phase as just about to be perceived as now. Thus, through its retention-protentional unification with other perceptual act-phases, a perceptual act-phase can both perceive a later worldly entity-phase as now and experience the just-previous worldly entity-phase as just having been perceived as now. This allows the perceptual act-phase to portray the worldly entity as passing through time: the worldly entity's earlier phases were present but are now past, its current phase is present but will be past, and its later phases are future but will be present.[18]

Retention and protention concern earlier and later phases of mental life. I have discussed these so far only in the context of Husserl's response to the problems of external time-consciousness. In addition to our awareness of intended objects, we always have a non-reflective awareness of the variety of our conscious orientation. Although our focus is upon the intended object, there is always a concomitant awareness of perceiving it or remembering it or actively imagining it or some other mental act. Since these mental acts are extended through time, our experience of them must itself be a type of time-consciousness.

A one-level analysis explains this inner time-consciousness by attributing a three-feature structure like that of perceptual acts to all phases of mental life. All temporally extended mental acts have phases that occur at different times. Since several distinct mental acts can occur simultaneously, many mental act-phases can occur simultaneously. The set of mental act-phases occurring simultaneously (in one consciousness) is a mental life-phase. Each mental life-phase has retentional, now-consciousness, and protentional features. (See Diagram A.7 in the Appendix.)

Since the retentional feature intuits the entire previous mental life-phase (as well as its objects), there is an awareness through retention of the types of mental acts in which we have been engaged. Since the protentional feature intuits the entire just-future mental life-phase (as well as its objects), there is an awareness through protention of the types of mental acts in which we will be engaged. There is even an awareness of the types of mental acts in which we are engaged *at this moment*, through the retention of the earlier mental life-phase's protention of the current mental life-phase. Thus, through the interlocking retentional-protentional structure, there is an awareness *both* of the types of mental acts and of their temporal extensions and simultaneity relations.

A one-level analysis has to explain our awareness of the temporal passage of our mental acts in terms of our awareness of the temporal passage of the intended objects of those acts. There is no additional feature that concerns just the awareness of the temporal passing of mental acts. A phase of a mental act is experienced as passing because it is correlated with (in the now-consciousness feature) an intended object-phase that is experienced as passing.

I indicated in section 5.1 that recollection or "secondary memory" is considered by Husserl not to be the basic form of awareness of *external* temporal features. Recollection is also not the basic form of awareness of *internal* temporal features. The main reason is that recollective memory is itself a temporally extended act whose phases need to be unified over time. This is accomplished through the retentional-protentional feature of each recollective act-phase (or of the mental life-phase of which it is a constituent). To be able to "re-live-through" (act) a former temporally extended experience (intended object), such as hearing a melody, the phases of the recollective act have to retain earlier recollective act-phases with their intended objects. Thus, we are aware of the temporal extension of the recollective act itself and are able to grasp at any given time an earlier temporally extended experience. Of course, *at* any given time we grasp the earlier experience from a particular temporal perspective: phases of it are grasped as already re-lived-through, one phase is grasped as being re-lived-through, and other phases are grasped as about to be re-lived-through.

There is another important way in which recollection is dependent upon retention. The intended object of recollection is something past. It is always a past experience of some sort, even though we may focus on what was perceived rather than on the (past) perceiving of it. The reference of recollection to the past is accomplished through the retentional-protentional structure of mental life. Any phase of recollection retains earlier phases of mental life that are past with respect to it. There is a chain of retentions extending backwards through mental life (and becoming less clear and distinct). The location of a recollected experience in the past depends upon this chain of retentions. As contrasted with an expected or merely phantasied experience, a recollected experience is intended as occurring earlier than the recollecting of it. This relative temporal location exists for consciousness by virtue of the intersection of the forward-directed horizon of the recollected experience with the backward-directed horizon of the recollecting act.

The preceding analyses involve one level of mental acts and two levels of time: (*a*) the temporal features of worldly entities that we perceive, and (b) the temporal features of mental acts (that compose mental life) of which we are non-reflectively aware. Mental life phases are considered to have a three-feature structure that explains *both* the perception of the temporal features of worldly things and the non-reflective awareness of the temporal features of mental acts.

In the manuscripts assembled in *Zur Phänomenologie des Inneren Zeitbewusstseins*, Husserl moved from a one-level account to a two-level account. There are two levels of mental acts (or its analogue) and three levels of time (or its analogue) of which we are aware:

(a)   the flow of worldtime, that is, the temporal features of perceived entities;

(b)   the stream of immanent acts and sensa, that is, the temporal features of mental entities (level one of mental acts);

(c)   the absolute self-constituting flux that also is aware of immanent time (level two of mental acts).[19]

The three-feature structure is here attributed to (c), the absolute flux. (See Diagram A.8 in the Appendix.) Any phase of the absolute consciousness has retentional, primal impressional, and protentional features. The absolute flux is able to be aware of itself ("self-constituting") by means of the interlocking retentional-protentional structure of its phases. Through its primal impressional feature, a phase of absolute consciousness intuits present (simultaneous) mental act-phases and sensa-phases. Through its retentional feature, a phase of absolute consciousness intuits earlier (simultaneous) mental act-phases and sensa-phases. Through its protentional feature, a phase of absolute consciousness intuits later (simultaneous) mental act-phases and sensa-phases. Through the unity of the phases of the flux, all internal mental life is intuited.

The absolute flux is supposed to constitute (provide for the awareness of) mental life. However, mental life is *not* posited as existing independently of the absolute flux. The absolute flux does not perceive mental life in the manner of commonsense realism. Rather, mental life is supposed to be *only* the intentional correlate of the absolute flux. Mental life exists *only as intended* by the absolute flux. Thus, mental life can have no features that are not experienced by the absolute flux. According to this conception, all features of mental life are transparent to the absolute flux. They are experienced, although not necessarily known.

The main reason that Husserl introduces the second level (c) is to account for the phenomenological fact that there is a non-reflective, non-focal awareness of the types of our mental acts. Instead of using the three-feature structure for this purpose (as in a one-level analysis), a special level of consciousness that intends mental life is introduced. The second level of consciousness explains our awareness of the temporal extension and temporal passage of mental acts on level one. However, there are other possible advantages of the two-level analysis. As developed by John Brough in "Husserl's Phenomenology of Time Consciousness,"[20] the distinction between level one and level two provides an account of *one identical constant* consciousness (the uniformly flowing flux) that has *many diverse* acts that *change at different rates*. The absolute flux is the main constituent of the ego.

> The absolute flow, of course, is a part, not the whole, of the ego. But it is the founding part, for through the flow the ego constitutes itself as one and the same in the face of the rich diversity and change of its own life on level one. Through its horizontal and vertical intentionalities, the flow supplies the consciousness of both dimensions, and there can be no ego without both, for in the ego sameness and difference play off against one another.[21]

Husserl considers the absolute flux itself to be non-temporal or perhaps quasi-temporal. The categories of time that apply to worldly entities or even to mental acts do not apply to the absolute flux. His main reason for this is that the absolute flux contains no content that could endure or persist. The primal impressions of each phase are not *qualitatively* distinct from each other; they differ only in that which they intend (the different phases of mental life). Because there is no content that could endure or persist, there could be no identical objects or processes through any stretch of the absolute flux itself. Without any enduring objects or processes to support them, alterations cannot exist either.[22]

This much of Husserl's thinking is clear. His reasons for taking the further step of denying that the absolute flux has temporal features are less obvious. Presumably he thought that because the absolute flux is so different categorially from enduring and changing things, the same temporal categories could not apply to both. Perhaps he thought that if time essentially includes change, as McTaggart[23] argued, but the absolute flux can not contain change, then the absolute flux can not be temporal. The legitimacy of Husserl's claims about the timeless character of the absolute flux will be examined in section 5.4.

When the two-level analysis is presented, there is no indication that the three-feature structure applies at level one in addition to level two. The main reason that Husserl introduces level two is to account for the phenomenological fact that there is a non-reflective, non-focal experience of the temporal features of our mental acts. If level one was self-constituting (provided for its own awareness of itself), there would be less reason to introduce a second level.

However, it is not totally clear from the published work how Husserl thought of level one or even whether he consistently advocated this two-level analysis. There are no clearcut references to the two levels in *Ideas*, and some passages there seem to ascribe the three-feature structure to mental acts themselves (level one).[24] There is one passage in *Cartesian Meditations* that clearly refers to two levels,[25] but it does not indicate whether the three-feature structure applies at level one. There are also passages in *Formal and Transcendental Logic* and *Experience and Judgment* that indicate two levels, although it again is not clear whether the three-feature structure applies only to the absolute flux.[26]

I have indicated previously why the three-feature structure might be thought not to apply at level one in addition to level two: if mental life at level one unified itself over time and provided for its own awareness of itself, an additional level would seem to be unnecessary. However, there is a converse problem if level one does not have the three-feature structure: phases of the same mental act would not *intrinsically* be unified with each other. There would be no intrinsic connection between the phases of one mental act. An earlier phase would not in any way influence the later ones. The only connections between these act-phases would be *external*. They would exist as a unified internal object for an observing absolute consciousness.

There is a possible rejoinder to this problem. Emphasizing that neither the absolute flux nor the stream of immanent acts is capable of independent existence, one could claim that phases of the same mental act "influence" each other through the unity of the diverse primal impressions that intend them. On this reading, absolute consciousness would not only intuit mental acts but also produce them (as unities) and their temporal features.

5.3   The Temporal Nature of the Experiencer

Husserl maintains that there is a transcendental ego that is conscious in and through each of the mental acts of one consciousness.[27] The three-feature structure is an important constituent of the transcendental ego on either a one- or a two-level account. On either interpretation human consciousness has some special temporal features in virtue of mental acts "reaching across" to other temporal locations. However, the one-level and the two-level interpretations are significantly different on the temporal nature of the experiencer; so I will discuss these separately.

5.3A   One-Level Account

The transcendental ego and its mental life occur within a real time, although they have some special temporal features. As depicted in Diagram A.7, phases of mental life *are actual at* moments of time. Perceptual acts of mental life portray worldly entities as occurring at the same times and for the same durations as the perceptual acts themselves.[28] Assuming that the world is not a "transcendental illusion" (see section 5.4), phases of mental life have real temporal relations with other entities in time, whether or not mental life is aware of these temporal relations. Furthermore, the interconnected continuum of phases that composes *one* mental life begins and ends in time. The ego is born and dies.

Mental life has special temporal features through its three-feature structure and through certain types of "time-spanning" acts that are based upon the three-feature structure. By its retentional and protentional features, any phase of mental life "reaches across" to other parts of time. Although the retentional and protentional features are *actual at* one time, they do not *exist completely at* that time because they are in direct contact with earlier and later moments. There is a sense in which they *exist across* stretches of time. For this reason, they cannot be located *at* moments of time as ordinary worldly entities can be, and stretches of mental life are not temporally divisible in the way that ordinary worldly entities are (see section 3.1). If Husserl is correct in thinking that recollective memory and attention to what has just happened are also types of direct contact with the past,[29] then these types of act would themselves exhibit these special temporal characteristics.

Since the direct contact of phases of mental life is always with *other* phases of the *same* mental life, the temporal extension of a whole stretch of mental life is basically standard, even though the temporal extension of any individual phase is non-standard. This one mental life exists during the entire period of time that is occupied by any of its constituent phases. Thus, the length of duration (temporal extension) of a complete stretch of mental life is also standard because it is comparable to the length of duration of ordinary worldly entities. The only complications concern the nature of a "complete stretch." Because of the "reaching across" of retentions and protentions, an arbitrarily selected segment of mental life is not a complete stretch. A complete stretch is one whose phases are in direct contact *only* with other phases of the stretch. If any moment of mental life (except the beginning and the end) has some retentions and protentions, only the entire lifetime of one mental life could be a complete stretch. If periods of unconsciousness (such as blackouts and dreamless sleep) are not reached over by retentions and protentions, then there could be shorter complete stretches.

The transcendental ego endures through time, is conscious through the phases of mental life, and possesses capacities and abilities.[30] There are many different types of potentiality that the transcendental ego possesses at any given time. There is the potentiality to experience as focal whatever is part of the horizon of meaning of that to which the ego currently attends. There are mental powers to think different things and to carry out mental operations, such as adding numbers or following an argument. There are bodily powers to affect the physical world, although Husserl says little about these. Most of these potentialities are unactualized at any given time and endure unchanged through time. Some of the potentialities exist even during periods of unconsciousness so that the transcendental ego may continue to exist even when no mental life is occurring. Heidegger and Sartre think that the possession of powers to affect the future are a special connection with the future. They claim that human consciousness has special temporal features in virtue of such powers, but Husserl himself does not make this claim.

5.3B   Two-Level Account

Husserl's two-level theory is similar to Kant's two-level theory in important respects. Kant claims that the transcendental ego is non-temporal but has time as a framework of consciousness. Husserl claims that the absolute flux is timeless or at best quasi-temporal; it supposedly does not have temporal features of any sort. Kant's transcendental ego depicts an ordinary knowing consciousness as being through time. Husserl's absolute flux intends ordinary mental life and its ego as being temporal. Mental acts and the ego's potentialities are experienced in inner time. Kant's non-temporal transcendental ego is part of a theory that denies that there is any mind-independent time. As I will argue in section 5.4, the non-temporality of the absolute flux also leads toward temporal idealism.

The absolute flux is the most basic "subject" of consciousness according to the two-level theory. The absolute flux is supposed to be composed of phases that have the three-feature structure and that intend ordinary mental life. Upon close examination, it is very hard to make sense of this two-level position. It is not clear that the structures of retention and protention can be applied non-temporally. The retentional and protentional features *are initially defined in temporal terms*. Retention is the direct impression of the past *as past*; protention is the direct impression of the future *as future*. How could we retain and protend phases of the absolute flux if these phases are neither past nor future?

One possible response would be to separate the double intentionality of retentions and protentions. Suppose that the retention of other phases of the absolute flux is *not* a direct intuition of these *as past* (or *as earlier*) but a direct intuition of these *as non-temporally ordered* with the operative phase. Suppose further that the retention of what is primally intended by these non-temporally ordered phases (namely, other phases of mental life) *is still a direct intuition* of these *as past* (or *as earlier*). (See Diagram A.9 in the Appendix.)

The problem with this distinction of two types of retention (and protention) is that it produces contradictory results concerning the retention of phases of the absolute flux. In order to be conscious of the non-temporal order of absolute flux-phases, we have to "look through" the retentional part of other phases. In the retention of retention, absolute flux-phase$_3$ retains (non-temporally) absolute flux-phase$_2$, which retains (non-temporally) absolute flux-phase$_1$. However, if we did indeed "look through" other non-temporally ordered absolute flux-phases, we would also "look through" their primal impressional feature, since retention is *of the whole phase*. Thus, absolute flux-phase$_3$ would retain (non-temporally) absolute flux-phase$_2$, which both primally intuited a mental life-phase *as now* and retained absolute flux-phase$_1$, which primally intuited a separate mental life-phase *as now*. There would be a non-temporally ordered set of primal impressional features, each of which intuited a different mental life-phase *as now*. Not only would this arrangement not provide for the experience of the temporal order of mental life-phases, but it would produce a temporally confused experience. If this arrangement did exist, we would always experience many non-temporally ordered primal impressions, each of which intuited its mental life-phase *as now*. The result would be a *temporal* confusion of "now" moments.

The problem in comprehending how the absolute flux could be non-temporal is compounded by Husserl's own expositions. Husserl describes the absolute flux in terms whose only straightforward meaning is temporal. The absolute flux is composed of phases that succeed one another. One phase is actual while other phases are not actual but have to be contacted by the actual phase. While Husserl recognizes that the only straightforward interpretation of these notions is temporal, he insists that we have to understand the absolute flux metaphorically.[31] The problem is that he provides no clues for this metaphoric interpretation and, as I will argue in section 5.4, no compelling reasons for denying temporality to the absolute flux.

If the absolute flux were temporal,[32] it would have the same special temporal features attributed to mental life in the one-level account. The three-feature structure, as incorporated in a temporal absolute flux, would provide for special forms of temporal location and temporal divisibility. Even if the absolute flux is non-temporal, however, special temporal features can exist at level one. If recollective memory and attention to what has just happened are types of direct contact with the past,[33] then these types of acts would themselves exhibit special temporal characteristics.

An interesting feature of the two-level analysis is that at the most basic level the transcendental ego consists solely of the absolute flux. The two-level analysis reduces the transcendental ego partly to the absolute flux itself, partly to features of inner mental life.[34] The unity and identity of one consciousness is attributed to the self-unifying absolute flux itself. On the other hand, mental abilities and capacities, which themselves can change over time, are attributed to the (constituted) ego of mental life at level one.

5.4   The Ontological Reality of Time

Most of Husserl's thought about the ontological realism or idealism of the experienced world supports the ontological realism of time. However, the notion that a non-temporal absolute flux is the most basic level of consciousness makes it very difficult for Husserl's position to endorse the consciousness-independence of time.

In phenomenological reflection the phenomenological investigator suspends *for himself or herself* (as reflector) any claims about independent reality in order to investigate how his or her first-order consciousness means anything. The phenomenologist examines how this first-order consciousness thinks of entities, what it conceives them to be, and what serves as evidence for or against first-order claims about the world. The first-order consciousness operates according to what Husserl calls "the natural attitude" or what is commonly called "commonsense realism."

According to the natural attitude, perception is the detection of what exists independently of consciousness. The conception of "independent existence" employed in the natural attitude is very complicated. It is probably an "open-textured" concept that has no precise set of necessary and sufficient conditions, although Husserl does not claim this. It is certainly a theoretical concept whose meaning is tied to other complex concepts. The concept "independent existence of a perceived entity" is *not reducible* to any ordered set of sensory givens. Among other things, the concept includes the ideas that an entity would be perceived by others even if I were dead and that it would affect other entities even if no consciousness were there to perceive it.

Despite the complications the phenomenological reflector can determine that it is possible to accumulate evidence for the independent existence of perceived entities. Husserl thinks that the ongoing experience of further self-given sensory data that accords with what is meant in the original perception provides evidence for the accuracy of the original perception. That some (apparently) perceived state of affairs does exist independently is partially confirmed by the occurrence of harmonious further experiences. However, in examining the relationship of meaning to evidence, the phenomenological reflector realizes that we can never attain absolute certainty about the independent existence of some specific state of affairs, although we can have very good reason to believe in it.

Not only might any specific (apparently perceived) state of affairs turn out not to be real, but it is conceivable according to Husserl that the whole world might turn out not to be real.[35] If the harmonious course of our perceptual experience were to disintegrate, the resulting confusion would provide no basis for believing in the reality of the world.

On the contrary, it is quite conceivable that it is not only in single instances that experience through conflict dissolves into illusion, and that every illusion does not as it were *de facto* proclaim a deeper truth, and every conflict in its proper place be precisely what is demanded by more widely connected systems for maintaining the harmony of the whole; it is conceivable that our experiencing function swarms with oppositions that cannot be evened out either for us or in themselves, that experience shows itself all at once obstinately set against the suggestion that the things it puts together should persist harmoniously to the end, and that its connectedness, such as it is, lack the fixed order-schemes of perspectives, apprehensions, and appearances—that a world, in short, exists no longer. It might happen, moreover, that, to a certain extent still, rough unitary formation might be constituted, fleeting concentration-centres for intuitions which were the mere analogues of thing-intuitions, being wholly incapable of constituting self-preserving "realities," unities that endure and "exist in themselves whether perceived or not perceived."[36]

The possibility of this disintegration means that we cannot know with absolute certainty that the world is ontologically real.[37] However, even if the world were to collapse, this would not prove conclusively that the world was ontologically dependent upon consciousness; it would only withdraw the grounds for believing in the reality of the world.

Husserl thinks that any evidence for the ontological reality of the world is also evidence for the ontological reality of time because time is a structure of the world. He regularly opposes the Kantian split between the thing-in-itself and the spatio-temporal qualitative objective world. He considers it nonsensical to attribute ontological reality to a thing-in-itself that is distinct from the world that first-order consciousness investigates and imperfectly knows.[38] Thus, the time of worldly entities has the same claim to ontological reality that the world does: we have strong evidence for its independent reality, but it is in principle possible that this evidence could be annulled.

5.4A   One-Level Account

Husserl's general views about the ontological reality of the perceived world accord with the one-level analysis of time-consciousness. According to this analysis, phases of mental life are actual at moments of time, and perceptual acts (and their phases) portray worldly entities as existing at the same times and for the same durations as the perceptual acts themselves. If any of these perceptual acts are in fact accurate detections of what exists independently of consciousness, then worldly entities exist in a real time that has the temporal features that are attributed to it. There would be a real time that had temporal locations that were related by earlier-later relations and in which temporal passage was real. Worldly entities would have temporal extensions that would be divisible into equally real subsections without any change in non-temporal properties, and there would be definite lengths to these temporal extensions.

When Husserl discusses time, he does not emphasize the special temporal nature of consciousness. He seems to assume that the same basic temporal features apply both to "immanent objects" (mental life) and to "external objects" (worldly entities). Nevertheless, as I explained in section 5.3A, the one-level analysis requires that phases of mental life and complete stretches of mental life have some special temporal features. Thus mental life would not have *all* the same temporal features as worldly entities. However, mental life would share some features with worldly entities: it would be actual *at temporal locations* (though not existing fully there), and its temporal extension and length of temporal extension would be categorially the same as that of worldly entities. With provisions for the differences in divisibility and existence across temporal locations, past-present-future and earlier-later features would apply equally to both. Thus, real temporal relations would exist between consciousness and other entities in time.

If the world were to disintegrate into an incoherent tumult, there would no longer be any evidence for the independent existence of what was sensed. Sensory data would still have a temporal order because the mental life of sensing it has a temporal order, but there would be no basis for attributing this temporal order to an independently existing temporal world. In this case, the only time would be the temporal features of mental life and the (derivative) temporal features of the sensed tumult that is the correlate of the sensory part of mental life. Although consciousness would still be temporal in the same way, there would be no evidence that it had *real* temporal relations with any other entities.

5.4B Two-Level Account

The introduction of a second level that was temporal in the same way that the first level is temporal (in the above analysis) would not affect the account of the ontological reality of time. However, if the absolute flux is non-temporal, there are serious problems with maintaining the same basic account of the ontological reality of time. The non-temporal absolute flux has to provide for the awareness of (constitute) a temporal mental life that is *only the flux's intentional correlate*. Mental life is *not* posited as existing independently of the flux. This temporal mental life has to provide for the awareness of (constitute) a temporal world of entities that *is justifiably taken* to exist independently of mental life. Because of its perception of this real world, mental life has to be taken to have real temporal relations with other entities. Since perceptual acts require that the acts themselves exist at the same times and for the same durations as the worldly entities that are perceived, mental life is portrayed as existing in the same ontologically real time in which perceived entities exist. Furthermore, to be consistent with his general position about the ontological reality of the perceived world, it must be possible for mental life to have its world disintegrate into a confusion of sensory data that provides no grounds for the reality of a world.

There are two reasons why all the above theses cannot be maintained. First, as I argued in section 5.3, a non-temporally ordered absolute flux cannot coherently be aware of a mental life that has past-present-future features. The reason is that each phase of the absolute flux intends a different phase of mental life *as now* or *present*. Since the absolute flux-phases are only non-temporally ordered, *only* a non-temporally ordered set of *present moments* of mental life can be intended. However, such a set of non-temporally ordered *present* phases of mental life is incoherent. A set could be coherent only if each were present *earlier* or *later* than the others.

Second, there is a conflict between temporal mental life being *only* the intentional correlate of the non-temporal absolute flux and temporal mental life being justifiably taken to exist in the same ontologically real time in which worldly entities exist. Although it is not known with absolute certainty, that temporal mental life has real temporal relations with perceived worldly entities is a very well justified belief, and it is an essential component of perception itself. If mental life does have real temporal relations with worldly entities, these exist *whether or not* they are intended by the absolute flux. Thus, real temporal features of mental life are not simply the intentional correlate of the absolute flux, and there may be some real temporal features of which the absolute flux is not aware.

Given these problems, the two-level account that maintains the non-temporal absolute flux as the basic level of consciousness (not just an adjunct to an independent mental life at level one) must make different claims about the ontological reality of time. The first problem could be eliminated by having mental life be temporal only in an earlier-later way. However, if mental life is to be *only* the intentional correlate of the non-temporal absolute flux, mental life cannot have real temporal features *of any sort*. Since perception includes real temporal relations between the perceptual act and what is perceived, perception as it is ordinarily understood could not occur. Since perception in the natural attitude is that which portrays worldly entities as existing independently and that which confirms their independent existence, mental life could no longer justifiably portray worldly entities as existing independently. Thus, the two-level account with a non-temporal absolute flux has to deny the ontological reality of time. Consistently with this account, neither mental life nor worldly entities can be justifiably believed to exist in a real time.

This result could be avoided if the absolute flux were temporal, particularly if the absolute flux existed (partially) in the same time as worldly entities. If phases of the absolute flux occurred at moments of time, then even though mental life-phases were only the intentional correlates of the absolute flux-phases, they might still occur at moments of time. They could thus have the temporal relations with worldly entities that are necessary for perception proper, and they could justifiably posit an ontologically real time.

In light of the difficulties, perhaps the non-temporality of the absolute flux should be abandoned. In section 5.2 I attempted to reconstruct Husserl's reasons for denying that the absolute flux is temporal. His thinking was that since the absolute flux contains no content that could endure, there can be no identical objects or processes within it nor any alterations. Presumably, he concluded that the same temporal categories cannot apply both to enduring and changing things and to the absolute flux (which supposedly neither endures nor changes). Perhaps he reasoned that if time essentially includes change but the absolute flux cannot contain change, then the absolute flux cannot be temporal.

An absolute flux must be categorially different from enduring substances and enduring processes with changing properties. However, this does not rule out all forms of change, and it does not make temporal features totally inapplicable. Whether Husserl recognizes it or not, the "flowing" of the absolute flux requires either temporal passage or an earlier-later sequence of temporal locations.

The absolute flux flows in that all its phases are *not actual together* (simultaneously); rather they are actual *one after the other*. For the absolute flux to be genuinely non-temporal, Husserl would have to provide an interpretation of "being actual in sequence" that was non-temporal. He has not done this, and I think that it could not be done.

5.5   Further Issues

Husserl's theory of time-consciousness is an improvement over Kant's partly because his theory of consciousness is more sophisticated. Kant neglected the mental act feature of consciousness. The three-feature structure of retention, primal impression, and protention, which is the major component of Husserl's theory of time-consciousness, exists at the level of mental acts or at level two, which is analogous to mental acts. It is the three-feature structure that provides both for the unity of consciousness over time and for the awareness of temporal extension and temporal passage in worldly entities.

Despite the elegance and disclosive power of Husserl's theory, there are a number of unanswered questions and potential problem areas.

First, Husserl simply *assumes* that only what is present can be actual. While past and future phases of consciousness can be contacted, the *contacting is actual only in the present* (or in some analogue for a non-temporal absolute flux). Although retention and protention may not exist *completely* in the present because they "reach across" to other times, they are nevertheless *actual only in the present*. This ontological assumption that only what is present can be actual is certainly plausible, but it does need to be defended. As I indicated in Chapter 1, there are alternative ontologies that allow for *actuality-as-past* and *actuality-as-future* (see theories 4 and 5). Two of these alternative ontologies, those of Heidegger and Sartre, will be examined in Chapters 6 and 7. By disclosing the problems that such ontologies generate, I will provide support for Husserl's assumption.

Second, Husserl conceives time to be composed of instants or infinitesimals (moments with a duration approaching zero). He emphasizes that time is continuous, and he seems to understand this continuity in terms of a dense continuum of points.[39] Such a conception of continuous points of time is probably necessary for a time that passes. A time that passes has to have *in itself* all the temporal divisions that a consciousness might ever make, because the "now" must pass through all the parts of time. These parts of time are not just the result of consciousness dividing time up. The passing "now" divides time up.

Although infinitesimals may be the correct analysis of real time, there are strong theoretical reasons to deny that mental life has infinitesimal phases and that experienced time has infinitesimal phases. Both of these would require that we have to retain an infinite number of previous phases in order to be aware of any finite temporal extension (see section 8.4).

Third, Husserl asserts the absolute certainty of retention (see section 5.2), but in fact retentions can be found to be mistaken. Husserl's claim that some form of direct contact with the past is necessary for time-consciousness is correct, but this direct contact cannot be such as to guarantee accuracy in all cases. Retention may sometimes portray experiences that *did not happen at all*. Particularly when occupied with many activities, a person may retain the experience of having just done something that she had intended to do, such as picking up her keys or dropping a letter in the box. When she turns more of her attention to the relevant circumstances, the error of the supposed retention can be discovered.

Fourth, Husserl considers time-consciousness to operate without interests or motivation, but retention seems in fact to be affected by the focus of attention. If I am listening to a symphony or watching a scene and an important message interrupts this, my attention may shift entirely to the message and to the situation that it concerns. In this case I do not retain the earlier experiences in the same way that I would if the perceiving had not been interrupted. There is no role for the previously perceived data in the present emergency situation, and the previous perceiving does not inform the present experiences in the way that it would under more ordinary conditions.

This difference might be accounted for by distinguishing two aspects of retention: retention-as-maintaining and the degree of prominence of what is maintained. The degree of prominence of what is maintained would vary according to our current interests and involvements.

Fifth, Husserl conceives protention to be direct contact with the future, but protention is so fallible that this is dubious. There are serious epistemological problems with any claim to direct intuition of what is to come. That we will perceive a specific object-phase in the next instant cannot be known with certainty. Even the anticipation that our mental life will continue in roughly the way that it is going can be rendered false if we are suddenly struck unconscious or dead. I explicated in section 5.2 Husserl's very sparse claims about protention. Protention is supposed both to be an intuition of the future and to portray the future as indeterminate and open. The most promising way to interpret these claims (see Chapter 1, theories 2 and 3) is to conceive the *future qua future* as a set of alternatives, only one of which will become present. Protention would then be direct contact with a set of alternatives *with one singled out*, probably without realizing that the one was only part of a set of alternatives. The problem remains, however, that we seem not to intuit *all the alternatives*. Even if we anticipate that one of a set of alternatives will happen, something entirely different that is not one of the alternatives may happen.

Sixth, Husserl does not sufficiently examine the details of the ontology of time. As I argued in Chapter 1, any theory of time-consciousness must at least implicitly take some position on many aspects of the ontology of time. Husserl's theory presupposes or requires many specific ontological positions (see the discussion under theory 3 in Chapter 1), but he does not examine and defend all of these. He says practically nothing about the being of the past and the future that allows them to be directly contacted through retention and protention. He is indefinite about the passage of time as it concerns levels one and two. Husserl does not provide any account of why there is change or flux in the most basic level of consciousness, whether this be mental life or the absolute flux. No account is given in terms of the internal nature of the absolute flux of why or how it flows.

Finally, there is no solid phenomenological evidence for level two, that of the absolute flux. I have never found it, or anything that indicates it, in my experience. If any level of consciousness is to be both self-aware and aware of other entities, the level of mental life is the obvious choice. There is good phenomenological evidence for the claim that mental acts are non-reflectively aware of themselves as part of mental life. In contrast, if it should be stipulated that mental life cannot be aware of itself, why should the absolute flux be able to be aware of itself?

In Chapter 8 I will defend a revised Husserlian theory of time-consciousness and respond to these issues.

6

Heidegger's Theory of Time-Consciousness and Temporality

Throughout his career the question of Being was the focus of Martin Heidegger's thought. He was concerned to elucidate what it is for something to be. Time in the sense of the temporal character of Being and beings (entities that are) was a fundamental theme of this thinking about Being. This chapter will examine Heidegger's views on time consciousness, temporal realism, and the temporal nature of the experiencer as they were presented in the late 1920s. Since Heidegger's thought concerning Being evolved during his lifetime, there is reason to think that his views concerning the relation of Being and time also evolved. However, Heidegger never explicitly revised the major positions that I will examine.

In *Being and Time* Heidegger proposed that the best way to investigate the Being of entities is by investigating the Being of human Being, since humans are those that encounter other entities. Human Being is distinctive in that its type of Being includes the understanding of Being. It is an intrinsic part of human Being both to encounter other entities in their Being and to operate out of some conception of its own existence and of the existence of other humans. Since the nature of human Being includes some understanding of the ways of existing (Being) both of non-human entities and of humans, Heidegger thinks that an elucidation of human Being will also clarify the Being of other entities.[1]

The procedure followed by Heidegger in elucidating human Being is hermeneutic phenomenology. Phenomenology is "to let that which shows itself be seen from itself in the very way in which it shows itself from itself."[2] As this iterative formulation emphasizes, something is to be "seen" or grasped as it shows itself to be, and this requires some activity ("to let") on our part. Heidegger's approach to human Being is phenomenological in that we are to *grasp* what actually shows itself (this corresponds to Husserl's reflective observation) and we can only do this if we refrain from premature categorizations of what appears (this corresponds to Husserl's suspension of the natural attitude and emphasis on presuppositionless observation and description). Through first-person observation of our own experiences and ways of living, we are to arrive at the way of existing (Being) of human beings.

Heidegger's phenomenological method differs from Husserl's in that Heidegger emphasizes that all observing, grasping, and understanding *necessarily* presupposes a system of meanings. Presuppositionless observation and description is impossible because all observation, even phenomenological self-observation, operates in terms of some system of meanings that could be otherwise. What appears is pre-structured by the system of meanings so that all observation is in some respects interpretation. However, this pre-structuring does not make further interpretation unnecessary. Rather, we have to develop our understanding of what appears by interpreting it in terms of further refinements of meaning. This more explicit and detailed interpretation can either bring out unnoticed features of what appears or distort what appears. Interpretations that bring out previously unnoticed features let an entity show itself more fully. Further interpretations that distort cover over what appears. It is this covering over that has to be resisted if we are to understand human Being as it shows itself to be.[3] Thus, the goals of hermeneutic phenomenology are, first, to let things appear without distorting them by premature and inappropriate categorizations and, second, to consider alternative interpretations of what appears in order to see what might have gone unnoticed.

Since Heidegger investigates the Being of humans and since all description already interprets, there is no sharp distinction in Heidegger's work between phenomenological data and ontological theory. The data of human experience and life are always already "seen through" the special way of existing that Heidegger claims is human Being. However, there are different "levels" of interpretation, and I will appeal to these in presenting Heidegger's positions.

6.1   Experienced Temporal Features

Heidegger was very impressed by Husserl's thinking about time-consciousness, and he adopted from Husserl two important notions: that we experience temporal features both in the objects of consciousness and in the conscious acts themselves, and that the experience of the temporal features of the acts is what makes the experience of the temporal features of the objects possible. However, since Heidegger understood consciousness essentially to include the motivational and power features that are necessary for agency, he conceived "objects of consciousness" and "conscious acts" differently from Husserl. Furthermore, unlike Kant and Husserl, the primary data on which Heidegger's theory of time-consciousness is based is the experience of the temporal features of conscious acts, rather than the experience of the temporal features of the objects of consciousness. The ontology of temporalizing consciousness that I will explore in sections 6.2, 6.3, and 6.4, is designed to explain how human acting consciousness can be what it is experienced to be.

In this section I will attempt to specify the experienced temporal features that are the basis for Heidegger's theory of time-consciousness and time. Because of his notion of hermeneutic phenomenology, Heidegger himself never distinguishes explicitly between experienced features and the structures of a theoretical account based upon the experienced features. According to Heidegger, the understanding of what features are experienced is always already an interpreting of those features in terms of some set of concepts. While I agree with Heidegger that description always itself operates with some classifications that affect what is described, I will nevertheless attempt to distinguish experienced temporal features from a more theoretical account of these for two interconnected reasons. First, I think that there are experiences (which themselves interpret what they encounter) that are independent of the description of the experiences. Second, I think that it is important to determine whether the interpretive classifications are really suitable to that which is interpreted. To determine this suitability, some provisional distinction between what is being interpreted and the interpretive classifications is necessary.

I will start by outlining Heidegger's notion of "the world" and then consider the characteristics of world-time. World-time will be distinguished from now-time, and Heidegger's claim that now-time is a distorted and derivative form of world-time will be examined. I will then turn to the experienced temporal features of non-conscious entities that appear "within the world" and to the experienced temporal features of human acting consciousness (Dasein or Being-in-the-world).

As a totality, world "is" no particular being but rather that by means of and in terms of which Dasein *gives itself to understand [signify]* what beings it *can* behave toward and how it *can* behave toward them.[4]

This understanding of the being of beings is connected with the *understanding of world*, which is the presupposition for the experience of an intraworldly being. But, now, since world-understanding is at the same time an *understanding of itself by the Dasein*—for being-in-the-world constitutes a determination of the Dasein—the understanding of being that belongs to intentionality *embraces* the Dasein's being as well as the being of intraworldly beings which are not Daseins.[5]

A "world" is a system of meanings in terms of which Dasein (Heidegger's term for human acting consciousness) encounters any entity. Heidegger borrowed and transformed Kant's notion that there are structures of meaning within which any entity must appear if it is to be available to knowing consciousness.[6] While he rejected the priority of knowing consciousness, Heidegger retained the notion that consciousness allows entities to be encountered by opening up (disclosing) a system of meanings that then pre-determines that which is encountered. From Husserl, Heidegger borrowed the notion that this system of meanings has the structure of focus-horizon. The world is a system of horizons that are necessary for and contribute to the meaningfulness of those entities with which we are primarily involved at any given time. In addition

Heidegger's conception of "the world" includes the following features.

1. While any specific world may change over time, there are essential features that all specific worlds must share.

2. This essence of world (the worldhood of any specific world) is part of Dasein's Being; Dasein exists necessarily as Being-in-the-world.

3. As a disclosed system of meanings with a focus-horizon structure, any specific world is *directed toward* the concrete entities that are discovered within it. Dasein's world could not exist without concrete entities that are encountered within the world.

4. Any specific world is dependent upon the community of Daseins that share and interact in terms of that system of meanings. Dasein's Being-in-the-world is essentially a Being-with other Daseins who share and interact in terms of a common world.[7]

5. A world is an action-oriented system of meanings in terms of which any entity is encountered and acted upon. Heidegger terms the structure of this system of meanings (world), "significance,"[8] As action-oriented, this system of meanings is structured in the following way (significance). First, the system includes Dasein's objectives and interests, that is, what we want, what we pursue and avoid, and what interests us. Second, the system includes our sense of our powers to bring about our projects, and our sense of the limitations on our powers. Third, the classifications or types of encountered entities are essentially connected with Dasein's objectives, interests, and powers. Heidegger adopted the pragmatist notion that the articulation of what we experience into differentiated but related entities is dependent upon human projects, human perceptual abilities, and human abilities to affect things.

The conjunction of features 4 and 5 indicates how the understanding of oneself, the understanding of other Daseins, and the understanding of non-conscious entities are interconnected, according to Heidegger. A specific world is an action-oriented system of meanings in terms of which we encounter and interact with any entity. The projects, powers, and actions that structure a specific world are those of the *community* of Daseins. Any individual Dasein will have only some of these objectives and interests, may have only some of the powers, and will be engaged in only some of the actions. Thus, what we might call an individual Dasein's "appropriated world" will encompass only a portion of his "public world."

Nevertheless, such an individual Dasein understands how other Daseins think and what they are doing. He understands other Daseins to have some objectives, interests, powers, and engagements that he does not have. Given this understanding of other Daseins, an individual Dasein can encounter entities in terms of a system of meanings that depend upon features *only some of which* belong to that individual Dasein.

Since *every* entity is encountered in terms of the world, an individual Dasein encounters herself in terms of her world. An individual Dasein understands herself through the same concepts or meanings through which she understands other Daseins. Thus, an individual Dasein always understands herself to be in general like the other individual Daseins who share her (public) world and with whom she interacts. Each Dasein initially and, with qualifications, constantly understands herself to be one of the public or "they" (Das Man). How an individual Dasein may *individualize* herself will be considered later.

The world, as it has been described above, has a "time structure." Time is an essential parameter of that action-oriented system of meanings through which we encounter non-conscious entities, other Daseins, and ourselves. Heidegger calls this basic time-structure of the world, "world-time." World-time is a pragmatic time. We encounter entities within world-time,[9] and world-time is the time with which we ordinarily concern ourselves, even though we do not explicitly comprehend this time in the right way. Whenever we "take time" for some activity, wait for the right time, do not have enough time, or schedule our day, we are operating in terms of world-time. Heidegger claims that world-time (like the world) has the character of significance. In ordinary language, this means that world-time should be essentially action-oriented. The most direct way in which world-time has the character of significance is that every moment of world-time is understood with respect to some actual or potential action. Every "now" is experienced as the appropriate or inappropriate time to do something.[10]

In conjunction with this "character of significance," Heidegger attributes "datability," "spannedness," and "publicness" to world-time.[11] Datability refers to the way in which moments of time are always understood with respect to what occurs "in time." "Every now dates itself as 'now, when such and such is occurring, happening, or in existence.' "[12] Temporal locations (in past-present-future time) and their distinctness from each other are meaningful only in terms of what occupies the locations and how these occupants are related (temporally) to each other.

Spannedness refers to the way in which moments of time have breadth or extension. The datable moments of time are never extensionless instants, but rather stretches of time during which events occur. Publicness refers to the way in which moments of time are accessible to everyone. Although different people may date a moment of time by means of different events that occur at that moment, each person's dated moment can be understood by everyone else.[13] "The accessibility of the now for everyone, without prejudice to the diverse datings, characterizes time as public."[14]

World-time is a past-present-future time. There is always a "temporal perspective" in world-time and always reference to the passage of time. The now that is present is consistently distinguished from the "at that time" (past) and the "then" (future). The passage of time is contained in each of these in that the "at that time" is a "now-no-longer" and the "then" is a "now-not-yet."[15] The temporal focus of experience (the now that is present) shifts in the world-time toward the "now-not-yet."

World-time is supposed to be *both* the time within which we encounter any entity *and* the time with which we concern ourselves and with which we reckon. It may not be apparent how these two characteristics of world-time are supposed to fit smoothly together. The first portrays world-time as a structural feature of our system of meanings. The most developed discussion of this characteristic is the *Grundprobleme* account of "praesens" as a horizonal schema (of enpresenting), that is, as the present-concerned time feature of the world.[16] The second treats world-time almost as if it were an equipmental entity that we use. In being concerned with how much time is available, it is almost as if we were concerned with a specific entity, one that someone *might not* be concerned with. How then can both of these be characteristics of one world-time?

This puzzle can be resolved by keeping in mind the nature of the world and clarifying what it is to "be concerned with world-time." As I have already indicated, the world is structured in terms of Dasein's objectives for itself, which are themselves a part of the world. Entities are always encountered in terms of humans' projects, powers, and limitations. Dasein's projects, in conjunction with its concrete environment, imply a large number of specific actions that are designed to bring about specific results. The accomplishment of most of these specific results requires that the actions be done "at the right time," that is, that Dasein's action be temporally coordinated with what is happening in the environment (as well as with its other actions). To adapt Heidegger's example, one cannot look for game while it is dark, and one must wait until the prey is within range before attacking. This temporal coordination of Dasein's action with what happens in the environment is the basic form of world-time. World-time is not a distinct entity that we use, but rather the temporal feature of any acting in an environment. We are concerned with time, because acting at the right time is necessary for successful action in a changing environment. Thus some form of world-time must be present in any acting consciousness that is to survive.

The world-time in terms of which we encounter any entity and with which we ordinarily concern ourselves is qualitatively different from our explicit commonsense conception of what time is like, which Heidegger calls "now-time." The explicit commonsense conception of the nature of time portrays it in the following way: "Time shows itself as a sequence of 'nows' which are constantly 'present-at-hand', simultaneously passing away and coming along. Time is understood as a succession, as a 'flowing stream of nows', as the 'course of time'."[17] Now-time is ordinarily thought to be a peculiar type of present-at-hand entity that intrinsically passes. Such time is composed of parts or "nows" that are sequentially ordered and that have a "privileged part" (the present), which constantly changes in the direction of later dates. This commonsense conception was formalized in Newton's theory of an absolute time that intrinsically passed independently of the material entities that existed within time.[18]

Heidegger notes that there have traditionally been many metaphysical puzzles about now-time.[19] There are problems about its continuity: Are the parts (nows) of time extended or non-extended like geometric points, and how do they form a continuous series? There are problems about the direction of time (its "irreversible succession"), about its passage, and about the existence of past and future. There are problems about time's infinity. He also notes that now-time lacks the references to human objectives, interests, powers, and actions that are essential features of the world, any specific world, and world-time.

Heidegger claims that now-time is *only a conception* (albeit a commonsense conception) of the nature of time. It is not a complete alternative temporal structure of a system of meanings. He claims that we never interact with things or live our lives in now-time terms. In everyday activity we do not treat time as such a "flowing stream of nows," and we do not actually perceive entities in terms of now-time. That time is a succession of nows is a theoretical conception that distorts the time that is actually experienced (world-time).

Heidegger supports this claim that now-time is a distorted form of world-time in two ways: first, by showing that real cases of "expressed nows" always actually contain the features of world-time,[20] and, second, by showing how the conception of time as a sequence of nows arises from thinking of time in terms of what is measured with clocks.[21]

Concerning the first point, Heidegger's idea is that "now" is a demonstrative term that is meaningful only in being used and that the "being used" presupposes a pragmatically structured system of meanings, namely, the world. He points out that whenever we pick out a "now," we do so in terms of our objectives, interests, powers, and engagements (significance: "now is the time for . . ."), and we do so by means of extended events (spannedness) that occur at that moment (dating). To quote one of Heidegger's examples, "then—when it dawns—it is time for one's daily work."[22]

Concerning the second, Heidegger argues that in the measuring with clocks of the time with which we concern ourselves (world-time), the standard unit (minutes, hours, etc.) that is used as a measure of the amount of time is understood as a present-at-hand thing that is repeated again and again. This counting of "now and now and now" is the basis for the conception of time as a succession of nows.[23]

6.1A   Experienced Temporal Features of Non-conscious Entities

The accounts of world-time and now-time are Heidegger's major phenomenological descriptions of the time-character of the "objects of consciousness." Since both these concern the world (in Heidegger's sense), however, it is important to supplement them with some consideration of the temporal features of "intraworldly" entities. Since Heidegger never analyzes the temporal features of other Daseins as encountered, I will restrict this discussion to the temporal features of present-at-hand (*vorhanden*) entities and ready-to-hand (*zuhanden*) entities.

Presence-at-hand is a way of Being. Being-present-at-hand means just that something is. The traditional ontological notion of existence is equivalent to presence-at-hand. The prime examples of present-at-hand entities are the substances with properties in causal interaction in space and time that Kant's metaphysics and modern physics describe. For such present-at-hand entities, to be is to be *in time* in a certain way. Heidegger claims that even non-temporal Being-present-at-hand is properly understood with respect to time. Given the focus of this chapter, I cannot examine whether this latter thesis is true or false.

Heidegger never provides a full analysis of the time features of present-at-hand entities, but these time features parallel closely the features of now-time. A present-at-hand entity can be understood as a past-present-future succession of states (of a substance) that follow each other according to a pattern (a rule, according to Kant). Each state exists fully *at and only at* its time (its now), and in conjunction with the states of the other substances with which it interacts, it gives rise (according to the rule or scientific law) to the following state (whether and how there are alternative states that might be brought about is a controversial issue). Present-at-hand entities have past, present, and future dimensions, and are immersed in the passage of time. Whether states are extended, how they can form a continuous series, what it is for states of substances to be past and future with respect to a present state, and how the present can shift from one state to another are ontological problems, just as they are problems for now-time.

Readiness-to-hand is another way of Being. Being-ready-to-hand is the type of existence of something that is defined by its functional role in a larger totality. The prime examples of ready-to-hand entities are equipment that humans have designed to be used in specific ways. That something *exists as equipment*, and what specific piece of equipment it is, are dependent upon: what it works together with (a pen with paper, ink, lighting, support, etc.), how it is used, for what objective it is used, and that someone has that objective.[24] This "equipmental contexture" is supposed to be definitive of the very existence (Being-ready-to-hand) of the piece of equipment. However, Heidegger never makes the boundaries of Being-ready-to-hand very clear. Is something that is *only potentially* a piece of equipment a ready-to-hand entity? Is something whose functional role has nothing to do with human objectives a ready-to-hand entity? When does a piece of equipment loses its equipmental nature? For example, is an entity of the right type, such as a pen, a piece of equipment if it is contingently removed from its equipmental contexture (while stranded on a desert island, one understands how to use pens but cannot use one's cartridge pen for lack of ink and paper)? Since Heidegger never answered these questions, I can only extrapolate what his position might be on the borderline cases.

The time features of ready-to-hand entities parallel closely the time features of world-time. As defined by their functional roles in larger totalities, ready-to-hand entities have a "with-which," a "for-which," and an "in-order-to" that specify their time features. The present of an equipmental entity is defined by its current "being used" with what it works together with. That temporal part of a piece of equipment that is being used is the present portion; this corresponds to the significance feature of world-time whereby each moment is understood with respect to some actual or potential action. Since this using is never instantaneous in nature, the present portion of an equipmental entity always occupies an extended stretch of time ("spannedness"). The use of equipment depends upon what has already occurred in the environmental context; this is the past portion of the equipmental contexture. It also depends both upon what will occur with the equipment and its context (this is the basis for the equipment's "in order to") and the objective that is to be brought about by the use of the equipment. These two factors are the future portion of the equipmental contexture. There is nothing in the equipment itself that accounts for temporal passage. This is entirely derived from the time features of acting consciousness itself.

6.1B   Experienced Temporal Features of Dasein (Human Acting Consciousness)

In addition to experiencing intraworldly entities, we also experience our own conscious life. We (non-reflectively) experience our own experiencing. While Husserl (and Sartre) claimed that this experience of our own conscious life was different in nature from our experience of other entities, Heidegger's position is less clearcut. Heidegger seems not to provide a single account of non-reflective self-awareness, but rather different accounts of our awareness of two different features of our experiencing. Both these accounts are connected with the world (in Heidegger's sense) but in different ways.

On the one hand, we are non-reflectively aware of ourselves as a structural feature of our appropriated specific world. As I explained earlier, our specific world is structured in terms of the projects, powers, and actions of the community of Daseins, and our "appropriated specific world" is structured in terms of our *individual* projects, powers, and actions too. Any Dasein is aware of the specific actions (from the set of possible actions available to a member of the community) in which he is engaged and the specific objectives for himself (from the set of possible objectives available for a member of the community) that he is trying to accomplish. In this respect we are always aware of ourselves within our specific world.

On the other hand, we are also non-reflectively aware of our freedom to transform our specific world and our "appropriated specific world." Insofar as our freedom to establish objectives for ourselves relies upon the possible objectives that are already specified by the community, this freedom itself is "within" the specific world, though not "within" the appropriated specific world. This freedom would be exercised by choosing among alternative lifestyles that are defined by the historical culture. However, Heidegger also thinks that we have the power to transform our specific world by choosing objectives that are not already *defined in detail* by the culture.[25] This type of freedom to transform our specific world is *not* itself within that world, but rather a partial ground of specific worlds. The special character of this power to transform our specific world is manifest in how we are non-reflectively aware of it. This freedom is revealed most explicitly in anxiety, which Heidegger portrays as the "breaking down" or dissolving of our specific world. Of course, this power exists constantly, not simply during bouts of anxiety, and so we are constantly aware of this power by the way in which anxiety haunts us. It is our fleeing from this haunting threat of anxiety that characterizes inauthentic living.

In attempting to specify the temporal features of Dasein that are experienced, there is the complication that human conscious life can be either authentic or inauthentic. According to Heidegger these variations involve some differences in Dasein's temporality.[26] However, the differences between authentic and inauthentic temporalizing do not make any difference for Heidegger's accounts of time-consciousness or the temporal realism question, and they affect the special temporality of the experiencer in only one way. Since inauthentic living is the more common, I will follow Heidegger in starting from the experienced temporal features of inauthentic existence.

Towards the end of division 1 of *Being and Time* Heidegger summarizes the Being of Dasein: "The Being of Dasein means ahead-of-itself-Being-already-in (the-world) as Being-alongside (entities encountered within-the-world)."[27] In division 2 and in *Grundprobleme*, the features of Dasein's Being are reinterpreted in terms of temporality. The "ahead-of-itself" is the ecstasis of the future. The "Being-already-in (the-world)" is the ecstasis of the past, and the "Being-alongside (entities encountered within-the-world)" is the ecstasis of the present. These classifications can serve as a framework for discussing the experienced temporal features of human acting consciousness.

Human conscious life is inherently "ahead-of-itself" in that at any given time its existing is defined by "being towards a future chosen from various alternatives." It is essential to a conscious agent that it care about its own future, that it be able to affect this future, and that its care about its future directs its affecting of this future. Since Heidegger usually discusses human Being through the use of reflexive expressions, some important distinctions are not explicitly made. Concerning this future dimension, there are at least two features involved. First, there is the fact that at any given time human conscious life is structured by a generalized concern for its own future that takes many concrete forms. Dasein is "for the sake of itself" and "an issue for itself." Second, there is the fact that at any given time human conscious life has two types of *powers* to affect its future (Dasein's "ableness-to-be"; Seinkönnen): the powers to act so as to bring about its objectives for itself, and the power (freedom) to change its objectives for itself. It may be that Heidegger does not distinguish care for oneself from power because he thinks that they are mutually implicative: that one can not care about one's own future unless one has some power with respect to it, and that to have a consciously exercisable power requires that one care about one's own future. Even if Heidegger does accept this as an essential connection, being-free (the power to determine the specific future toward which it is directed) would not be included. In any case Heidegger appeals to both features in characterizing Dasein's Being as Being-possible (*Möglichsein*) and as "able-to-be toward itself" (*Seinkönnen zu ihm selbst*).

To provide a phenomenological grounding for the Being of Dasein, these futural features have to be experienced. If acting consciousness is in fact able-to-be toward itself, we should always in some way experience our own care about our own future and our power to affect this future. It is important to emphasize, however, that these are not supposed to be special *distinguishable* experiences that accompany our other experiences. Rather, they are supposed to be structural features of all our experiences that are experienced with them. Heidegger's claim is that all perception, cognition, feeling, and action include these structural features, which can be located by careful observation within them. Even the power to transform its objectives for itself is regularly experienced through the way in which anxiety haunts our everyday activities.

Human conscious life is essentially "already-in-the-world" in that at any given time its existing is defined both by its cultural and its personal past. Heidegger always discusses Dasein's past in terms of how it contributes to Dasein's world. He does not discuss how the specific facts of a person's previous environment and her previous life are related to her current life, because the Being of such facts is usually thought to be presence-at-hand.[28] Rather, Dasein's past is characterized as "thrown facticity" to emphasize the way in which we do not initially have power over its contribution to our system of meanings (this is the basis for guilt). We find ourselves experiencing and living in terms of a system of meanings that is shared with the people in our community. That this world *has already been* (and is experienced as having already been) is the primary way in which Dasein is defined by its past.[29]

Although Heidegger discusses Dasein's past in terms of the historical culture that contributes (along with Dasein's free projecting of its objectives for itself) to the world, his approach to pastness *could* consistently consider the specific facts of a particular person's previous environment and previous life so long as it did so with reference to the person's ongoing action to accomplish his objectives for himself. Insofar as a person's previous life was partly determined by that person himself, this previous life is not something into which the current person is *thrown*. Nevertheless, if one's previous life is considered as earlier steps (in an earlier factual environment) in a currently continuing program of action to accomplish its (continuing) objectives for itself, this past is both within the world and essentially connected to Dasein's current Being. One of the deficiencies of Heidegger's analyses is that he does not consider how such specific past factors might contribute to the disclosing of the world.

Dasein's Being-already-in-the-world is supposed to be experienced. However, as with the experience of the futural feature, our experience of our thrown facticity is not supposed to be a special distinct experience. Rather, we are supposed to experience our special type of pastness as a "pastness parameter" of all our experiences. Yet there is, according to Heidegger, a commonsense category of experiences that emphasizes our experience of our pastness. In the "finding itself" (*sich befinden*) feature of moods and emotions, Dasein's thrown facticity is experienced as such. In moods and emotions we find ourselves living, conceptualizing, and evaluating according to our historical culture. Since all conscious life has some "affective" dimension, in all conscious life we have the experience of being subject to a historically given system of meanings.[30]

The way in which human conscious life is present is the most easily understood "ecstasis" of temporality. Humans are "alongside entities within the world" by being involved in acting to accomplish their objectives. At any given time we are encountering and using equipment within an equipmental context, all of which is experienced within the world as a system of meanings. Ordinary perception is an interested "circumspection" of this equipmental context; that is, we perceive things with reference to their relevance to actual and potential actions. Even theoretically concerned regarding of entities as objects of knowledge, which Heidegger rightly considers to be a motivated activity, is a form of being-alongside present-at-hand entities within the world.

That this present dimension of human conscious life is experienced is also easily understood. Along with our awareness of other entities, we always have some sense of our own present being-aware. We experience diverse types of involvement in the world so that we are aware of the differences between them, for example, that we are now "watching and waiting" or now intensely engaged in repairing a car or now planning a future course of action.

Heidegger considers the usual forms of the present dimension of human conscious life to be inauthentic. Ordinarily we are *so involved* with entities within the world that we pay no attention to, in fact even run away from, our power to change our specific world and our objectives for ourselves. Our "fleeing from" our freedom to transform the world is an unthinking embracing of the public world with its pre-established alternatives for living. Even this "fleeing from" our authentic way of existing reveals, however, that our authentic way of existing is disclosed for us. We have to have some awareness of what it is freely to project our world and objectives for ourselves in order to run away from authentic existing.

The exact nature of authentic existing is complicated and will not be explored in any detail here. My concern is with the peculiar temporal features of authentic existence. Heidegger describes authentic existence as anticipatory resoluteness. Resoluteness is resolving upon our specific world and objectives for ourselves with a full realization of our thrownness into a historical-cultural world and into being a specific individual.[31] Anticipation is explicitly Being- towards-death, that is, projecting our specific world and objectives for ourselves with a full realization that we are essentially finite and that we might die at any time. What is *temporally* significant about authentic existence is the explicit realization of the essential finiteness of human conscious life. We live and experience in light of the fact that we might die at any time and must die at some time. This finiteness is an essential feature of human Being of which we are always in some way aware, although usually we flee from it.

6.2   The Awareness of Experienced Temporal Features

Heidegger's theory of human Being is designed primarily to explain Dasein's *experience of itself*, rather than Dasein's experience of other entities. While the ontology of human Being is certainly supposed to account for our experience of present-at-hand and ready-to-hand entities, the distinctive features of Heidegger's ontology of human Being come from the attempt to account for Dasein's experience of itself. It is Dasein's experience of having-been, being-ahead-of-itself, and being "anticipatorily resolute," that is the source of and justification for the ontology of temporalizing temporality. As I noted earlier, Heidegger's hermeneutic phenomenological approach means that he does not distinguish sharply between the description of Dasein's experience of itself and the theory of Dasein's Being. The description is already mediated through his theory of Dasein's Being, so that much of the same terminology is employed "at both levels." Nevertheless, I think that an intelligible distinction can be made between the description of Dasein's experience of itself and the ontology of Dasein that is supposed to explain how Dasein is able to experience itself in the ways that it does.

I explained in section 6.1 that our non-reflective awareness of our own experiencing is complex according to Heidegger. For this reason it is simpler to start with Heidegger's account of how we are able to experience the temporal features of non-conscious entities. Heidegger's ontological account of this time-consciousness is an "ecstatic-action" account (see Chapter 1). Like Husserl's theory, it requires that the "mental act" feature of experience be intrinsically related to earlier and later "mental act" features. The present phase of acting consciousness is what it is only through its unity with past and future phases. This unity of the temporal features of consciousness is what makes possible the experience of temporal extension and temporal passage in the objects of consciousness.

However, this is where the similarity with Husserl ends. For Husserl this unity is provided by consciousness' "transverse intentionality," that is, by the interlocking retentional-protentional structure of all phases of consciousness. For Heidegger the unity is not a matter of phases quasi-intending each other, but rather a matter of consciousness "being outside of itself" or ecstatic. Although the futural and past dimensions of acting consciousness are "outside" the present dimension, all three ecstases form an intrinsic unity. All three dimensions contribute to our current experiencing because our current experiencing is not itself something that exists solely *in* the present. Thus, the futural and past dimensions of acting consciousness are as operative in our current experience as the present dimension is. All the temporal ecstases "operate together." In my terminology from Chapter 1, the futural dimension is *operative-as-future*, the present dimension is *operative-as-present*, and the past dimension is *operative-as-past*.

Heidegger's difference from Husserl concerning the unity of the temporal features of consciousness also requires a difference concerning non-reflective self-consciousness. In Husserl the interlocking retentional-protentional structure that unifies consciousness also explains how we experience our own experiencing. Since Heidegger's account of the ontological unity of the temporal features of acting consciousness does not employ transverse intentionality, his account of self-awareness has to be different.

It might appear that Heidegger's conception that human acting consciousness is "outside of itself" (ecstatic) by being a unity of past, present, and future dimensions, would have some difficulty in explaining what makes the current experiences at different times distinct from each other. Since past, present, and future dimensions *operate together* (without being simultaneous), current experience cannot be defined as the experience that is present. Yet current experience must be distinct from previous and later cases of current experience if we are to experience ourselves as "in process." Heidegger's theory can explain this distinctness perfectly well by distinguishing different modes of being operative. A temporal portion of Dasein contributes to experience differently when it is operative-as-future than when it is operative-as-present. This is just to say that the future-as-future is different from that same future-as-become-present, and the same goes for all the temporal ecstases. Thus, although one temporal portion of Dasein may contribute to two distinguishable instances of "current experience," these instances are distinct because the contributions are different.

There is a good deal more to the "ecstatic unity" of human acting consciousness than the "operating together" that I have so far described. In terms of the theories of time-perception in Chapter 1, I have discussed Heidegger's theory only in so far as it is a case of theory 4. Not only do the ecstases of time operate together, but there is an intrinsic movement to human Being that is the source of temporal passage. Human Being is an *active* process of projecting its objectives for itself (and its specific world) and of moving toward this future. Human Being is not only being-possible, but also the actualization of its potentialities. The exercise of Dasein's powers is essential to human life. Since Dasein has two types of powers, the power to change its objectives for itself (freedom) and the powers to act to bring about its objectives for itself, the exercise of its powers takes two forms. The exercise of the power to maintain or to change its objectives for itself is the projecting of its specific future. The exercise of the powers to act to bring about its objectives for itself is the *active making present* of this specific future. This active making-present is the source of the passage of time.

Heidegger explains our experience of the temporal features both of non-conscious entities and of ourselves in terms of Dasein's Being as temporalizing activity.[32] Temporalizing activity is the unity of "coming towards itself," "having been," and "making-present," which are the three ecstases of temporality. As diagrammed by Heidegger, human Being as temporalizing activity both "goes forward" to its future and "comes back" from it.[33] Dasein is futural as coming toward itself from its future. The past dimension of Dasein is its having been, which is that to which one comes back in coming toward itself. The present dimension of Dasein is its making-present the entities of the world with which it is involved. The activity defined by these three dimensions of Dasein's "outside of itself" existence is the temporalizing of temporality.

The temporalizing of temporality is supposed to disclose or "open up" the time-structured world that is a feature of Dasein's Being. It is because Dasein's Being is temporalizing activity that we experience world-time. The portion of human Being that might be said to exist "at any given time" is defined (ecstatically) by the earlier and later portions. This makes possible the experiencing of temporal extension in other entities within the world.

The active process of "coming towards itself" and the difference between the three ecstases are supposed to make possible the experiencing of past-present-future features, including the passage of time, in world-time and in worldly entities. While it is clear that temporalizing activity as an active process must *include* temporal passage, Heidegger does not explain how it provides for the *experience of* temporal passage of the world or of worldly entities (or of Dasein itself). Presumably, "at any given moment" of the active process of "coming towards itself," the previous portions of the process not only operate (as past) together with the present portion (as present), but they also reveal their "having been present." Presumably, the future portions of the process not only operate (as future) together with the present portion (as present), but also reveal their "going to be future." Exactly how these revelations of passage exist is not clarified by Heidegger.

Temporalizing activity is supposed to open up the world-time within which all other entities are encountered. As explicated in section 6.1, we experience temporal features in both ready-to-hand and present-at-hand entities. The experienced temporal features of both of these are supposed to derive from temporalizing activity.[34] It is fairly clear how *in general* this is supposed to work. The experienced temporal features of ready-to-hand entities depend upon our specific world, our objectives for ourselves, and our acting to bring about our objectives, all of which are components of temporalizing activity. Thus, the present feature of ready-to-hand entities is defined by our *using* of equipment in the equipmental context. This present is a "span" or extended period, rather than an extensionless moment, because our using (which is a component of temporalizing) "stretches itself out." The past feature of ready-to-hand entities is what has already occurred in the equipmental context; it is the past *as relevant* to our ongoing action. As defined by its contributing to what is currently being done, the past of the ready-to-hand derives from Dasein's having been. The future feature of ready-to-hand entities is what will occur with the equipment and its context and the state of affairs that is to be brought about by the use of the equipment. This future feature is essential to our current acting and is supposed to derive from Dasein's futural "coming towards itself." As I will explain in section 6.5, there are serious problems with

Heidegger's contention that the being-future of the ready-to-hand derives entirely from the futural feature of temporalizing activity.

The experienced temporal features of present-at-hand entities are dependent upon world-time, according to Heidegger. I explained in section 6.1 how now-time is a distorted form of world-time. In a similar fashion, the experienced temporal features of present-at-hand entities are supposed to emerge through the subtraction of the value and use components from ready-to-hand entities.[35] The temporal features of present-at-hand entities are supposed to have their origin in the world, which is itself the result of temporalizing activity.

Temporalizing activity as both going forward from its having been to its future and coming back from its future to its having been is supposed to explain Dasein's experience of itself as temporal. As I explained in section 6.1, Heidegger has different accounts of our non-reflective awareness of two different features of our experiencing. We experience ourselves both as within our specific world and as able to transform our specific world. Both of these ways of experiencing our own experiencing are supposed to be based in temporalizing activity. However, Heidegger never makes the temporalizing of the difference between these forms of self-awareness very clear. Roughly speaking, this difference is supposed to correspond to the difference between authentic temporalizing and inauthentic temporalizing. Authentic temporalizing projects its future from out of its past with an explicit sense of its power to transform its inherited historical-cultural world. However, even in inauthenticity we are aware of our freedom, even though we flee from it. There is thus an important way in which inauthentic temporalizing depends upon authentic temporalizing. Heidegger recognizes this but never makes the ontological dependence clear.[36]

That Dasein goes forward to its future and comes toward itself from its future is the ontological ground for Dasein's experience of itself as "ahead of itself." As explicated in section 6.1, all experience is supposed to contain the structural features of caring about our own future, being able to change or maintain our specific world and our objectives for ourselves, and being able to act to bring about our objectives for ourselves. These experienced structural features are made possible by and dependent upon temporalizing activity. Dasein's concern for its own future, Dasein's projecting of objectives for itself (which it is able to project differently), and Dasein's projecting of a specific world are together dependent upon (and constitute) the way in which temporalizing activity is ontologically "stretched forward" into the future, that is, the way in which the present portion of Dasein is ontologically dependent upon future (possible) portions. Temporalizing activity "comes back" from this future in understanding its specific world in terms of the range of objectives that are socially available, in understanding its appropriated specific world in terms of its objectives for itself, and concretely in acting to bring about its objectives for itself. The exercise of its concrete powers to affect worldly entities through action is made possible by (and constitutes) temporalizing activity as the *process* of the futural dimension of Dasein "coming back" to the present dimension.

That Dasein both goes forward to its future *from* its having been and comes back *to* its having been is the ontological ground for its experience of itself as defined by its personal and cultural past. As I indicated in section 6.1, Heidegger always considers Dasein's pastness in terms of its contribution to Dasein's specific world and to its ongoing action within the world. The role of our personal and cultural past in the projecting of our specific world and our objectives for ourselves is made possible by (and largely constitutes) temporality's "going forward from." In the continuous development of our foresight concerning what means to follow to our objectives, there may also be a "going forward from where it already is in ongoing action." The *reinterpretation* of our personal and cultural past in terms of our projected specific world and projected objectives for ourselves is made possible by (and partly constitutes) temporalizing activity's "coming back to" its having been. Heidegger may also have in mind that the "adding on" of completed steps to our ongoing action within the world is dependent upon (and partly constitutes) temporalizing activity's "coming back to" its having been.

The making-present feature of temporalizing activity is the ontological ground for Dasein's experience of itself as "alongside entities within the world." Our experiencing of diverse types of (present) involvement with entities in the world is dependent upon (and constitutes) the making-present of ourselves as interacting with other things.

The essential finiteness of human Being is something of which we are always aware, even though we usually flee from it. Both this finiteness itself and our awareness of this finiteness are supposed to be components of temporalizing activity. There are unclarities about the temporalization of each of these. Our awareness of our finiteness is our awareness that we will inevitably die and that we might die at any moment. We have this awareness in the fullest sense only when it is embedded in our projecting of our future, that is, when we project our future as finite. Such a future as finite is one that is not just a chosen possibility amongst unchosen alternatives, but also a possibility that might be cut off by death. Thus, we project our specific future objectives *as* possibly cut off by death. This is what we do in authentic temporalizing that is "anticipatorily towards death." The problem with the temporalization of this awareness of finiteness is, as I pointed out above, that we are also aware of our finiteness when we are inauthentic. Inauthentic temporalizing is ontologically dependent upon authentic temporalizing in a way that Heidegger never makes clear, and this makes the temporalizing of our awareness of our finiteness unclear.

Humans are thrown into being finite, according to Heidegger. It is just an existential fact that our temporalizing activity is itself finite in nature. *How* the temporalizing activity itself is finite is never made clear by Heidegger. There should be something about the temporalizing activity that *requires that it not continue* indefinitely. Although a Heideggerean position on this issue can be constructed based on the notion that having projects at all depends upon being finite (this position is developed and criticized in section 10.3), Heidegger does not explain what it is about temporalizing activity that requires that it not go on and on.

Temporalizing activity can be either authentic or inauthentic. Although both of them are activities, authentic temporalizing includes a sense of being active with respect to time and its passage, whereas inauthentic temporalizing includes the usual sense of being immersed in a time where events pass independently of us. Thus, our attitude toward our projects and toward worldly states of affairs is different in inauthentic temporalizing where we consider the past to be "over and done with" and the future to be that for which we can only wait. Since I have already indicated the problematic character of their relationship to each other, I will close this section with a summary of their different characters.

General	Authentic Form	Inauthentic Form
Futural (*Zu-kunft*) (coming-towards-itself)	Anticipation (*vorlaufen*)	Awaiting (*Gewärtigen*)
Making present (*gegenwärtigen*)	Moment of vision (*Augenblick*) (instant)	Waiting-toward (*Gegen-wart*)
Having been (*gewesen*)	Retrieve (*wiederholen*)	Forgetting (*vergessen*)

6.3   The Temporal Nature of Dasein

In sections 6.1 and 6.2, I have already discussed how Heidegger conceives human Being to have a special type of temporality. Human Being is the temporalizing activity that explains how we are able to experience the temporal features both of ourselves and of other entities. All that remains to be done in this section is to explicate more fully some of the special temporal characteristics of human Being that have already been discussed.

Heidegger emphasizes that human Being is not temporal in the way that present-at-hand entities are temporal.[37] The ordinary notion of existence, which Heidegger calls "presence-at-hand," gives priority to *present* existence. For ordinary thinking, existence as present is the paradigmatic case of being; only what is present is actual and fully real. Existence as past and existence as future are understood from it, and what is past and future is thought to be less than fully real. Although Heidegger does not expressly say this, these views about existence represent our past-present-future perspective on time.

Heidegger claims that for human Being the future dimension has priority. Human Being is most distinctively able-to-be; this emphasizes being-possible rather than being-actual. However, this notion of possibility is not the notion of possibility in logic.

> As a modal category of presence-at-hand, possibility signifies what is *not yet* actual and what is *not at any time* necessary. It characterizes the *merely* possible. Ontologically it is on a lower level than actuality and necessity. On the other hand, possibility as an *existentiale* is the most primordial and ultimate positive way in which Dasein is characterized ontologically.[38]

It is not that Dasein's future is possible in the sense of not now actual and perhaps never actual. It is rather the case that what Dasein is now is defined by this future in special ways. One main way is that Dasein's powers *have to be exercised*. Dasein's powers to affect its future cannot fail to be exercised because they are not dependent upon anything else, and Dasein does not have the power not to exercise its powers. Hence, this is a somewhat different notion of "power" than that of "dispositions" that can be triggered or not. It is in part because Dasein now is defined by some exercise of its power to affect the future that Dasein now is "ahead of itself." However,

Dasein's future is also open in that there are different possibilities that Dasein might select and "be toward." Heidegger thinks of humans as always toward some possibility that is maintained as a possibility with reference to other alternatives.

Another distinctive feature of human Being is its intrinsic finiteness. According to Heidegger, humans are not contingently finite in the sense that they might die or might just live on and on. Rather, human existence at any given time is defined by its temporal finiteness; humans are always "towards-death." When a person's death will occur is rarely known, but that a person will die is a necessary feature of human existence.

The notion that Dasein might die at any time seems to conflict in one way with the notion that Dasein is "ahead of itself" and able-to-be. Despite Heidegger's insistence that authentic projecting of our specific world and objectives for ourselves must be *in light of* the facts that we will die and that we might die at any time, there is a definite difference between future objectives that we have an opportunity to attain and those that are cut off by death. Heidegger neither explains how both of these "futures" can have the same ontological standing nor provides a different ontological account of each.

Along with essential finiteness and the priority of the future dimension, human Being has a special temporal nature in many other ways. Human Being does not occur together with other entities in an ontologically real time. Rather, as I will discuss in section 6.4, temporalizing activity is the most basic form of time and seems to be the ontological ground of all forms of time. This temporal idealism means that the standard temporal features of entities that occur *within* time do not apply to humans.

Although there is a sense in which a phase of human acting consciousness defines a temporal location by its existence there, the standard notion of temporal location does not apply for two reasons: because human Being is essentially being-possible, not just being-actual, and because temporal locations are defined by human acting consciousness existing there, not vice-versa.

The standard form of temporal extension does not apply to human Being because of its ecstatic nature. The temporal extension or duration of human Being is not a matter of occupying contiguous points of time, but of being ecstatically "outside of itself" and of "stretching itself along." All three ecstases of temporalizing activity form an intrinsic unity and operate together in producing the passage of time. For this same reason the period of a human life is not divided or divisible in the standard way. No "time slice" of human conscious life is independent of the other temporal "parts."

The intrinsic finiteness of human Being introduces a special feature into the length of duration of a human life. A *completed* human life from birth to death does have a length of duration that is comparable to the lengths of duration of other entities. What is special about a human life is that it is necessarily finite rather than contingently finite.

The ecstatic character, the way in which the present portion of human conscious life is dependent upon the past and future portions, and the active "stretching" character also make a difference to earlier-later relations and past-present-future features. Both earlier-later relations and past-present-future features do characterize Heidegger's human Being, but because of the ecstatic and "stretching" characters, they have to be interpreted in special ways. One important example of this is Heidegger's conception of the future of human Being, not as what will become present, but as that "towards which" we currently are. Another important example is Heidegger's notion that the passage of time is dependent upon the stretching activity of "coming towards itself" from its future.

6.4   Temporalizing Activity and the Denial of Temporal Realism

It is difficult to formulate a consistent Heideggerean position on the general issue of metaphysical realism versus idealism. On the one hand, Heidegger frequently criticizes the traditional realism-idealism debate as not being well formulated. On the other hand, he frequently adopts a realistic position concerning some natural entities and an idealistic position concerning others. In this section I will explore Heidegger's temporal idealism, which is different in important respects from traditional idealism. Heidegger portrays time as dependent upon human temporalizing activity, but with a different type of dependence from that of traditional idealism. As I will also indicate, Heidegger admits that many entities have some type of independent existence, although this cannot be a temporal existence.

Heidegger has two interconnected criticisms of the traditional realism-idealism debate.[39] First, human Being has been misunderstood. Human conscious life has been considered to be something present-at-hand that either is or is not related in a present-at-hand way to "independently existing" (present-at-hand) entities. Humans have been thought to be Cartesian mind-substances that are directly aware only of their own ideas so that they can worry about whether there is a world independent of their ideas. According to Heidegger, human conscious life is Being-in-the-world; that is, humans exist only as aware of and interacting with other entities within the world. For humans as essentially in a world along with other entities, the question of metaphysical idealism or realism may not even make sense.

Second, the notion of reality has never been adequately clarified. To be real, entities must exist as present-at-hand and must not be dependent upon human existence. According to Heidegger, the notion of "present-at-hand existence" is meaningful only *within* Dasein's world. Within a specific historical-cultural system of meanings, there is a notion of "independent existence," but this is not the purported metaphysical notion of "independent existence." Dasein can not make meaningful to itself the purported metaphysical notion of reality, and so cannot meaningfully argue about metaphysical realism or idealism.[40]

Despite this critique, Heidegger does claim in many places that some entities are not dependent upon human Being.

Entities *are*, quite independently of the experience by which they are disclosed, the acquaintance in which they are discovered, and the grasping in which their nature is ascertained.[41]

As we have noted, Being (not entities) is dependent upon the understanding of Being; that is to say, Reality (not the Real) is dependent upon care.[42]

Beings are in themselves the kinds of beings they are, and in the way they are, even if, for example, Dasein does not exist.[43]

Intraworldliness does not belong to nature's being. . . . Of nature *uncovered*—of that which is, so far as we comport toward it as an unveiled entity—it is true that it is always already in a world; but being within the world does not belong to the *being* of nature.[44]

This last quotation is particularly important because in this section Heidegger is quite explicit that natural entities "enter into the world" but can exist without any world. This notion runs directly contrary to the second argument, that "being outside the world" is a meaningless idea.[45]

Although Heidegger is a realist concerning some things, he is an idealist concerning time. While he never exactly argues that time *in general could not* exist independently of human Being, he does argue that time as commonsensically conceived, now-time, could not exist independently (see section 6.1). Furthermore, he consistently claims that time exists most basically as the temporalizing activity of human Being,[46] and he sometimes expressly denies that time exists independently.[47]

> There is no nature-time, since all time belongs essentially to the Dasein.[48]

> We must first understand that temporality, as ecstatico-horizonal, temporalizes something like *world*-time, which constitutes a within-time-ness of the ready-to-hand and the present-at-hand. But in that case such entities can never be designated as 'temporal' in the strict sense. Like every entity with a character other than that of Dasein, they are non-temporal, whether they Really occur, arise and pass away, or subsist 'ideally.'[49]

The form of temporal idealism that Heidegger embraces includes two components. First, time exists most basically as the temporal features of human Being. Temporalizing activity has past, present, and future dimensions, all of which operate together in the activity of "going forward" from its having been to its future and "coming back" from its future to its having been (see section 6.2). These temporal features of temporalizing activity are how time exists. Time has no other independent existence, so that temporalizing activity does not occur in a time that would exist without it. One way to understand this dependence of time on human Being is in terms of the notion that time exists only if change exists. The temporalizing activity of human Being is that which changes, so that the existence of time is dependent upon this changing that is built in to human Being.

This way in which time is dependent upon human Being is different from the traditional forms of dependence. (See section 2.2 on these different forms of dependence.) Time is not an idea in the mind of a non-temporal consciousness nor even a necessary framework through which a non-temporal consciousness experiences.

Time is rather the ontological structure of human Being. This different type of dependence is consistent with the first criticism of the traditional realism-idealism debate.

The second component is that temporalizing activity "opens up" the time (world-time) that is experienced and within which all entities are experienced. As I have explained in section 6.2, all experienced temporal features are supposed to derive from temporalizing activity. Temporalizing activity is not just a necessary condition for the experiencing of temporal features; it is the *sole source* of the experienced temporal features of entities. Although experienced entities do have some type of real existence so that they bring something to the encounter with human acting consciousness, their experienced temporal features are not brought to this encounter because the temporal features do not have real existence.

All experienced time and temporal features of entities are supposed to be productively dependent upon temporalizing activity. Since Heidegger never discusses what natural entities are like "outside world-time," I can not give any authoritative account of how temporalizing activity could be the *sole source* of their temporal features *as experienced*. The most plausible account would be along Kantian lines: that real entities have some type of non-temporal order that is experienced by Dasein as a temporal order. Even with the most favorable assumptions, however, there are serious problems with the notion that all experienced temporal features derive exclusively from human Being as temporalizing activity.

6.5 *Problems*

Heidegger's thought has an impressive scope. Despite my focus upon those portions of his thought that concern the relation of time and human Being, I have touched upon many other controversial issues. I will not critique these other issues, but will consider only the problems in the accounts of experienced temporal features, temporalizing activity, and temporal idealism.

First, Heidegger draws the wrong ontological conclusion from his insightful analysis of now-time (our explicit commonsense conception of what time is like) as a derivative form of world-time. He is quite right that we do not and could not experience simply in terms of now-time. As interested acting consciousnesses, we always encounter other entities in terms of our action-oriented world with its world-time. However, even though now-time must be conceived by a consciousness whose system of meanings is structured in world-time terms, this does not make now-time dependent upon world-time. Only the conception of now-time is dependent upon a lived world-time. It is perfectly possible that a real now-time could exist independently of our conceptualization.

It is curious that Heidegger fails to realize this point since he sometimes makes a very similar point concerning Being-present-at-hand: that our conception of it is derivative, but that it itself may not be dependent upon Being-ready-to-hand. I think the reason is that he connects now-time too strongly with measuring activities, which do seem to be dependent upon an interested acting consciousness. However, we can conceive of now-time as the time of the succession of states of substances in causal interaction with each other. This conception of now-time does not depend upon any measuring activities.

Second, Heidegger's analysis of the past dimension ("at that time") of world-time needs to be supplemented. With his notion of world- time as the time of our action-oriented system of meanings, Heidegger overemphasizes the type of immediate contribution of the past to our experience that Husserl calls "retention." The past is considered only in terms of its immediate contribution to our ongoing action and thought. I do not deny that this is the most important way in which the present dimension of human Being is connected with the past, but it is not the only way. Explicit remembering of the past is not, I think, entirely dependent upon or reducible to this pragmatically oriented "retention" of the past. With the notion of retrieving "covered-over" cultural meanings, Heidegger himself recognizes that there is an important place for thinking that *focuses on* the past as past. Such other ways of relating to the past should be incorporated in the analysis of the world-time that is temporalized.

Third, Heidegger's analysis of temporalizing activity does not distinguish relationships of meaning from relationships of production or causation. The "going forward" from its having been to its future and "coming back" from its future to its having been includes: the grasping of meaning relationships, particularly, how the present phase of any entity is defined by earlier and later phases; the maintaining or changing of a specific world and objectives for oneself by the exercise of freedom; and the producing of later states of affairs by the exercise of powers to act. As I indicated in section 6.1, it is not clear why all three of these features should be united in one temporalizing activity.

Fourth, Heidegger's theory that temporalizing activity is the sole source of the experienced temporal features of entities within the world is incapable of explaining the differences between what we take to be the future features of worldly entities and what actually becomes present. In using equipment in an equipmental context, we depend upon what will happen. We exercise our powers to act with an understanding of the future states of the equipment and its equipmental context. However, things may happen that are completely different from that which we understood. The future features of equipmental entities on which we depended may not in fact become present. This is easily explained if the equipmental entities themselves have real temporal features. The difference can be explained as a difference between what we humans thought the future features were and what they *really* were.

However, if ready-to-hand entities (or present-at-hand entities) have temporal features *only* within world-time that is temporalized by temporalizing activity, the difference is not explainable. If the future of ready-to-hand entities derives entirely from temporalizing activity "going forward" to its own future and "coming back" from it, there is no place for this difference. There *is* a place for our portraying the future features of worldly entities to be a range of alternatives only one of which becomes present, but there is not a place for a discrepancy between how we portray the future and what actually becomes present.

Fifth, Heidegger's theory that temporalizing activity is the sole source of experienced temporal features does not give an adequate account of the experience of passage. I pointed out in section 6.2 that although temporalizing activity is an active process that must *include* temporal passage, it does not explain how the passage of time is experienced. In Husserl's theory of time-consciousness, this is accomplished by the "double intentionality" of retention and protention. In Heidegger's theory, the past, present, and future ecstases of temporalizing activity "operate together" to disclose the world and world-time, and they intrinsically change together. However, the change in temporalizing activity does not by itself explain the experience of change. Although Heidegger's theory could be expanded so as to explain the experience of temporal passage, in its present form it does not explain how we experience ourselves and other entities as moving through time.

Sixth, at the end of section 6.2 and in section 6.3, I pointed out some unclarities about the notion that temporalizing activity is essentially finite. Heidegger never makes it clear what it is about temporalizing activity that requires that it not go on and on. In addition there is the apparent conflict between "being ahead of itself" and being subject to death at any time. Heidegger never explains how it is possible that a person is defined by her future (not just her present conception of the future) in those cases where that future is cut off by death.

Finally, I have referred several times to the problem of the relation of authentic temporalizing to inauthentic temporalizing. Since we are always aware of our freedom even when we flee from it, there is an important way in which inauthentic temporalizing is supposed to be dependent upon authentic temporalizing (see section 6.2). Heidegger never makes this ontological dependence clear.

Heidegger's important insights are (1) that human Being must be temporal in order to experience the temporal features of entities, (2) that the temporal features of human Being are different from the temporal features of natural entities, and (3) that there are special temporal features necessary for human action. However, his claim that the temporal features of human Being are in some ontological sense the basic form of time are unsubstantiated. While there is a type of epistemological *equip*rimordiality in the sense of (1), namely, that we have to experience our own temporality in order to experience the temporal features of other entities, this does not establish any ontological priority. Furthermore, there is no argument, other than the first argument critiqued above, for the claim that there is no independently real time. Heidegger probably thought that if there were an independently real time, human Being would have to occur within it and so claims (2) and (3) would be impossible. I will argue in Part III that a special temporal nature for human Being is consistent with an ontologically real time.

7
Sartre's Theory of
Time-Consciousness and Time

Jean-Paul Sartre's primary concern at the time of *Being and Nothingness*[1] was to make people responsible for themselves. Since Sartre believed that free will was necessary for responsibility, his ontology of human being was designed to explain how humans can be free and responsible for themselves. Following in the Kantian tradition, Sartre thought that if human life occurred in a real time, free will would not be possible. Thus, his ontology portrays time as entirely dependent upon human being. As in Heidegger's philosophy, human being is a temporalizing activity that produces the time of worldly entities.

Sartre's philosophy was very strongly influenced by both Husserl and Heidegger. While his conceptions of human existence, of time, and of time-consciousness are similar to Heidegger's, his conception of phenomenology is more Husserlian than Heideggerean. Sartre claims that in *pure* reflection we have a direct, absolutely certain awareness of our own conscious life.[2] In contrast with Heidegger, Sartre does not maintain that this awareness operates through a system of meanings that pre-structures what is experienced. Rather, *pure* reflection is something like an extension of the pre-reflective cogito that is an essential feature of any conscious act.[3] In *pure* reflection the reflecting act is so intimately connected with the reflected-on conscious life that this conscious life is known without being made into an object. This pure reflection provides the phenomenological basis for Sartre's ontology of human being.

Sartre emphasizes that pure reflection is very different from ordinary reflection, which he calls "impure." Impure reflection on our conscious life does not straightforwardly reveal that conscious life, but rather *transforms* it. Reflection "is a stage of nihilation intermediate between the pure and simple existence of the for-itself and existence for-others."[4] Since conscious life (Being-for-itself) is literally transformed by the "look" of the Other, there is a way in which impure reflection also objectifies our conscious life into enduring psychic facts. Psychic entities that simply continue to be the same through time (endure), such as the Ego, personality characteristics, continuing emotions, and long-term actions, are created by impure reflection and do not exist independently of its objectifying regard.[5]

7.1 Experienced Temporal Features

Sartre's phenomenological descriptions of the experienced temporal features of entities focus primarily on human acting consciousness, which in ontological terms Sartre calls "Being-for-itself." Sartre is mainly interested in the ontology of human being, rather than the ontology of what exists independently of human being (Being-in-itself), because he thinks that all the interesting features of the objects of experience are productively dependent upon human being. His phenomenological descriptions of the basic structures of human acting consciousness are supposed to reveal the ontological structures of Being-for-itself.

Sartre's phenomenological descriptions of the experienced temporal features of entities are sometimes hard to separate from the ontological arguments with which they are conjoined. This is not because phenomenological (pure) reflection necessarily interprets the reflected-on. It is just that all too frequently Sartre claims to be doing phenomenology when he is actually arguing ontologically that things must be a certain way, such as arguing that since the Being of the object of consciousness is Being-in-itself and Being-in-itself contains no internal relations or negations, the object of consciousness cannot contain some specific internal relation or negation, such as quality or potentiality. Nevertheless, Sartre does offer an extensive phenomenological description of the experienced temporal features of acting consciousness itself and, to a lesser extent, of the objects of acting consciousness. Like Heidegger, Sartre claims that these temporalities are different in important ways, and as earlier noted he considers the experienced "time of the world" to be derivative of the "original temporality of the For-itself." Reversing this order of ontological dependence, I will start with Sartre's limited phenomenological description of the temporal features of the objects of consciousness.

7.1A   Experienced Temporal Features of Instrumental-Things

Sartre borrowed from Heidegger the notion that we (acting consciousnesses) encounter other entities in terms of a system of meanings or "world." His conception of the world is very similar to Heidegger's. The world is productively dependent upon human existence (Being-for-itself). Any specific world is *directed toward* the concrete entities that are discovered within it because Being-for-itself (with its world) exists only as the nihilating of what exists on its own (Being-in-itself). The system of meanings is essentially tied to the In-itself because this system of meanings exists only as an essential feature of consciousness' both separating itself off from and relating itself to (by being conscious of) what exists in-itself.

Like Heidegger, Sartre conceived consciousness to be essentially an *agent* that acts upon things, and so the world is an action-oriented system of meanings in terms of which any entity is encountered and acted upon. As action-oriented, this system of meanings includes the following structural features. First, a person's projects, that is, what he wants to make himself be. The correlates of a person's projects in the world are what he wants and desires, what he pursues and avoids, and what interests him. Second, a person's sense of her powers to bring about her projects, and her sense of the limitations on her powers. Third, a set of classifications or types of encountered entities. These types are essentially connected with a person's projects and powers. Sartre adopted the pragmatist notion that what we experience is "divided up" into differentiated but related entities on the basis of our projects, our perceptual abilities, and our abilities to affect things.

Sartre's conception of the world differs from Heidegger's concerning the priority that each ascribes to the individual versus the community. Heidegger's world is dependent upon the community of Daseins that share and interact in terms of that system of meanings. An individualized system of meanings for a specific person develops only when that person becomes authentic. Sartre adopted the more traditional view that communities are composed of interrelated and interacting persons, so that the individual consciousness is more basic than the community. Any individual consciousness initially has a somewhat individualized system of meanings that is modified by its interactions with other individual consciousnesses. Shared community conceptions are adopted by an individual consciousness only through these interactions. Although there is always in fact a dialectical interplay of Being-for-itself with Being-for-others and thus a dialectical interplay of a For-itself's individualized system of meanings with a community system of meanings, an individual person's world can continue without any *further* interaction with other people. The meaningfulness of a For-itself's world is not strictly dependent upon community interactions, even though in fact these regularly occur and affect the meanings in a person's world.

According to Sartre, the objects of experience are "instrumental-things," that is, distinct enduring things with qualities that are related to each other in terms of their possible instrumental uses together in achieving some desired state of affairs (composed of instrumental-things) through action. Although Being-in-itself has no temporal characteristics, the In-itself appears in the For-itself's world as temporal. Instrumental-things are experienced as extended through time, as being (at any given time) past, present, and future, and as being immersed in the passage of time from future to present to past. Sartre's account of the experienced temporal features of instrumental-things can be presented in outline form (Outline 1). Many of the temporal features of the instrumental-thing require little explication.

A1(*a*). It is obvious that a past state has been present, and it is experienced as formerly being present.

A1(*b*). The past states of instrumental-things affect what the thing now is in at least two ways. First, it makes a difference that there are past states at all; otherwise the current state would be that of a newly existent thing. Second, the specific past states make a difference concerning whether the current state is usual or unusual and whether it is an enduring characteristic or part of a process of change. For example, if brightly colored autumn leaves dangling from a tree were always that way, trees and leaves would be quite different things. That trees undergo seasonal (and quicker) changes make a large difference to what trees and their leaves are.

Outline 1

A. Instrumental-things as past, present, and future.
    1. Instrumental-things as past
        (a) having been present[6]
        (b) contributing to the meaning of what is present[7]
        (c) being completely determinate and without possibility[8]
        (d) cannot be used as an instrument or perceived
    2. Instrumental-things as present
        (a) presence to perception either as focus or as background[9]
        (b) presence to action (part of the instrumental complex being used)[10]
        (c) being in motion[11]
    3. Instrumental-things as future
        (a) what will be present (determined future)[12]
        (b) what might be present[13]
        (c) what is to be made present[14]
    4. Categorial connections of instrumental-things as past with instrumental-things as present.
    5. Categorial connections of instrumental-things as future with instrumental-things as present.
B. Instrumental-things as immersed in the passage of time.
    1. Instrumental-things as present becoming past
        (a) displacement of what is present by the new present (which was future)
        (b) becoming fully determinate and without possibility[15]
    2. Instrumental-things as future becoming present
        (a) "slipping by of In-itself instants"[16]
        (b) what is lacking in the present situation being made present[17]

A1(c). The past of instrumental-things is completely determinate and without possibility. States of things and states of affairs that could have been different are now fixed and unalterable.

A1(d). Sartre does not discuss the notion that instrumental-things as past cannot be used instrumentally or be perceived, but these features follow from the fact that the past is no longer present.

A2(a). States of instrumental-things and states of affairs involving several instrumental-things are present insofar as consciousness is present to them either as the focus of perception or as the context (ultimately including the entire world) from which the focus stands out.

A2(*b*). States of instrumental-things and states of affairs involving several instrumental-things are present insofar as acting consciousness uses them in its simple action to attain its goals.[18] A simple action is one that is experienced as an undivided unit, as not composed of a series of shorter-term actions. What is used in such shortest-term actions is present. What is used in the course of a longer-term action (which is composed of a series of simple actions) need not be present.

A2(*c*). Sartre also claims that the present of universal time is defined by the motion of enduring things from place to place. The basic idea seems to be that motion takes place *only* in the present. In the section "The Time of the World," Sartre does not explicitly claim that motion occurs only in the present, but this seems to be the starting point for his discussion.[19] Thinking that motion essentially takes place in the present and so can be used to define the present of an instrumental-thing, he notes that an enduring thing's "being in motion at point *a*" is different from simply "being at point *a*." The "being-of-passage" from point *a* to point *b* cannot be analyzed in terms of simply *occupying* all the points between *a* and *b* in succession. From this he concludes that there is a difference in the *being* of an instrumental-thing between its "being in motion" and its "being at rest." "Being in motion" involves a type of "exteriority-to-self" because the enduring moving thing both is and is not at a particular point. This "exteriority-to-self" is then claimed to be the appropriate reflection onto Being-in-itself of the For-itself's present. The "exteriority-to-self" of a moving thing is experienced to be temporal because the experiencer (the For-itself) is temporal (the ecstatic nature of the For-itself).

The ontological claim about the derivativeness of the temporal features of the objects of consciousness will be examined in section 7.4. I want to note here that the phenomenology of the present of instrumental-things is suspect. It is dubious that in any *experiential* sense a thing's motion takes place only in the present and so can be used to define a thing's being present. We both perceive and conceive things to be continuously in motion for a period of time, such as ten minutes or ten years. Although, "being in motion at point *a*" is certainly different from simply "being at point *a*," there is no experiential basis for thinking that "being in motion at point *a*" cannot become past in the same way that any other quality becomes past.

A3(*a*). The essence of an instrumental-thing includes all the characteristics that it will have (assuming that it is not destroyed by human agency). What will be present includes both those characteristics that are permanent through time and those characteristics that result from inevitable change. However, none of these characteristics really exist according to Sartre until they are present; they are "being beyond being."

A3(*b*). Within the essence of the instrumental-thing there is also a range of possibilities concerning characteristics of things and states of affairs. One or another of these possibilities will come about, either through human action or through the mere passage of time.

A3(*c*). Humans experience instrumental-things as composing a "world of tasks" where certain states of affairs are to be brought about through action. What is to be made present is that which the present states of affairs lack.

A4. Since Sartre's main objective is to show that instrumental-things have a hybrid temporality that derives from the a-temporality of the In-itself and the ecstatic temporality of the For-itself, he does not consider the "temporal parts" of the instrumental-thing to be *internally related* to each other. Nevertheless, in terms of the above features of instrumental-things as past and as present, there do appear to be some obvious categorial connections between them (supposedly deriving from the temporality of the For-itself). Pastness is partially defined by having been present (A1(*a*)), and what it is that is present is partly defined by its past (see A1(*b*)). Furthermore, being completely determinate and without possibility (A1(*c*)) seems to characterize the present as well as the past of instrumental-things.

A5. There also appear to be some obvious categorial connections between instrumental-things as future and as present. All three features of futurity are defined with respect to the present. Conversely, the future characteristics of a thing seem to affect its present by partially defining what it is that is present (by defining the essence, just as a thing's past does). Furthermore, present states of affairs are lacking only in contrast with future more perfect totalities, and instrumental complexes are used and usable only in order to bring about future states of affairs.

B. According to Sartre, there is very little to be said about instrumental-things as immersed in the passage of time other than that they do change from future to present to past. There is nothing in the instrumental-thing itself to require or to make intelligible this becoming. The future states of instrumental-things just "slip by" into the present and thence into the past. The passage of time is dependent entirely upon the activity of acting consciousness.[20]

B1(a).States of instrumental-things and states of affairs become past by being displaced from the present by new present states. What is displaced does not disappear entirely but slips by into the past.

B1(b). The transition from present to past is the acquisition of the distinctive characteristics of being past. Sartre describes consciousness' transition from presentness to pastness as a matter of becoming factual, that is, fully determinate and without possibility. However, instrumental-things are already factual in the present. For instrumental-things, becoming fully determinate and without possibility (A1(c)) best describes the transition from future to past, since both the present and the past are factual. The inability to be used as an instrument or to be perceived (A1(d)) best distinguishes the past from the present.

B2(a). States of instrumental-things and states of affairs also become present through the apparently external "slipping by" of instants. What will be present (A3(a)) and part of what might be present (A3(b)) move from the future to the present in this way.

B2(b). However, there is a second type of transition from future to present, that in which acting makes some desired state of affairs present. The "lack" relation between present and future *does* provide some basis for the transition from future to present. However, if value is indeed consciousness-dependent, both this "lack" relation and the action motivated by it derive from consciousness as Sartre's thesis claims.

7.1B   Experienced Temporal Features of Acting Consciousness

Sartre's phenomenological descriptions of human acting consciousness are supposed to reveal the fundamental ontological structures of Being-for-itself. With respect to time, Sartre's descriptions are supposed to reveal Being-for-itself as "outside of itself" ("ecstatic" or "diasporatic") in that each of its temporal dimensions (past, present, and future) is internally related to the other temporal dimensions. Furthermore, Being-for-itself is supposed to be revealed as essentially an *activity* that is the ground of the passage of time.

As I noted at the beginning of this chapter, Sartre distinguishes pure (phenomenological) reflection from ordinary (impure) reflection, which distorts the object of reflective consciousness. Ordinary, impure reflection portrays human acting consciousness to have a continuing nature; it consists of psychic entities that either endure unchanged through time or follow a necessary course of development. Sartre calls the temporal features of such psychic entities "psychic temporality." The impure reflective act objectifies the reflected-on consciousness and thereby creates psychic temporality. Psychic objects are created by construing the past of acting consciousness as determining its future. "The reflective projects a psychic object provided with the three temporal dimensions, but it constitutes these three dimensions solely out of what the reflected-on *was*."[21] Such psychic temporality is a distorted form of original temporality, and in many ways it is similar to the derivative temporality of instrumental-things. Because of its derivative character, I will not examine psychic temporality any further in this chapter.

Outline 2

C. Acting consciousness as past, present, and future.
    1. Acting consciousness as past
        (a) having been present in perceiving or using to ———[22]
        (b) acting consciousness as fact (ontologically: the For-it-self-become-In-itself)[23]
        (c) having to be its past; responsibility[24]
    2. Acting consciousness as present
        (a) being present perceptually to ———[25]
        (b) being present through action to ———[26]
    3. Acting consciousness as future
        (a) having projects; what I am to be[27]
        (b) projects as possible (freedom)[28]
        (c) possible presence to ———[29]
    4. Categorial connections of acting consciousness as past with acting consciousness as present.
    5. Categorial connections of acting consciousness as future with acting consciousness as present.
D. The basic activity of consciousness as the source of time's passage.
    1. Acting to bring about projects is the part of the activity whereby the future becomes present.[30]
    2. Displaced presence to ——— becoming consciousness-as-fact is the part of the activity whereby the present becomes past.[31]

Sartre's phenomenological descriptions of the temporality of acting consciousness reveal that there is necessarily a pastness, presentness, and futurity of acting consciousness and an activity wherein the futurity is becoming present and the present is becoming past (see Outline 2).

C1. Sartre does not explicitly distinguish three forms of pastness, but it is important that they be distinguished in order that the question of their interrelations can arise. I will indicate how the three forms can be interpreted so as to be mutually consistent.

C1(*a*). Having been present to ———, which Sartre also describes as "past presence to a past state of the world,"[32] is Sartre's replacement for Husserl's retention. It refers to our previous experiences of things *as informing* our current perceiving and acting. It is the understanding of what things are like *through* our prior being present to them. For example, in order to perceive the eighth chime *as* eighth when a clock strikes eight o'clock, we have to be conscious of the present chime as following in sequence seven other chimes, each of which is present when it occurs. Sartre's phenomenological claim is that acting consciousness is *still conscious through* each of the former acts of being present to one chime but in the mode of "having been." We are present to the eighth chime and have been present to the seventh, sixth, fifth, and so on. All practical or empirical knowledge of what things are like, for example, that an automobile endures relatively unchanged through short stretches of time or that it will crush a leaf in its path, is based on having been present to ———,[33] as is all extended action (where we *have been* the earlier steps of an extended action).

C1(*b*). There is a second type of pastness of acting consciousness, its solidifying into facticity. Acting consciousness-as-fact is our former perceiving, thinking, or acting as viewed externally, rather than being conscious through it (C1(*a*)). It is past actions, thoughts, emotions, and so on as facts back behind the present, as past episodes in which we no longer participate.

Ontologically, Sartre describes acting consciousness-as-fact as "the For-itself-become-In-itself." If this feature of the pastness of acting consciousness is to be made consistent with the "having been present to ———" feature, many of our past experiences must be still in the process of solidifying. Given Sartre's ontological account of consciousness in terms of nihilation, there must still be nothingness in the For-itself-become-In-itself if we are to be *conscious through* former acts of presence to ———.

C1(c). The third form of pastness, having to be its past, is the way that at any time acting consciousness is defined by its *attitudes toward* its past-as-fact (C1(b)). Having to be its past is an obligation or responsibility to appropriate past actions, thoughts, emotions, and so on. We appropriate them as something *outside of* our current consciousness. They are factual episodes of past acting consciousness toward which we now take some stance (which stance affects our current action and outlook on the world). Sartre is rather vague about what various forms of appropriation are available to us. Presumably, attitudes such as "being ashamed of" or "being proud of" or "being guilty for" or "feeling entitled to something because of" are what he has in mind. Even considering our current self *not to be responsible* for parts of our past is claimed to be a form of appropriation.[34]

It is obvious that this third form of acting consciousness as past depends upon the second. What is less obvious, although I think that Sartre intends this, is that the second form itself depends upon the third. What I think that Sartre wants to maintain is that acting consciousness-as-fact is the past of current acting consciousness *only if* the current acting consciousness has to be this past, and is thus partially constituted by these past facts. It is the obligation to appropriate these past facts that makes them the past of the current consciousness.

C2. Presence to —— is the basic form of intentionality according to Sartre. Rather than things being "present in consciousness," acting consciousness is present to things in the sense of being in contact with them. The very basicness of "being present to ——" makes it difficult to describe phenomenologically, and Sartre says very little specifically about it.

C2(a). Perceptual presence to —— is the awareness of some appearance (profile of an enduring thing) or set of appearances against the background of the less determinate field of other (present) appearances. Sartre's analysis of perception is like naive realism; perception includes a direct contact with what exists on its own. The experience of this direct contact is of "not-being" or of standing over against the appearance-in-context.

Sartre claims that in any conscious experience there is a double awareness: an awareness of the object and a self-conscious awareness of the *type* of awareness of the object. This self-conscious awareness of the mental act, which Sartre sometimes calls "the pre-reflective cogito," does not posit the act of awareness as an appearing object, but nevertheless experiences it non-thetically. Hence, this non-thetic awareness (of) the type of not-being the appearance-in-context is a part of being perceptually present to ———. This non-thetic self-consciousness is also the phenomenological basis for Sartre's ontological thesis concerning the "reflection-reflecting" form of nihilation (see section 7.3).

C2(*b*). Since Sartre conceives perceiving and acting to be inter-defined, there should be a type of being present through action to ———. Our making use of something or acting upon something to attain our goals seems also to be a form of presence to it.

C3. Sartre portrays the futurity of consciousness in several ways without explaining in detail how these are related to each other. In discussing each form of futurity, I will indicate briefly how that form relates to the other forms.[35]

C3(*a*). Having projects, that is, conditions or states of acting consciousness that are *to be attained*, is one form of the futurity of consciousness. In being defined by its projects for itself, acting consciousness is "ahead of itself" in the future. The present phase of acting consciousness is defined by this future, and acting consciousness is in the process of uniting itself with this future through its acting. The ultimate project of consciousness is to be an In-itself-For-itself, but short of this there are "qualified futures" that consist of consciousness being in a certain state or condition, such as being dancing, being generous, or being successful. Projects provide the ends or goals of action; their reflection onto the object of consciousness is "what is to be made present" in the world.

C3(*b*). Once acting consciousness has a future to be attained, it is not forced to continue to pursue it. Freedom possibilizes the projects of consciousness. The future that we are currently acting to unite ourselves with need not remain our future over time, because we are always free to develop new projects. The futurity of acting consciousness is essentially possibility because being free requires that any project can be revised or abandoned before being attained. Thus, there is a difference between the future *qua* future (the chosen possibilized projects that define current action and experience) and what eventually becomes present ("the For-itself that is to-come"[36]).

C3(*c*). Possible presence to ——— (being beyond being) describes the future of acting consciousness as present to ———. It depends upon both C3(*a*) and C3(*b*). Since consciousness is essentially intentional, the future condition of consciousness that is to be attained is also present to ———. However, since the future condition of consciousness is only possible because of freedom, possible presence to ——— results. Which appearance-in-context we will experience is now undetermined because our future courses of action (including how we align our senses) are now only possible.

That our future presence to states of the world is *only* a *possible* presence to states of the world raises some serious questions both about a really future dimension in time-consciousness and about the ontological dependence of the future of instrumental-things on the future of the For-itself. I will address these issues in sections 7.2 and 7.5.

C4. The pastness and the presentness of acting consciousness are mutually constitutive. The past is defined by formerly being present and exists only in virtue of its intrinsic connection with the present of an acting consciousness.[37] The present of acting consciousness is affected in three ways by its past. First, having been present to ——— (C1(*a*)) affects being perceptually present to ——— (C2(*a*)) by partly defining *what it is* (the essence of) that we are perceiving. What we have just perceived affects the meaning of what we are presently perceiving. Second, having been present (through action) to ——— affects being present through action to ——— (C2(*b*)). What we have already done qualifies what we are now doing. Third, the attitudes toward our past consciousness-as-fact that are required by having to be our past (C1(*c*)) affect our present action and outlook on the world. All these effects of its pastness on its presentness are instances of how "surpassed facticity" provides a point of view.

C5. The presentness and futurity of acting consciousness are also mutually constitutive. All the forms of futurity are defined with respect to presentness, as either what is to be made present or what might possibly be present. The presentness of consciousness is itself defined with respect to futurity as *lacking* the qualified completeness that the attainment of a project would accomplish. The present of consciousness is deficient with respect to the future condition of consciousness with which we are to unite ourselves. This deficiency is the motivation for action; present acting is to attain a future goal.

D. For Sartre the passage of time is equivalent to the basic activity of consciousness that he describes phenomenologically. This basic activity can be divided for explanatory purposes into two parts.

D1. Acting consciousness is always engaged in pursuing its projects, that is, in uniting itself with some more ideal state or condition of consciousness that its current presence to ——— lacks (see C5).

The process of making the future condition of consciousness present is how the future becomes present.

D2. In making its own future present, the basic activity displaces its lacking presence to ———. This former present does not disappear entirely but becomes factual; a special type of fact, consciousness-as-fact, results. In ontological terms, the presence to ——— is reabsorbed by Being-in-itself, which produces the For-itself-become-In-itself.

7.2   The Awareness of Experienced Temporal Features

Like other phenomenologists, Sartre claims that in any conscious experience there is a double awareness: an awareness of the object and a self-conscious awareness of the *type* of awareness of the object. This self-conscious awareness of the type of awareness, which Sartre sometimes calls "the pre-reflective cogito," does not posit the act of awareness as an appearing object, but nevertheless experiences it non-thetically. We are aware of our acts of awareness without thematizing them, while we are thetically aware of intentional objects.

Acts of awareness are only abstracted features of a more wholistic acting consciousness. Acting consciousness is essentially temporal. Our awareness of the experienced temporal features of acting consciousness occurs through acting consciousness' non-thetic awareness of itself. We are non-thetically aware of our acting consciousness in all its temporal dimensions.

That we are both positionally aware of the objects of consciousness and non-thetically self-aware explains how we can experience both the temporal features of instrumental-things and the temporal features of acting consciousness. These two temporalities are always *coordinated* with each other. We are positionally aware of the temporal features of instrumental-things while being non-thetically aware of the temporal features of acting consciousness itself.

The temporality of acting consciousness (the For-itself) is what makes possible the awareness of the temporal features of instrumental-things. Sartre's analysis of time-consciousness, like that of Heidegger, is an ecstatic-action account (theory 5 in section 1.3). We are able to be aware of the past, present, and future of instrumental-things only through the past, present and future of acting consciousness.[38] Since acting-consciousness is always intentional, the past of the For-itself is a (C1(*a*)) "having been present to ———," the present of the For-itself is a "presence to ———," and the future of the For-itself is a (C3(*c*)) "possible presence to ———." The *unity* of these temporal dimensions of the For-itself explains our awareness of instrumental-things as temporal. This unity is ontological, rather than, as in Husserl, based on mutual reference. It is because the present of the For-itself is "outside of itself" in being defined by its future and its past that we can experience the future and the past of the world of instrumental-things as the horizon or context of the present state of the world. All three temporal dimensions of the For-itself contribute to its current awareness: past presence to ——— is operative-as-past; presence to ——— is operative-as-present, and possible presence to ——— is operative-as-future (see Diagram 7.1).

Acting consciousness is essentially a process because it is always engaged in pursuing its projects and displacing its present into the past. Our experience of the temporal passage of instrumental-things depends upon the For-itself's active changing of itself. In making its future become present, acting consciousness makes the intentional correlate of its future presence to ——— become present and it displaces its lacking presence to ——— into the past. Since acting consciousness not only produces change in what it is present to, but also is non-reflectively aware of itself as changing, we can experience the passage of time in worldly entities. We can experience the past of the world as that *to which we were present* and the future of the world as that *to which we will be present*.

Sartre emphasizes that the future of the For-itself is possibilized because we are always free to abandon a project or course of action before completing it. Our future presence to states of the world is only a "possible presence to ———." As I indicated concerning C3(*c*), this raises some serious problems concerning a future dimension of time-consciousness. Although our present perceiving and acting includes an anticipated future of what we perceive and what we act upon, this anticipated future of the world is, according to the thesis in question, *only possible* because the presence to it is only

Diagram 7.1

Past presence to (operative-as-past) ——→ past of the world
Presence to (operative-as-present) ——→ present of the world
Possible presence to (operative-as-future) —→ future of the world

possible. Because of freedom, there is no future presence to (states of the world) that will inevitably become present. Thus, in the commonsense meaning of "future" as "what will be present," there is no direct awareness of future states of the world.

The position that the future of the For-itself is never more than possible so that there is never more than "possible presence to future states of the world" runs counter to Sartre's recognition that acting consciousness realizes that some states of the world will inevitably come to pass (see A3(*a*) in section 7.1A). Most of our actions are undertaken with an understanding that the future world will have certain definite characteristics. This definite future world is the context for the continuation of and the results of our present acting. Sartre's account of "possible presence to ———" needs to be supplemented by the thesis that there are states of the world that must occur in *all possible* cases of "possible presence to ———." If all possible cases of "possible presence to ———" are present to the same states of the world, there would be a type of direct awareness of future states of the world.

7.3 The Temporal Nature of the For-Itself

The basic ways of existing according to Sartre's ontology are Being-in-itself and Being-for-itself. Being-in-itself is pure positive "being what it is" without any differentiation of "parts" or qualities or any relations between these.

> The result is evidently that being is isolated in its being and that it does not enter into any connection with what is not itself. Transition, becoming, anything which permits us to say that being is not yet what it will be and that it is already what it is not—all that is forbidden on principle.[39]

All differentiation, of qualitative differences, of temporal moments from each other, and of spatial locations from each other, requires negation. Being-for-itself is what introduces negation into being and forms a world from the undifferentiated mass of Being-in-itself. Being-for-itself is itself defined by two types of mutually constitutive nihilating activity: the non-temporal negation of "reflection-reflecting" and temporal negation.

Being-for-itself is the being of acting consciousness. As I indicated in C2 of section 7.1B, consciousness separates itself off from and relates itself to the In-itself. Even within an instant, consciousness exists as this nihilation of the In-itself. Consciousness of the In-itself, however, must be non-thetically aware of itself. The non-temporal nihilation of reflection-reflecting is what is supposed to explain this non-thetic self-awareness. This nihilation is the continuous back and forth movement between consciousness of the world and non-reflective self-consciousness (of) this consciousness of the world. "Each of the terms refers to the other and passes into the other, and yet each term is different from the other."[40]

Aside from the possibility of bad faith, all Sartre's interesting analyses operate in terms of the temporal form of nihilation. Being-for-itself is "diasporatic"; it separates itself into "parts," but the "parts" have an essential unity with each other. Temporality is the most basic form of this diasporatic being. The For-itself is "distant from itself" or "ekstatic" by dispersing itself into the three temporal dimensions, but each of these temporal dimensions of the For-itself is internally related to and dependent upon the others. The For-itself both is and is not its past, its present, and its future, and it is continuously changing itself by moving beyond what it has been toward its future that it is to be (projects).

The For-itself is a temporalizing activity that is supposed to be the basic way in which time exists (see 7.4). For this reason, the For-itself does not have the standard temporal features that natural objects are ordinarily thought to have. By being temporal, acting consciousness defines temporal locations rather than occurring at pre-existent temporal locations. Furthermore, since the For-itself has nothingness in its very nature, it is never simply actual at a standard temporal location; it always "is and is not."

The standard form of temporal extension does not apply to the For-itself because of its ecstatic character. The duration of the For-itself is not a matter of occupying contiguous moments of time, but rather of being outside of itself and of surpassing its facticity in projecting itself into the future. For this same reason the For-itself is not divided or divisible in the standard sense. Any phase of the For-itself is internally related to other phases.

Earlier-later relations apply to the past of the For-itself but not to its future. Because the For-itself is inherently free, there are not fixed and fully determinate states of the For-itself *later than* the present. As I have explained in sections 7.1B and 7.2, past-present-future features do characterize the For-itself.

7.4   Sartre's Temporal Idealism

Sartre is quite clear that time is dependent upon acting consciousness. Time exists most basically as a structural feature of Being-for-itself and appears in the objects of consciousness only as a reflection from the temporality of the For-itself. He has two arguments in support of this temporalizing view of time. One is an ontological argument based on the Being of time. The other is a phenomenological argument designed to show that the temporality of the instrumental-thing, which I described in section 7.1A, reveals itself as a hybrid of the a-temporality of Being-in-itself and the ecstatic temporalizing of the For-itself.

First, Sartre's ontological argument is that time must both separate and unite things. Sartre claims that traditional conceptions of time have emphasized the separation without explaining the unification. Temporal locations (instants) have been taken to be distinct from each other, and the temporal relations between locations have been conceived to be *external* relations. They do not define the things related, but rather exist only "in the eyes of" an external witness, such as an a-temporal god or transcendental ego.

Sartre claims that "before-after" relations between temporal locations are internal relations; they define the temporal locations. "If then we grant *a priori* being in-itself to A and B, it is impossible to establish between them the slightest connection of succession."[41]

> The before and after are intelligible . . . only as an internal relation. It is there in the after that the before causes itself to be determined as before and conversely. In short the before is intelligible only if it is the being that is *before* itself. This means that temporality can only indicate the mode of being of a being which is itself outside itself. Temporality must have the structure of selfness.[42]

Time requires that each temporal location be defined (as part of a temporal series) by other temporal locations that it is not. Each temporal location "is what it is not" because it is both distinct from and defined by other temporal locations. Since Being-in-itself is what it is, time cannot be a characteristic of the In-itself. Rather, time is the basic ontological structure of the For-itself, which is essentially "outside itself." The Being of time turns out to be only an essential feature of the Being of the For-itself.

Second, Sartre's phenomenological argument that the temporality of the instrumental-thing can be seen to be entirely derived
from the temporality of acting consciousness starts with the analysis
of the instrumental-thing into a series of appearances (appearings of
the In-itself). Each individual appearance will show itself to be
a-temporal and to be just what it is, and the seriality or temporal
relations of appearances to each other will show themselves to be
external relations that do not define the appearances themselves but
that are the mere reflection onto what exists In-itself of the temporality of the For-itself. The temporal relations between appearances
are supposed to show themselves to be derived from the temporality
of acting consciousness; they exist only *for* an observing consciousness.[43]

> Permanence, as a compromise between non-temporal identity
> and the ekstatic unity of temporalization, will appear therefore
> as the pure slipping by of in-itself instants, little nothingnesses
> separated one from another and reunited by a relation of simple
> exteriority on the surface of a being which preserves an a-tem-
> poral immutability.[44]

> The cohesion of Time is a pure phantom, the objective reflection
> (*reflet*) of the ekstatic project of the For-itself towards itself and
> the cohesion in motion of human reality. But this cohesion has
> no *raison d'être*. If Time is considered by itself, it immediately
> dissolves into an absolute multiplicity of instants which consid-
> ered separately lose all temporal nature and are reduced purely
> and simply to the total a-temporality of the *this*.[45]

The phenomenological argument for the derivativeness of the
time of the instrumental-thing starts from presentness. The present
of the instrumental-thing is defined directly in terms of consciousness being present to the thing.[46] Given Sartre's claims in his Introduction that the object of consciousness is a series of appearances
(appearings of the In-itself), that the essence of the object is just the
principle of the series, and that the mode of existence of the appearance is Being-in-itself, it is plausible to claim that the presentness of
the instrumental-thing consists of consciousness being present to an
a-temporal appearance. If each appearance is a-temporal and exists
as self-contained, the series of appearances that constitute an object
should be a series of self-contained, a-temporal "atoms." We thus

arrive at time as a series of instants (a-temporal "atoms). Since each appearance is self-contained (not defined by relation to anything else), the appearances themselves do not provide for their being related in a temporal series. The seriality of the appearances is external to the appearances themselves. The source of the temporal relations between instants must be elsewhere; these relations derive from the temporalizing activity of acting consciousness.

The argument continues by claiming that according to the phenomenological description of the time of the instrumental-thing, its past is external to its present. The present of the instrumental-thing does not "have to be its past." Whereas the present of acting consciousness is defined by its past, which it has to be (see C1(c)), the past of instrumental-things just exists as a self-contained fact behind the present. The present of the instrumental-thing is connected with its past only by the experiencing consciousness that brings past appearances together with present appearances into a series. The temporal relation of the present of instrumental-things to its past exists *only for* acting consciousness. It is constructed out of the a-temporality of the appearances and the temporality of acting consciousness.

Similarly, the future of the instrumental-thing is external to its present. The present appearance does not "have to be its future"; it does not strive to unite itself with its future, as the present of acting consciousness does. Not only is the future of the instrumental-thing dependent upon acting consciousness to unite it in a temporal series with the present, but it is totally dependent upon acting consciousness for its being. Whereas past states of instrumental-things exist on their own, though not *as past*, future states do not exist at all until they are present. *Qua* future, they exist *only for* an experiencing that is defined by its future. Temporal relations again appear to be derived from the temporality of acting consciousness.

There is a feature of instrumental-things as future that essentially connects the present and the future, namely, what is to be made present (A3(c)). Present and future states of affairs of instrumental-things are mutually defined by the "lack" relation. However, as I have already indicated under B2(b), this "lack" relation is itself consciousness-dependent. It too is derived from the temporality of acting consciousness.

The final point of the deriviation argument focuses on the passage of time. Since the past, present, and future of instrumental-things are all external to each other, there is nothing in the instrumental-thing as past or as present or as future to account for its transition to being more past or just past or present or less future. The passage of time is an external flow in which the self-contained appearances slip by. This passage of time is dependent upon the basic activity of acting consciousness. It is only as a reflection of consciousness' changing what it is present to through making its future present that present appearances become past and future appearances become present.

7.5   Problems

Sartre's philosophy speaks to an enormous number of philosophical issues that I do not discuss in this chapter. The criticisms that I raise concern his accounts of experienced time, of time-consciousness, and of the ontology of time. I focus on his arguments for the ideality of time because these are the central supports for the notion of the For-itself as a temporalizing activity.

First, in section 7.1B I noted that Sartre employs three notions of the past dimension of acting consciousness and explained briefly how these could be interpreted so as to be consistent with each other. The *prima facie* problem is the consistency between "having been present to ———" (C1(*a*)) and "acting consciousness as fact" (C1(*b*)). The first requires that there still be nothingness in former states of consciousness in order that we can be conscious through them. This retention-like awareness of former experienced features of the world is supposed to be how our accumulated "practical knowledge" contributes to our current experiences. The second requires that former states of consciousness lose their nothingness by becoming facts that exist as In-itself.

My resolution of this problem appealed to the notion that there can be degrees of nothingness and factuality. The past of acting consciousness becomes *more factual* the farther it is from the present, and, concomitantly, we are less conscious through it. This fits nicely with Husserl's observation that experiences "fade out" from retention as they become more past. However, there is an additional problem about the status of our accumulated empirical knowledge. Empirical knowledge should itself "fade out" according to this account. If accumulated empirical knowledge depends upon our still being conscious of the evidence for the empirical generalizations (by being conscious through those earlier conscious states that are present to the evidence), then empirical knowledge would "fade out" as the conscious states that are present to the evidence become more past. That this "fading out" of empirical knowledge does not uniformly happen indicates that some other factors must be involved.

Second, a major source of problems in Sartre's philosophy is his notion that Being-in-itself cannot contain any negations, relations, or differences. Being-in-itself, which is the way of existing of whatever is independent of consciousness, is supposed to be pure positivity. Thus, any distinctness of "this" from "that" is supposed to be foreign to Being-in-itself. Since such differentiations are experienced in the objects of consciousness, Sartre regularly claims that Being-for-itself is the complete source of these differentiations.

Sartre's ontological argument for the ideality of time (see section 7.4) relies upon the notion that whatever exists on its own independently of consciousness (the In-itself) cannot include negations, relations, or differences. Thus, having shown that time includes temporal locations that are both distinct from each other and defined by each other, Sartre thinks that this establishes that time cannot exist on its own. While it is true that time includes internal relations between temporal locations and that time both separates and unites entities in time, there is no reason that such characteristics cannot exist on their own independently of consciousness. There is no reason that what exists on its own cannot contain differences and relations, and no reason that time cannot be real.

Third, in his account of the For-itself as temporalizing activity, Sartre claims that the passage of time has its complete source in the For-itself's basic activity of making its future become present and displacing its present into the past. However, the "becoming past" of the For-itself raises questions about this. That consciousness' "presence to ———" is reabsorbed by Being-in-itself seems to require some activity or force on the part of Being-in-itself. Rather than Being-for-itself just ceasing to separate itself off from the In-itself, the In-itself seems to act upon and to transform the For-itself. If consciousness simply disappeared *as consciousness* in being displaced from the present so that a past consciousness was an In-itself *no different from* other In-itselfs, there would be no reason to think of the In-itself as acting upon consciousness. However, in being displaced from the present, consciousness becomes a special type of fact, namely, facticity (see C1(*b*)). The transformation from "presence to ———" to facticity is not explicable solely in terms of the For-itself's own activity. Nihilating activity does not explain the transformation into consciousness-as-fact. Whatever does help to explain this transformation, whether it be the action of the In-itself or something else, would point toward an ontologically real time.

Fourth, Sartre's phenomenological argument for the derivativeness of the temporality of the instrumental-thing requires that the essence or seriality of the series of appearances (appearings of the In-itself) *not be based* in the appearances themselves, which are supposed to be self-contained and non-relational (see section 7.4). However, the phenomenological evidence does not support this claim. The experienced instrumental-thing does not fall apart into self-contained a-temporal "atoms" that are only externally related.

In section 7.4 I noted that Sartre claims that the past of the instrumental-thing is external to its present because the present of the instrumental-thing does not "have to be its past." While this is true, there is another way in which the past of an instrumental-thing defines its present, namely, by partially defining the essence of what is present.[47] As described in A1(*b*) and A4 of section 7.1A, there is a categorial connection between the past of an instrumental-thing and its present appearances. What it is that appears in the present appearance is partly defined by the past. If that past were different, what is presently appearing would be different.

Similarly, Sartre claims that the future of the instrumental-thing is external to its present because the present appearance does not "have to be its future." Despite this, the future of the instrumental-thing does partially define the present appearance. What characteristics of the thing will be present (A3(*a*)) and the range of possible characteristics of the thing that might be present (A3(*b*)) affect what it is that is now present. Even assuming that the essence of the instrumental-thing is consciousness-dependent, the present appearance is itself defined by the essence, which depends upon the past and the future of the thing.

Since the appearances that constitute an instrumental-thing are internally related in terms of their essence, there is no phenomenological evidence for the "a-temporality of the In-itself" in the object of consciousness. The result is that at the phenomenological level there is an essential *correlation* between the temporality of acting consciousness and the temporality of the object of consciousness. In this correlation, neither is more basic than the other. There is no indication that the temporality of consciousness is *more basic than* and the *sole source for* the temporality of the object, which on its own would be a-temporal.

Fifth, the phenomena of "abolitions and apparitions"[48] create a second problem for Sartre's claim that the temporality of the instrumental-thing is entirely derived from the temporality of the For-itself. Abolitions and apparitions indicate that there is some type of temporality to what exists independently of consciousness.

Apparitions and abolitions are the coming into existence and the passing into complete pastness (or passing out of existence, in ordinary language terms) of instrumental-things, conceived as containing within their essence the whole sequence of their appearances (appearings of the In-itself).[49] Sartre himself admits that the beginning and the end of the sequence of appearances that constitute an object is not brought about solely by the temporality of consciousness. In effect, this is to introduce a basis *within the appearances-as-transcendent* for the uniting of individual appearances into a temporal series to form an object. The beginning and the end of the series of appearances is not totally dependent upon consciousness because there is this basis in the appearances-as-transcendent for their being united with other appearances in a temporal series to form one object. Although there are alternative ways of conceptually structuring the world into objects, there are constraints in the appearances-as-transcendent upon which other appearances they can be united with in a series to form a temporally extended object.

This characteristic of individual appearances that makes them "fit together" in a temporal series with some other appearances but not "fit together" with others is the reason that the beginning and end of things seem to derive from the In-itself. Sartre recognizes that the In-itself *as he has portrayed it* cannot contain such temporal features. Yet he admits that abolitions and apparitions do involve a "quasi-after" and "quasi-before" within what appears. The "quasi-temporality" of abolitions and apparitions is claimed to be a contingent metaphysical fact that is not explainable in terms of the ontology of Being-in-itself and Being-for-itself. This is to admit the failure of the program of tracing all temporal features of instrumental-things to the temporalizing activity of Being-for-itself.

Sixth, a third problem concerns the derivativeness of the futurity of the instrumental-thing from the futurity of acting consciousness and the ability of the For-itself to affect states of the world by its action. Sartre's conception of the futurity of the instrumental-thing vacillates concerning the Being-in-itself character of future states. On the one hand, as I noted in section 7.2, Sartre frequently claims that such future states are *only possible*. While what consciousness is "present to" exists on its own, what consciousness is only "possible presence to" does not simply exist on its own. The future of instrumental-things is a "being beyond being" because this experienced future is not what inevitably becomes present (what is the case a-temporally). "Being beyond being" seems to be entirely dependent, even for its content, upon the futurity of consciousness.[50]

However, Sartre also recognizes that the In-itself is experienced in terms of all three temporal dimensions and that many future states of the world will inevitably become present. As I explained in section 7.2, this indicates that some future states of instrumental-things are (already) an In-itself to which the For-itself has a "future presence to." Much of the future of the world is Being-in-itself, not "being-beyond-being." Only those parts of the future of the world that are brought about by human action would be at present a "being beyond being."

Both of these positions concerning the ontological status of the future of the instrumental-thing produce serious problems. The first does not explain why the specific future characteristics of instrumental-things are destined to be the way they are or why these specific characteristics and states of affairs should become present. It is plausible to think that both the determined future of a thing (A3(a)) and the determined range of its possibilities (A3(b)) have some basis in the In-itself. More damning is the fact that almost all the specific characteristics of the future of the world seem to become present independently of human action. This indicates that what exists on its own is temporal in that it is something temporal about independent things that accounts for the determined future of an instrumental-thing (A3(a)) becoming actual.

The second position raises questions about the compatibility of Sartre's notion of the a-temporal In-itself with his notion that the For-itself affects states of the world by its acting. Sartre claims that the future of the instrumental-thing becomes present only because it is the correlate of the futurity of consciousness that is made present through acting. According to this position, both the determined future of a thing (A3(a)) and the determined range of its possibilities (A3(b)) would be based in the In-itself. Assuming that there is this In-itself component of many future states of the world, how is it that the For-itself is able to determine by its action some states of the world? The notion of an In-itself that can be changed by human agency seems to be incompatible with an a-temporal In-itself. If there are alternative states of matter that can be made present by human agency, particularly free agency, does this not require that states of matter exist in time? The In-itself would be changed by human action from a condition that supported a set of alternatives to a condition of simply being one alternative. This *change* in the In-itself would require that the In-itself have temporal features.

Part III

The Temporality of Experience

8

Time-Consciousness

In developing the phenomenological basis for my theory of time-consciousness, I should first state what my conception of phenomenology and of a phenomenological basis is. As envisioned originally by Husserl, phenomenological method is a special type of reflection upon our being conscious. Reflective awareness of conscious life is different from just "living through" that conscious life. Reflection is a particular, second-order mental act in which we observe our first-order conscious life and its intended objects.[1] Phenomenological reflection suspends for itself any claims about independent reality in order to observe without presuppositions and to describe our first-order consciousness. Husserl thought that through mental discipline the observing could be kept free of presuppositions, and that we could then describe the phenomena purely as they appear. Heidegger claimed that *all* conscious experience necessarily operates with "fore-structures" so that we cannot unmediatedly encounter an entity. It must always appear to us through our "disclosed world," that is, our conceptual framework that is oriented around action. An action-oriented conceptual framework is necessary for any (mature) encountering because it "opens up" the logical space within which an entity appears. However, since alternative action-oriented conceptual frameworks are possible, an action-oriented conceptual framework also "closes off" certain features of entities for which there is no place within it.

The above notion of an action-oriented conceptual framework is similar to Husserl's notion of the (forward) horizons of experience, except that Husserl does not require the connection to action. Husserl and Heidegger differ most markedly not with respect to first-order, outward-directed consciousness, but rather with respect to second-order, reflective consciousness, which Husserl thought could be rendered free of pre-structuring influence upon what it observed. Heidegger denied that phenomenological reflection could simply mirror what occurred in first-order consciousness, and for this reason phenomenology had to be hermeneutic. It had to keep in mind that its framework inevitably limits what can appear, and that the framework partially determines what does appear.

I think that Heidegger is correct about phenomenology having to be hermeneutic. Our conceptual framework does limit and partially determine what we find when we reflect upon our own mental life. As contemporary cognitive theorists might state this point, we introspect in terms of commonsense ("folk") psychological categories, and we portray the objects of our experience in terms of commonsense categories for worldly entities. Furthermore, our linguistic categories are more limited than our conceptual framework. We cannot describe in our familiar language some things that we can recognize and identify. Since phenomenological *descriptions* are made in language, our linguistic categories are a further impediment to simply mirroring conscious experience in phenomenological descriptions. This latter impediment can be partially overcome by expanding and revising our familiar language.

Even within one conceptual framework, the results of phenomenological reflection are not absolutely certain. Since there are other types of evidence about our conscious experience besides reflective evidence, it is possible in some cases for these to outweigh epistemologically our first-person reflective observations. That it is possible for even careful phenomenological reflection sometimes to misidentify mental acts and their intended objects is suggested by several things. In ordinary life we sometimes infer, despite a person's sincere denial (although this is rarely based on reflection), that she must have perceived certain environmental features because her behavior adapted to the features. Psychological experimentation on perception has shown that people are sometimes unaware of some of the environmental factors whose detection is influencing their beliefs and actions.[2] "Unconscious" desires, beliefs, and emotions, that is, desires, beliefs, and emotions that are not available to reflection, are accepted by many people in explanations of their own behavior. Psychological experimentation on evaluational and motive states has shown that in certain types of cases people's supposed introspective reports are not accurate and may even be unconscious fabrications.[3]

Despite these complications, reflection does provide the best and most reliable access to our conscious experience. Our conceptual framework already includes many alternative and conceptually overlapping categories for mental life and other categories may be added. In reflecting upon our mental life we can adopt different standpoints and assume different theories to see what each of these discloses; for example, we can reflect upon our experience using a cognitive science rather than a "folk psychological" framework. Any set of categories that we find to be revelatory of something about mental life can be added to our conceptual framework. All these reflections could still be considered to be phenomenological insofar as they continue to suspend any reflective claims about independent reality.[4] Insofar as the reflector *is able* to transfer himself out of this attitude in order to act upon the world, there is never a complete suspension of reality claims, but there can be a type of suspension that is sufficient for the epistemological purposes that it is to serve.

Within our multifaceted conceptual framework, reflection provides very strong evidence for specific claims about experience. The experimental evidence from cognitive psychology that challenges the accuracy of introspection is limited to certain types of mental processes and mental conditions. There are no experimental grounds for a general rejection of careful reflective claims about one's own experience. Although reflective claims are not in all cases absolutely certain because other types of evidence might outweigh them, they nevertheless provide reliable and readily accessible evidence that is very hard to outweigh. It would be impossible in a practical sense to accumulate in any other way the necessary amount of evidence about the *details* of our temporal mental life. We have to rely upon first-person reflective evidence.

The phenomenological basis for a theory of time-consciousness is the experienced data that the theory must explain. In section 8.1 I start with a discussion of the basic temporal features of non-conscious entities *as these are experienced*. These temporal features of intended objects are present in consciousness without reflection (in the intended objects of first-order mental acts), but they cannot be thematized *as they are present in consciousness* without reflection. In section 8.2 I discuss perception as a representative way of experiencing these temporal features, and consider the experienced temporal features of the perceiving itself. The experienced temporal features of perceptual acts are also present in first-order perception, but again they cannot become the focus of awareness without reflection. These two sections provide the initial data for which a theory of time-consciousness has to account. In sections 8.3 and 8.4 I defend a type-3 theory of time-consciousness that incorporates the insights of the theories examined in previous chapters.

8.1   The Basic Experienced Temporal Features

Since all non-abstract entities exist in time, there is a great wealth of types of characteristic that involve time in some way. If there is to be such a thing as "time-consciousness," time must be a fairly well-defined parameter of entities. If the exceedingly diverse "time involving" characteristics did not all share some core temporal features (which make them "time involving"), there would be no distinct time-parameter and no generalized issue about time-consciousness.

In the following analyses, I will be dealing only with *ordinary* experienced temporal features, that is, with the temporal features of entities *as these are ordinarily experienced*. I am not making any claims here about the ontologically real temporal features of entities, only about their ordinarily experienced ones. I am also not claiming that these are the *only* temporal features of entities that can be experienced. In non-ordinary experiences, such as dreams, religious experience, or perhaps experiencing hermeneutically through scientific theories, other temporal features might be experienced. However, the ones that I am discussing are basic in that they should be locatable even in non-ordinary experiences. Even in a dream in which the present of experience jumps (inconsistently) from one date to another, there will be a sense of pastness, presentness, and futurity for local periods. Even in a religious experience in which a current (re)enactment of a holy event is not experienced as distinct from the holy event (so that the notions of temporal location and of earlier-later relations between these are disturbed), there will be some local sense of earlier and later.

Among the *basic* experienced temporal features of entities are five of the temporal features that I discussed in Chapter 3. Our commonsense conception of time attributes six standard temporal features to entities that exist in time: (1) temporal location—that any non-conscious worldly entity exists at some definite location in one temporal coordinate system in which all other worldly entities exist; (2) temporal extension or duration—that any non-conscious worldly entity occupies some point or set of contiguous points of this coordinate system; (3) length of duration—that there is a definite size to the temporal extension of an entity and that its size can be expressed as a multiple or fraction of any arbitrarily selected temporal extension; (4) temporal divisibility—that any non-conscious worldly entity's duration that occupies more than a single point can be divided into equally real temporal parts without any change in its non-temporal properties; (5) earlier-later relations—that the temporal parts of an entity are temporally related as earlier or later than each other and that the temporal parts of any two entities are temporally related as earlier, later, or simultaneous with each other; and (6) past-present-future features—that if there is a date at which a temporal part of an entity is present, there is an earlier date at which it is future and a later date at which it is past and that it passes from being future to being present to being past.

Our commonsense conception is accurate in that we do experience five of these temporal features (1, 2, 3, 5, 6) in some non-conscious worldly entities, and we do experience something that indicates the other one (4). The temporal location of entities is experienced in experiencing them to be simultaneous or not. With the experience of temporal location comes the experience of earlier-later relations between locations. Of course we do not experience the entire system of these earlier-later temporal locations that we understand to exist, but only a portion of it. The temporal extension of entities is experienced in taking them to have temporal parts, that is, in taking one portion of the entity to succeed another portion.

Some thinkers may deny that we regularly experience the length of duration of temporally extended entities. They think of length of duration as dependent upon the use of clocks, and the use of clocks as dependent upon a more basic experienced time. However, there is good reason to reject this. Although length of duration is comparative, we directly experience the comparative length of duration of two entities when they occur "side by side," that is, when the temporal extension of one is wholly contained within that of the other. It is when the temporal extension of one is not wholly contained within that of the other that we can experience their comparative lengths only indirectly, usually through comparing each to a repeat-

ing occurrence used as a measure. Even in the case of indirect comparison, however, most of the comparing activity is automatic, and
we do experience the entity as having a definite length of duration.

That we experience the "passage" portion of past-present-future
features may be controversial. Defenders of B-series (earlier-later)
time admit that ordinary experience includes the "past, present, and
future" portion of A-series (past-present-future) features; it is these
for which they want to provide token-reflexive definitions. However, since they deny that passage is real, they usually also deny
that the passage of entities is actually experienced. Temporal passage is considered to be at best a feature of a particular picture or
theory of time. Since this theory is to be replaced by a more accurate
theory of time that is more scientifically justified, it is denied that we
ordinarily experience temporal passage. We just mistakenly think
that we do.

The controversy here is a very basic one that concerns the fundamental idea of an experiential grounding for any claim. The B-
series theorist is denying that we experience temporal passage in
entities. At the reflective level, we think that the experiences reflected upon are experiences *of* passage in entities, but this is a result
of the framework or theory from which reflection operates. Our reflective observations are distorted by the theory so that they do not
reveal what we actually experience. Thus, a reflector can make false
claims about her own first-order experiences.

As I indicated at the beginning of this chapter, I agree that reflection (whether strictly phenomenological or not) operates from its
own framework, so that it does not simply mirror its intended object, but rather pre-structures it. I further agree that reflection does
not provide absolute certainty for its results. Nevertheless, it does
provide strong, although defeasible, evidence for claims about experience. It would require very strong counterevidence to overrule its
findings. I do not think that B-series theorists have provided sufficiently strong counterevidence. They have directed their arguments
against the *real existence* of temporal passage, not against the fact
that we experience temporal passage in things. Even if temporal
passage does not exist independently, we still experience it, since
our first-order time-perception operates through the same A-series
(past-present-future) framework that B-series theorists claim that our
reflection does. In the absence of good reasons for disputing the
specific findings of reflection, that we experience temporal passage
in entities should be accepted.

The one standard temporal feature that we do not directly experience is temporal divisibility. While we can and do experience an actual "being divided up," a "capability of being divided up" is not the right sort of thing to be directly experienced. Divisibility is a susceptibility that we conceptually understand, but that we do not perceive or experience in things.

Nevertheless we *do* experience a form of "temporal dividedness" of entities that *indicates* other possible divisions. In experiencing the passage of any temporally extended entity, the continuous extension (duration) of the entity is divided into contiguous temporal parts. The flow of time is experienced as the successive presence of these temporal parts. There is no obvious element of this flow, that is, no obvious atomic unit that occurs one after the other in the flow of all temporally extended entities. In some cases, such as continuous motion in space that is not too rapid, we experience a succession of temporal parts that are extremely short (because we experience the moving thing to pass through all the parts of the space in its path). In other cases, such as watching a red stoplight turn green or hearing a sequence of musical notes, we experience an unchanging condition (the light temporarily being red or the sounding note) to be an undivided temporal part; that is, we do not distinguish earlier or later parts of it. If such unchanging conditions are experienced *together with* more rapidly changing conditions, however, the unchanging condition is experienced to have earlier and later parts. That an unchanging condition could be experienced either to be itself an undivided temporal part or to be composed of smaller temporal parts is the experiential basis for temporal divisibility.

In addition to these standard temporal features, there are some special temporal features that are experienced in *some* non-conscious worldly entities. For an acting consciousness worldly entities are encountered differently than they would be in interestless perception. Worldly entities are experienced (or practically perceived) with respect to their relevance to potential action and to what we want. As Heidegger and Sartre claim, we frequently experience worldly entities as instruments or equipment. Equipment and other functionally defined entities have some special temporal features that are different from the more standard temporal features above.

Any implement that was constructed for a particular use or any functional part of a larger system (for example, a fuel injector in an engine or the respiratory system in an organism) must exist *for a certain period of time* if it is to be able to be used for the purpose for which it was designed or if it is to be able to fulfill its function in the larger organization. Equipment has a special form of length of duration. It must endure for a particular period of time if it is to be the equipment that it is.

This requirement that equipment endure for a period of time specified by its equipmental function also affects its temporal divisibility. Any temporal part of a piece of equipment that is *shorter* than the time span required to fulfill the equipment's equipmental function *cannot* fulfill that equipmental function. Thus, a relevantly short temporal part of a piece of equipment *does not have* all the same non-temporal properties as the piece of equipment itself has. Thus, equipment or any functionally defined entity is not temporally divisible in the standard way.

8.2   Interested Perceiving of the Basic Temporal Features

The basic temporal features of worldly entities can be experienced in more than one way. Different types of mental acts can have these basic temporal features within their intended objects. It would be simple and elegant if there were *one* way of experiencing these temporal features that was *basic* in that all the other ways depended upon it and it did not depend upon them. A theory of time-consciousness would have to explain only this basic way without worrying about other ways. It is even possible that perception (however this is analyzed) is such a basic form of time-consciousness. It is arguable that because perception is the basic form of awareness of external entities, it is the basic form of awareness of the temporal features of external entities. A case could be made that other forms of intending and knowing external entities all rely upon the basic data provided by perception and that other types of mental acts that expressly concern external temporal features themselves presuppose perception; for example, recollective acts concerning past occurrences are analyzable as the remembering of the perceiving of the occurrence. However, because there are difficult cases, such as hoping that future generations will live in a better world, I am not going to argue that perception is the single basic form of time-consciousness. It is sufficient for my purposes if perception is a *representative* form of time-consciousness, that is, if the same account of how it is able to be aware of the basic temporal features of external entities applies to other mental acts that concern external temporal features.

In the preceding chapters, I have considered two different analyses of perception. The interestless analysis considers perception to be a relatively autonomous experiencing of presented content as the properties of appearing worldly entities. Interestless perception does not include parameters for motivation and for powers to act. On the other hand, the analysis of perception as essentially interested claims that perception is only an aspect abstracted from an acting consciousness. As such, perception is essentially affected (through our action-oriented conceptual framework) by our motivations, our powers to act, and the concrete doings in which we are engaged. Our perceiving always includes these parameters, although they may not be obvious in all cases.

The significance of these different analyses of perception for theories of time-consciousness is that proponents of acting consciousness think that it requires a different account both of the temporal parts of consciousness and of the connections of these temporal parts. They think that a temporally extended action has a special *unity through development over time* that a temporally extended interestless perceptual act would not have. The reason is that each of the parts of the action is teleologically directed toward the completion of the entire action. Each part of the action is intended only as a step toward the whole action, not for itself alone, and each part is intrinsically in process toward the completion of the whole action. If then all types of mental act, particularly perceptual ones, are essentially only aspects abstracted from an acting consciousness, and temporally extended action has a different unity over time, then all types of mental act have a different type of unity over time.

This notion that acting consciousness has a special type of unity over time is the basis for the ontology of time that does not limit actuality to the present but rather includes actuality-as-past (being operative-as-past) and actuality-as-future (being operative-as-future). Acting consciousness is thought to be able to engage in temporally extended action and to perceive (interestedly) temporally extended worldly entities only because its past is operative-as-past and its future is operative-as-future. It is particularly the actuality of its future that is supposed to provide for the intrinsic process of acting consciousness. Acting consciousness continuously develops toward its future self because this future self is operative-as-future. The temporal parts of acting consciousness are thought to be defined by the natural divisions in this acting development. When conjoined with the claim that all time is dependent upon consciousness (temporal idealism), these notions yield the view that time passes only because acting consciousness is making its future present and displacing its present into pastness.

The nature of perception is an immensely complicated issue. There is good experiential evidence that perception is interested in many complex ways. In addition to perceiving worldly entities in terms of their possible relevance to what we are now doing, there is the cognitive interest in what is the focus rather than the background of perception, the way emotions and moods "color" what we perceive (dispose us to have certain types of factors stand out or be salient), and the effect of earlier interests on the development of the concepts in terms of which we now perceive.

However, the fact that perception is interested in these and perhaps other ways does not have the importance for theories of time-consciousness and for ontologies of time that thinkers such as Heidegger and Sartre thought that it did. As I argue in section 8.3, a revised type-3 theory of time-consciousness can perfectly well accommodate the interested nature of perception. So long as there is an ontologically real time in which mental life (partially) occurs, there is no need for a type-5 theory of time-consciousness or for the very problematic ontology of time with which it is conjoined.

Whatever account is given of interested perception, it should be capable of perceiving the six standard temporal features (with the qualification concerning temporal divisibility) and the two special temporal features that are basic in ordinary experience. There should be no controversy about interested perceiving of the special forms of length of duration and of divisibility; these are temporal features of functionally defined entities such as equipment, and equipmental entities can be encountered only by an acting consciousness.[5] That there can be interested perceiving of the standard forms of length of duration and of a type of dividedness that indicates temporal divisibility might initially appear to be more of a problem. If interested perceiving could encounter *only* equipmental entities, it would not perceive these standard temporal features.

There is no reason that perception that is essentially oriented toward potential action would not perceive enduring worldly things that have standard temporal features. Many enduring worldly entities have no *single* use. We may use an enduring thing for *many* different purposes or we may have no current specific use for it. Nevertheless, we can and do identify such an enduring thing at a time and over time. Independently of some specific equipmental function, we perceive an enduring thing *as* one enduring thing with changeable properties. In perceiving such an enduring thing we perceive its standard temporal features.

Interested perceiving is itself experienced to be temporal. The perceiving of any worldly process itself takes time and is experienced to be temporally extended, temporally divided, and temporally passing. Although there are ontological differences between the temporality of consciousness and the temporality of worldly entities, the general experienced temporal features are similar, though not exactly the same. Perceptual acts are experienced as spread out through time and so as in some way divided into somewhat distinct temporal parts which form a continuous sequence. Perceptual acts are experienced as passing in that some temporal part (phase) is experienced as occurring *now* while other phases are experienced as having just occurred and still other phases are experienced as about to occur. Finally, there are experienced temporal relations between the perceptual act and its intended object. The present phase of perceiving is experienced to be simultaneous with the present phase of its intended object. The past and future phases of perceiving are experienced to be simultaneous with the past and future phases of their intended objects respectively.

8.3   A Theory of Time-Consciousness

The theory that I defend is an account of how phases of consciousness are unified through time so as to produce our experience of the temporal features both of intended objects and of mental acts. Although I focus on interested perceiving, this theory explains the unity through time of all types of mental acts. Recollective memory and explicit expectation depend upon this form of time-consciousness, but are not reducible to it.

In section 1.1 I distinguished time-perception, the perception of the temporal features of the objects of perception, from some other forms of time-consciousness. It is important to keep time-perception distinct from our *understanding* of the *unperceived* temporal features of worldly entities. We understand that many occurrences are past, present, or future, and are earlier, later, or simultaneous with other occurrences, even though we do not and have not perceived these temporal features. The understood temporal features of entities are important factual details in the framework of meaning through which we experience anything, but they are largely distinct from and epistemologically dependent upon time-perception. In contrast with the Kantian account of the representation of objective temporal order through understanding the necessary order of data, the perception of temporal order has consistently shown itself in psychophysical studies to be relatively direct, that is, not to be a matter of constructing order from some other clues.[6] This agrees with what we would expect on epistemological grounds. Perceived temporal order is epistemologically more fundamental than understood temporal order, because perceived temporal order is what provides the initial grounds for formulating the laws through which we understand what happens outside our perception.

We do interpret what we perceive. We understand what we perceive in terms of larger patterns, parts of which we may not have perceived. The Kantian conception is right in thinking that we continuously acquire new perceptual data that agree or disagree with our continued application of some one of these concepts covering a larger pattern; for example, we may take a few notes to be part of a familiar melody but discover that the succeeding notes do not fit into that melody. In this case (disconfirmation) our understanding of what we are perceiving changes, but the already perceived elements with their durations and temporal order do not in general change (because these are the basis for the new pattern).[7]

Any theory of time-perception makes certain ontological assumptions about the nature of time, as I explained in section 1.4. In explicating my theory of time-consciousness, I assume some things about real time, and I anticipate some conclusions that will be reached in Chapters 9 and 10. Specifically, I rely upon the following propositions that will be established later: that there is a real time, that consciousness has some special temporal features and shares some standard temporal features with real worldly entities, and that consciousness has some real temporal relations with real worldly entities. I assume that real time might either include temporal passage or not, that past or earlier entities are amenable to being contacted by later phases of consciousness, and that real time is composed of relatively small elements (real time may or may not be a dense continuum).

The theory of time-consciousness that best explains how interested perception is able to perceive the basic experienced temporal features is a variant on Husserl's one-level analysis. According to Husserl's theory, all phases of mental life have a three-feature structure. They consist of a "now-consciousness feature," a retentional feature, and a protentional feature. (See Diagram A.7 in the Appendix.) The now-consciousness feature consists of all those components of mental life through which consciousness is now focusing, that is, those features (of the simultaneous mental act-phases that compose a mental life-phase) that intend what is temporally central or focal in conscious experience, rather than what is part of the temporal background. In the case of perception the now-consciousness feature is the original sensing of the present state of the world. At any given time we perceive a wealth of data through several different sensory modalities. In terms of mental acts, there are several simultaneous perceptual act-phases at the specific time. The now-consciousness feature of these simultaneous perceptual act-phases is that which perceives the present phase of their intended objects.

The retentional feature is the direct awareness of the entire previous mental life-phase. There are two important aspects of retention. First, retention grasps *as just-past both* the earlier mental life-phase and this phase's intentional correlates (Husserl calls this "the double intentionality of retention"). Second, retentional awareness "looks through" the earlier mental life-phase to its intentional correlates; that is, it portrays the intentional correlates by means of the mental act-phases that intend them. Since each mental life-phase has its own retentional feature, in "looking through" an earlier phase, we are directly aware of the phase that preceded it. Thus, a temporal series of earlier phases of mental life along with their intentional correlates is intended by any phase of mental life. As a greater number of mental life-phases intervene between a retained phase and the retaining phase, the retained mental life-phase tends to become less clear and distinct for the retaining phase.

The protentional feature is supposed to be the direct awareness of the entire later mental life-phase. As I explained in section 5.2, Husserl is unclear about the details of protention. On the one hand, he thinks of it as like retention except that it concerns the future; on the other hand, he realizes that our grasp of even the just-future is more indefinite and fallible than our intuition of the past. Insofar as we are aware of a temporal series of later phases of mental life along with their intentional correlates, this would have to be accomplished by the current protentional feature "looking through" later phases' protentional features.

There is an immediately anticipative feature to our mental life. We anticipate the continuation of our mental acts and of the exercise of our powers. With respect to perception, we anticipate the appearance of specific phases of worldly entities. However, as I argue in section 8.4, this protentional feature is not a direct contact with the just-future and does not unify earlier and later phases of mental life. Hence, in the following discussions I employ the term "protention" to mean *only* this portraying of what is expected to happen.

This theory of time-consciousness explains well how interested perception is able to perceive all eight basic temporal features of worldly entities. Of the standard temporal features, temporal location, duration, and earlier-later relations are perceived by a perceptual act-phase that *grasps together* simultaneous worldly entity-phases *as simultaneous* (through the now-consciousness feature) and earlier and later worldly entity-phases *as earlier and later* (through the retentional and protentional features). Length of duration is perceived by perceiving together the durations of two or more entities that occur concurrently (the duration of one is wholly contained within that of another). The temporal divisibility of entities is not perceived, but is indicated by the perception of a dividedness (the duration of a worldly entity is divided into perceived phases) that indicates the possibility of other divisions.

The theory provides a particularly insightful account of the perception of the temporal passage of worldly entities. The temporal passage of a worldly entity (or entity-phase) is perceived by means of the "look through" feature of retention. Retention is directly aware of the just-previous mental life-phase, portrays it as just-past, and "looks through" this mental life-phase to its intentional correlates. Each mental life-phase has a now-consciousness feature. In both portraying a previous now-consciousness feature *as just-past* and "looking through" it to its intentional correlate that is experienced as now for the now-consciousness feature, retention is able to experience a worldly entity-phase as just having been perceived as now. Through its retentional unification with other perceptual act-phases, a perceptual act-phase can both perceive a worldly entity-phase as now and experience the just-previous worldly entity-phase as just having been perceived as now. This allows the perceptual act-phase to portray the worldly entity as passing through time: the worldly entity's earlier phases were present but are now past, and its current phase is present but will be past.[8] I should also note that in virtue of its protentional feature, a perceptual act-phase portrays what is expected to happen. Through the retention of this earlier protention, there is an experience of the future becoming present, even though strictly speaking we do not perceive the future.

There is more controversy concerning this theory's ability to accommodate interested perception and the two special temporal features of functionally defined entities. As summarized in section 8.2, the interested nature of perception has been thought to require different accounts both of the temporal parts of consciousness and of the unity of these temporal parts. Heidegger, Sartre, and others think that the temporal parts of acting consciousness are unified in the way a temporally extended action is and that a temporally extended action has a special unity through development over time.

My Husserlian theory analyzes the unity of the temporal parts of consciousness that is necessary for time-consciousness in terms of the three-feature structure, which is not in the relevant way interested in nature. Although the now-consciousness feature is usually interested, retention and protention are basically interestless types of awareness. Retention unifies the phases of mental life, but this unification is not an *action* and does not contain the parameters of action. The occurrence of retention is "passive" or automatic. It is not motivated and it does not involve the conscious exercise of powers to act.

My theory of time-consciousness can accommodate interested perception even though it unifies the phases of mental life in terms of a basically interestless retention. The interested nature of mental acts can be included in the now-consciousness feature. Since the interested nature of perception is a thesis about the awareness of external, worldly entities, there is no inconsistency between such an interested perception of external entities and an interestless awareness of earlier phases of mental life. Perception is interested in that its intended objects are related to possible actions. What we perceive is categorized in terms of its relevance to our motivations, our powers to act, and our current activities. This categorization, like the application of other concepts in perception, does not imply that the perceiving itself be an action. We perceive things in terms of a framework of meaning that includes these parameters concerning action. The categorization does in fact require a large amount of "internal processing," but this processing is unconscious. Like the processing of other sensory cues, only the results, not the processing itself, is given in consciousness.

The compatibility of interested perception with an interestless unification of mental life can be highlighted by considering the unity through time of an intention. Action is movement (either bodily or mental) that is governed throughout by an intention. A temporally extended action requires an intention that endures through time. Such an intention generally includes some type of action-plan that specifies the overall objective as well as the individual steps to be taken in bringing about the overall objective. Each individual step is enacted when it is determined that the preceding step has been accomplished. A temporally extended intention that is effective throughout a temporally extended action must itself have a unity through time. The three-feature structure of my theory can provide this unity. At any given time, we retain our earlier intending to do the previous steps of the action, we are aware of what we are now intending to do, and we protend our continued carrying out of the intention. Since my theory can explain the unity through time of the major conscious feature of actions (see section 10.3 concerning additional factors in the unity of actions), it should be able to explain interested perception.

The special forms of length of duration and temporal divisibility are features of functionally defined entities, particularly equipment, and equipmental entities can be encountered only by an acting consciousness. My theory of time-consciousness allows consciousness to be essentially an actor, even though it does not require it. Thus my theory can easily accommodate an interested perception that perceives worldly entities that have to endure for a specified period of time (long enough to fulfill their equipmental function) in order to be instances of an equipmental type.

Another advantage of this theory is its treatment of the multiple concurrent mental acts that compose mental life. As I indicate in Diagram A.7 (in the Appendix), not only can multiple perceptual act-phases involving different sensory modalities occur concurrently, but different varieties of mental act-phases can occur concurrently. Since the theory unifies consciousness over time in terms of mental life-phases that may contain many different mental act-phases, act-phases of other varieties of mental act are unified over time in the same way that perceptual act-phases are. By "looking through" the earlier phases of these different varieties of acts in retaining them, we are able to experience temporally extended intended objects of different modal types; that is, we can experience some entities *as perceived*, some entities *as imagined*, and some entities *as remembered*. Furthermore, since the temporal features of these intended objects are experienced *through* the temporally extended mental acts that intend them, these temporal features can be distinct. While a perceptual act and an imaginative act may occur concurrently and be experienced as such, their intended objects need not be intended as occurring concurrently. The imagined entities need not be intended as occurring in the same worldly time as the perceived entities.

Although imagined, remembered, and perceived entities need not be intended as occurring at the same time, my theory explains how we can concurrently experience temporal passage in each. The unification of mental life-phases is what provides for the experience of temporal passage. In both portraying a previous now-consciousness feature *as just-past* and "looking through" it to its intentional correlate that is experienced as temporally focal for the now-consciousness feature, retention is able to experience an intended entity-phase as just having been intended as focal. Thus, we can experience temporal passage in imagined or remembered entities as well as in perceived entities.

I noted in section 8.2 that interested perceiving (and other mental acts) is itself experienced to be temporally extended and temporally passing. My theory explains our experience of this "inner" temporality of mental life, as well as our experience of the temporal features of worldly entities. Perception (and other mental acts) is experienced to be spread out through time by means of retention and protention. At any given time, we are aware of earlier perceptual act-phases through retention and through protention we portray perception as continuing. At any given time there is no additional awareness of the act-phase that is happening at that time; that is, there is no feature that is directly aware of the present perceptual act-phase. Our experience at any given time of the varieties of mental act in which we are then engaged occurs through something like protention. With reference to the variety of the intended object-phase, we presume the continuation of the mental acts that we are retaining (they are retained as protending their continuation). If we are intending a real world event and we have just been seeing that event, we experience ourselves to be seeing now. If we are intending an imagined scene and we have just been imagining that scene, we experience ourselves to be imagining now.

Our experience of our mental life as passing from future to present to past is, according to my theory, dependent upon the correlation of phases of mental life with phases of intended objects that are experienced as passing. There is no additional level of mental life that "observes" the passage of a perceptual, imaginative, intending, or desiring mental act. Even if our consciousness is "moving itself" into the future through action (see section 10.3), the *experience* of this "moving" depends upon our experience of intended objects as passing. With respect to interested perception, at any given time we experience an earlier perceptual act-phase to be passing because we retain that phase and that phase is experienced to be perceiving an intended object-phase that is passing through time. We also protend the continuation of the current perceiving into a future-become-present. With respect to intentional action, at any given time we experience an earlier phase of the intention that governs the action to be passing because we retain that intention-phase as governing phases of behavior (bodily or mental) that are passing through time. We also protend the continuation of the current intention and of the behavior it governs into a future-become-present.

8.4   Refinements in the Theory of Time-Consciousness

There are some further refinements and modifications that need to be made in the original Husserlian theory. Several of these modifications are made possible or required by my positions in Chapters 9 and 10 concerning real time and the temporality of consciousness.

1. The phases of mental acts, mental life, and worldly entities are extended in real time. They endure through real time, so that there are earlier and later temporal parts of these phases. However, the extension through time of these phases is not experienced.

Husserl conceived phases to be instantaneous or infinitesimal, that is, to have a duration approaching zero. Infinitesimal phases were not observed in phenomenological reflection, but were introduced for theoretical reasons. He seems to have thought that since time was both *continuous* and *passing*, it must be divided up into infinitesimal parts, each of which is present successively. Since Husserl did not locate mental life in a real time, he thought of the phases of mental life as being infinitesimals. Since time consisted of infinitesimals, and time was nothing more than the process of phases of mental life and phases of intended objects, these phases were thought to be themselves infinitesimal.

It may be that a real time that passes has to have infinitesimal parts. Nevertheless, there are strong theoretical reasons to think that the phases involved in my theory of time-consciousness must be temporally extended.

For one thing, concerning mental acts and mental life, infinitesimal phases of mental life would introduce an infinite complexity into any mental life-phase. If there were infinitesimal phases, the retention of even one second of our past mental life would involve the retention of an infinite number of previous infinitesimal mental life-phases. Since the experienced continuity of mental life can be explained in another way, the experience of past durations of mental life should not be made dependent upon an infinite capacity.

The continuity of mental life means that there are no gaps in it. Mental life can be continuous even though the phases that are unified by the three-feature structure endure unchanged through periods of real time. Such enduring mental life-phases retain other temporally extended mental life-phases. Although the duration of such an extended three-featured phase could be divided into smaller temporal parts, these would not retain *each other*.[9] Rather, each smaller part would participate in the retention of the same temporally extended phase that precedes the larger phase of which it is a portion. Thus, there would be a continuous mental life composed of temporally extended three-featured phases that retain each other.

Although mental life may fail to be continuous in real time, the experienced continuity of mental life always exists in a consciousness that is unified by retention. Experienced continuity means that there are no *experienced* gaps in mental life. It requires that retention always find a mental life-phase at any moment of time that it contacts. Since retention by its very nature is of a previous mental life-phase, this condition is always satisfied; so it is satisfied by mental life-phases that endure unchanged through periods of real time. Individual mental acts, however, could be experienced to be discontinuous because retention could contact a mental life-phase from which the act-phase was missing.

Experienced continuity could exist even if there were gaps in mental life in *real time*. If the gap was undetected, as in some cases of short blackouts, there would be an experience of continuity.

A second reason to think that the phases must be temporally extended is that, concerning experienced worldly entities, we perceive their temporal extension by perceiving all the entity-phases that compose the extension. If perceived entity-phases were infinitesimals, we would have to perceive an infinite number of them to perceive an entity to exist for one second. There is no good reason to place such a burden on perceiving temporal extension. The only advantage of infinitesimal phases is that they would make instantaneous changes in perceived worldly entities possible. Studies of perception have proven that the human sensory modalities have limited powers of detection with respect to time. Very quick events and very quick interruptions (for example, an object is removed for an instant and then returned) are not detected at all. Since the scientific data show that we do not in fact perceive such instantaneous changes in content, there is no reason to make it possible for them to be perceived.

Perceived worldly entity-phases endure through real time but are not perceived *as* enduring because there are no smaller perceived entity-phases that compose them. Although the enduring entity-phases can in principle be subdivided, these smaller temporal parts are not distinguished in perception. The perceived continuity of entities through time requires only that there be a distinct worldly entity-phase that is perceived by the now-consciousness feature of every perceptual act-phase. Since perceptual act-phases also endure through real time, this condition is easily satisfied.

Perception does not portray continuous worldly entities as filling all the infinitesimal moments of time because it does not portray time as composed of infinitesimals. While we may *understand* temporal durations to be infinitely divisible and thus to be composed of infinitesimals, this is not something that is intended by perceptual acts.[10]

2. The identifying characteristics of retention need to be made more specific. Since retention is so central to this theory, it is important to clarify how we identify cases of retention and how the characteristics of retention differ from similar phenomena. An experientially based theory needs a strong grasp on any distinctive experiential characteristics of retention in order to make justified claims about the structure of retention.

The paradigm case of retention is our awareness, at any given moment of a temporally extended mental act, of the preceding moments of that mental act. Suppose that we see a ball roll across the floor from the door to the chair to the wall. When we see the ball approaching the wall, we are still aware of having just seen the ball rolling through the other positions. As proponents of the "specious present" emphasized, the ball's rolling through the earlier positions (and our *seeing* of the ball's rolling) is still "before the mind" in some way. It informs our current experience in a way that is experientially different from recollective "thinking back" to this earlier experience (see section 1.1). This same "holding before the mind" of the preceding moments occurs in all temporally extended mental acts; it occurs in perceiving, imagining, remembering, calculating, abstract thinking, desiring, intending, and emoting.

The paradigm case is the retentional awareness of the just-previous portions of one mental act, but there are natural extensions from this case. Since several mental acts may occur concurrently, at any given moment of consciousness there is the "holding in mind" of the just-previous portions of *all* these diverse mental acts. In addition, our mental life is not neatly divided into separate mental acts; there is a continuous quality to most of it. Within one perceptual modality, such as vision, everything that is seen at one moment might be considered to be the intentional correlate of *one* perceptual act. Furthermore, the temporal extension of such an encompassing visual perceptual act is not fixed by nature. Rather, we specify the temporal extension of perceptual acts according to our interests in *what is perceived*. It is possible to ascribe the perception of an entire movie or an entire symphony to one temporally extended act, because the movie or the symphony has a unity of meaning. However, even if we do not think of a period of mental life as occupied by one temporally extended mental act, there is still a "holding in mind" of the just-previous mental acts with their intentional objects. If we see one ball roll from the door to the chair and strike another ball that rolls from the chair to the wall, while we are watching the second ball's movement, we usually are still aware of having just seen the first ball's movement.

This non-segmented character of mental life, which Husserl described in terms of the notion of horizons, indicates that retention is more complicated than it might appear to be from the paradigm case. The just-previous moments of mental life are most clearly and distinctly "held before the mind," while the earlier moments are less clearly and distinctly maintained. There is a "fading out" of moments of mental life as they become more past with respect to the present moment.[11] This "fading out" is not what characterizes them as past, but it does occur in all human (finite) consciousnesses.

Given that earlier phases of mental life are retained with decreasing degrees of clarity and distinctness as they become more past, how should the informing of our current experience by relatively distant previous experiences be analyzed? Many experiences that occurred five hours ago or yesterday form part of the horizon of

meaning (background) for our current perceptions, thoughts, emotions, and actions. That the earlier experiences occurred does affect
the meaning of what we now perceive (and our emotions, thoughts,
and actions). This influence is both more than merely causal and not
a matter of explicit recollection either of the earlier experiences or of
what occurred in them. For example, if we are reading a story and
put it down for five hours, we generally can pick right up where we
left off. What we read is understood in light of what we read some
time ago, but we do not have to recollect either our reading or what
was read (as in a synopsis of the plot up to this point). Similarly, if
yesterday we saw John punch Bill and run off with his wallet, today
we immediately understand what Bill is up to when we see him
lying in wait for John. Are such cases instances of retention?

The phenomenological data is not sufficient to answer this question. Since information from the previous experiences is part of our
current horizon of meaning so that it immediately informs our current experiences, it may be that it is retained. There is no *experiential*
difference between the above cases and cases of retaining similar
information from one minute ago. However, previous experiences
can contribute to our horizons of meaning in many ways. In addition to retention and recollection, previous experiences may influence current experiences by giving rise to new concepts, new generalizations, a new "file" for a particular enduring entity, or the
attribution of different characteristics to some particular entity. Sets
of concepts, generalizations, conceptions of individual enduring entities, and conceptions of the specific characteristics of entities are all
constituents of our current horizon of meaning. They all automatically contribute to the meaning of our current experiences. Hence,
the phenomenological fact that previous experiences immediately inform our current experiences *does not differentiate* between retention
and the operation of these other cognitive features. The empirical
investigations of cognitive psychologists would be necessary to decide in such cases whether it is through retention or through these
other cognitive features that previous experiences inform our current experience.

3. Retention is fallible but does directly contact the past. Husserl
thought of retention as being infallible because it contacts just-past
phases of mental life, but in fact retentions can be found to be mistaken. It is thus necessary to clarify how retention can contact just-
past phases of mental life yet still be capable of inaccuracy.

It is difficult to describe more fully the notion of "contact" employed here. That retention "contacts" just-past phases means that it touches them or reaches across to them. Retention is like a ray of light that illuminates something at a location different from the source of the ray. Retention is aware of just-past phases in a way similar to the way that consciousness is aware of external entities in commonsense realism accounts of perception (although this position on inner awareness does not imply anything about external perception).

That the contact is direct means that it is unmediated. Nothing comes between. In a strict sense this applies only to a mental life-phase's retention of the just-previous phase. Although any mental life-phase retains a whole series of previous mental life-phases, the retention of any phase other than the just-previous phase is *mediated* through the just-previous phase. Hence, although there is a transitivity of contact (phase $_3$ contacts phase $_2$ which contacts phase $_1$), there is not a transitivity of direct contact.

It might be thought that retention can be inaccurate by misportraying how far past a previous experience is in objective worldly time. Gaps in consciousness sometimes occur without being noticed, such as when a person falls asleep or blacks out for a few moments without realizing it. When such a gap occurs, the person usually retains the experiences on the other side of the gap without initially realizing that they are not just-past.

That retention directly contacts the just-previous mental life-phase is not challenged by such experiences once it is understood that the intentional correlate of retention is the mental life-phase that precedes the retaining phase. Retention does not contact the just-previous moment of time per se. It contacts the just-previous phase of mental life, which normally is in the just-previous moment of time. Strictly speaking, retention is not inaccurate in these cases of gaps in consciousness. What is inaccurate is our assumption that the just-previous mental life-phase occurred in the just-previous moment of objective worldly time.

Retention can be inaccurate by portraying as having occurred experiences and actions that did not in fact occur. When we are engaged in many mental acts at one time, we may later (even moments later) retain an experience or action that we were expecting to happen but that never did happen. This sometimes happens when we have regularly perceived some type of occurrence, and we are busy at the time of today's token of that occurrence. Although we do not misperceive today's token when it happens (recollective memory can reveal that our perception was not inaccurate), we do not pay any attention to it. Even immediately afterwards, we may retain the perception of the token *with all its familiar properties* even though these did not occur. For example, suppose that Mary always wears a blue suit to work; I see her today wearing a gray dress, but I take no particular notice of this because I am very busy with other activities. Even immediately afterwards, I may think and act on the basis of having just seen Mary wearing a blue suit. As I noted in section 5.5, discussing the third issue, the very same sort of error in retention can occur when we retain having done some action that we intended to do.

One possible response to these types of cases would be to deny that they are really cases of retention. As I noted above in point 2, experiential data provide necessary but not sufficient conditions for retention of relatively distant previous experiences. It would be possible to deny that experiential data provide sufficient conditions even for the retention of *just-past* experiences. Thus, one might *stipulate* that inaccurate portrayings cannot be instances of retention even though there are no obvious experiential differences between these portrayings of recent past occurrences and legitimate retentional portrayings. This would be to abandon (or at least to downgrade seriously) the experiential criterion of retention in order to make epistemological certainty an essential feature of retention. Rather than following this line, I will keep the experiential criterion for retention of the recent past and claim that contact with a previous phase of mental life that contains much complexity is consistent with not grasping accurately all of that complexity.

As previously explicated, retention is awareness of previous mental life-phases that are grasped as past and through which retention "looks" to their intentional correlates. In order both to retain a phase of mental life and to misportray some intentional correlate of that mental life-phase, we must fail in some way either in contacting or in "looking through" the mental act-phases of the phase of mental life. Although we could not retain the mental life-phase *at all* unless we successfully contacted and "looked through" some of its components, it does not seem to be necessary that we successfully contact and "look through" all its components. We can contact a phase of mental life even though we are not aware of all its acts and their intentional correlates.

In the above example, this would account for our *not* retaining Mary's gray dress, but it would not explain our sense that she was wearing the customary blue suit. This latter bit of information is not retained in the strict sense but added on in some other way. The possibility of such additions that are not *experientially different* from legitimate retentions means that retention (as determined experientially) cannot provide epistemological certainty concerning all its apparent content. Nevertheless, the retentional feature of experience does provide extremely strong and reliable evidence.

4. Our current focus of attention affects our experience of the just-past, but this can be made consistent with a basically interestless retention. A distinction between retention-as-maintaining and the degree of prominence of what is maintained is necessary.

The retentional unification of mental life-phases is basically interestless. However, retentional awareness does sometimes seem to be affected by our current focus of attention. When previously perceived data are irrelevant to that to which we are presently attending, they do not usually inform our present experience in the way that they would if they were relevant. For example, if we are listening to a recorded symphony or thinking through a theoretical problem and an important message interrupts us, the earlier moments of the symphony or steps of the theoretical problem do not significantly inform our attention to the message and the situation that it concerns. In the experiential sense of retention, these earlier moments certainly do not contribute to the meaning of the current experience in the way that they would if we had not been interrupted. If our attention then shifts back to something to which the previously perceived data are relevant, this data may then inform our experience in a way that they did not moments earlier. For example, if the message turns out not to be so pressing, we may pick up the symphony or the problem at the point where we left it, relying upon our retention of the earlier moments.

Retention of any mental life-phase other than the just-previous one operates through the just-previous one, which operates through the phase just-previous to it, and so on. Because of this and the fact that we cannot change the past, we cannot retain an experience that occurred two minutes ago *unless we have retained it all along*. This means that if at any time our present experience is informed by the retention of an earlier experience, we must have been retaining it throughout the entire period since its occurrence. The changes in retention in the type of cases mentioned above present a problem because it appears that we *resumed* the retention of the experience after a period during which we were not retaining the experience.

Since there definitely is some experiential difference in this type of case, and it seems to be a difference in the retentional feature, some aspect of retention must account for it. The simplest and most direct explanation is to postulate two essential aspects of retention: an automatic interestless "maintaining" or keeping available for consciousness (in its horizon), and a degree of prominence or importance of what is retained to present experience, which can vary according to our present involvements and understandings of what is perceived. The maintaining aspect of retention would operate independently of interests and would be that which unifies phases of mental life. The maintaining would have all the structures of retention as previously described. However, whatever was maintained could inform our experience to different extents ranging from having very little prominence to being an essential part of the meaning of our current mental acts and their intentional objects. Some degree of prominence would have to exist if retention is to be a feature of *conscious* experience, but a retained mental life-phase could inform present experience to a minimal extent insofar as we have some background sense of where we are and what we had just been doing.

With the distinction of these two aspects of retention, the previously mentioned type of cases no longer presents a problem. There is a continuous retention in these cases but a variation in the prominence of what is retained.

5. Protention requires an analysis that is different from that for retention. There are insurmountable problems with any conception of protention as a form of direct awareness of just-future mental life-phases with their intentional correlates.

Commonsensically, we think of the future as being open and at least partially indeterminate and the past as being fixed and fully determinate. On this version of a past-present-future time, protention cannot be just like retention because there is not a fixed and fully determinate future mental life to be contacted.

Protention could be analyzed in the same way as retention if three conditions were satisfied: (*a*) mental life and worldly entities exist in an earlier-later time so that there is (tenselessly) at any given date a definite mental life-phase with its intentional correlates, (*b*) this earlier-later time allows some mental entities to exist across temporal locations, rather than having to exist completely at a temporal location, and (*c*) protention has the same very high degree of accuracy as retention. Condition (*a*) would eliminate the asymmetry between the past and the future, and condition (b) would allow protention to "reach across" temporal locations. At any given time there would be a fixed and fully determinate future capable of being contacted by protention.

Condition (c) presents a problem on any ontology of time, however. Our protentions are far more fallible than our retentions, and it seems to be possible to be mistaken about all the components of a future phase of mental life, even one that is not very far from the present. Assuming that there were fixed and fully determinate future mental life-phases, it does not seem possible that a protention could contact such a future phase in the way a retention contacts past phases yet still be mistaken about all its components. If the protention does not contact and "look through" any of the future mental act-phases that compose the mental life-phase, it is not clear of what a supposed contact with the mental life-phase could consist. If, then, protention does not contact future phases of mental life in these cases, it is unlikely that it contacts future phases in other cases when it is not completely mistaken. There is no experiential difference between the protentions that turn out to be accurate and those that turn out to be completely mistaken.

The fallibility of protentions remains a problem even if a past-present-future ontology of time is assumed. As I indicated in section 1.4, the most promising way to interpret protention as direct contact in a past-present-future time is to conceive it as contact with a set of alternatives. In a past-present-future time the future-as-future can be conceived as a set of relatively determinate alternatives only one of which will become present. Protention can then be contact with a set of alternatives *with one singled out*. This might appear to resolve the problem of fallibility because only the singled-out phase of mental life fails to become present. One of the other alternative phases of mental life does become present, and protention is in contact with it, although as a non-singled-out alternative.

There are three problems with this purported solution. First, there is no experiential evidence that protention grasps a set of alternatives. Our immediate anticipation of our just-future mental life and its correlates is of single courses of perception, thought, and action. The notion that protention really is aware of a set of alternatives does not have any phenomenological basis and seems to be simply *ad hoc*. Second, even if protention is allowed to be contact with a set of alternatives, there is no reason to think that we immediately anticipate the *right set* of alternatives. Events that are complete surprises to us do happen. It is hard to understand how this could be the case if we regularly contacted the real future alternatives. Third, in cases of unconsciousness or death, we protend the continuation of mental life, but it does not continue at all.

In light of these difficulties in any analysis of protention as similar to retention, I think that protention should be analyzed as a complex projection into the future of patterns discerned in the past. Some version of the present representation theory is probably accurate for protention. Since these projections into the future are not cases of contacting fixed and fully determinate future phases of mental life, they can be mistaken in the way that any prediction can be mistaken.

6. Because protention does not directly contact later phases of mental life and their intentional correlates, the unification of mental life-phases necessary for time-consciousness is accomplished primarily by retention. In contrast with the Husserlian theory's interlocking retentional-protentional structure, I think that the real unity can extend only in the "backward" direction.[12] Only present and past phases of mental life are involved in the genuine perception of the temporal extension and the temporal passage of worldly entities. Of course, through protention there is an anticipation of the phases of mental life and their intentional correlates to come, and these are generally accurate. However, these depictions of what is expected to come do not qualify as perception of future phases of worldly entities. The depicted mental life-phases and their intentional correlates are ontologically distinct from the phases that become present.

7. I have to admit to uncertainty about one aspect of the experience of temporal passage. My theory of time-consciousness explains the experience of temporal passage in worldly entities by means of the three-feature structure of consciousness. At any given time the now-consciousness feature of mental life intends its intentional correlates as present, while the retentional feature grasps as past earlier mental life-phases (with their now-consciousness features) and "looks through" them to their intentional correlates. This theory is consistent with either a passing or a non-passing real time (see section 9.4). What this theory does not address is whether the now-consciousness feature intends its correlates as "becoming" or "in transition."

There is a difference between an entity-phase's simply "being at time t" and "being in transition at time t," just as there is a difference between "being in motion at point a at time t" and simply "being at point *a* at time *t.*" "Being in transition at time *t*" would be an irreducibly past-present-future property. An entity-phase's "becoming at a time" could not be analyzed in a reductive way. When a phase of mental life perceives (through its now-consciousness feature) a worldly entity-phase as present, does it also grasp a basic "becoming" in the entity-phase? Are worldly entity-phases perceived as having this irreducibly past-present-future feature?

My theory does not require the perception of an entity's "being in transition at a time," but it does allow for it. The type of perception of temporal passage that my theory explains is necessary for the meaningfulness of "being in transition." Only if we can experience full-fledged temporal passage can we make sense of "from what" and "toward what" an entity is "in transition." "Being in transition" would be meaningful only as connected to the "from what" and "toward what" that are experienced through retention and protention.

I think that the experiential data are just not definite on whether "being in transition at a time" is experienced, so that I am content with a theory of time-consciousness that does not take any specific position. If any phenomenological data were to reveal irreducibly past-present-future features, I think that they would be data about mental life itself rather than about experienced worldly entities.[13]

The result of incorporating these modifications into the theory of time-consciousness is depicted in Diagram A.10 in the Appendix. Mental life consists of phases that endure through periods of real time. Each later phase directly contacts the just previous one and "looks through" it to its intentional correlates. Each earlier phase also depicts what it expects the just-later one and its intentional correlates to be like. Through this revised three-feature structure, interested perception is able to perceive all eight basic temporal features of worldly entities, and we can experience the temporal extension and passage of the perceiving itself.

9

Temporal Realism

None of the phenomenological theorists that I examined in Part II were idealists in general, but most and arguably all of them were temporal idealists.[1] Their theories of time and time-consciousness were such that the temporal features of worldly entities and of mental life did not exist independently of consciousness. Human consciousness was the foundation of all time and temporal features of entities.

The theory of time-consciousness that I presented in Chapter 8 relied upon the existence of an ontologically real time. Phases of mental life and experienced phases of worldly entities were portrayed as existing in and enduring unchanged through periods of real time. In developing this theory of time-consciousness, however, I did not defend the existence of an ontologically real time or the existence of real temporal relations between consciousness and real worldly entities. In this chapter I will examine some of the evidence for an ontologically real time and for real temporal relations between mental life and other entities.

9.1   Real Worldly Entities and Real Temporal Features

There are many reasons to think that some non-abstract entities exist independently of consciousness. Since I want to focus on temporal realism, I will be very brief concerning realism in general. I will discuss two arguments that support the independent existence of something. These make a strong *prima facie* case for some independent existence, but they would require a great deal of further argument to refute decisively a philosophical defense of idealism. My objective is to show that realism is highly plausible and that if one accepts either or both of the two arguments for realism concerning something (as do all the temporal idealists), then one should also accept the reality of time.

1. Perception is commonsensically understood to involve the detection of what exists independently of consciousness. One main component of this conception is the sense that sensory information is received "from outside." There seems to be *input* into consciousness, whether this involves consciousness contacting external entities or the entities contacting consciousness. This notion that perception receives information from outside is grounded in our lack of control over what we perceive. In contrast with the intended objects of imagination or even of memory, there is little control over what is perceived. The combination of the information of kinesthesia and of the external sensory modalities is almost totally outside our conscious control. Specific sensory information (in regular patterns) seems to be *imposed* upon us in perception, whether we want it or not. To a very limited extent, we can control the concepts that we apply in recognizing types, but assuming a fixed set of such concepts and a fixed orientation of our sense organs, the individual entities that we perceive is set.

That specific sensory information (in regular patterns) seems to be imposed upon us in perception is the main reason for thinking that it comes from outside consciousness. Although the regularity and connectedness of the patterns of sensory information also play a role, lack of control is the most basic factor.[2] Our lack of conscious control over what we perceive does not prove that the sensory information is actually received, but in the absence of contrary evidence it does provide good grounds for believing that it is. Paraphrasing Descartes, our perceptions seem to come from outside the mind, and in the absence of contrary evidence we have no way of discovering that they do not. Certainly, scientific accounts of our perceptual processes confirm this sense that information is received (from outside the brain rather than the mind). There are very complex causal chains connecting perceived worldly events with neural states and processes.

2. There is a great deal of evidence that the existence and functioning of first-person consciousness is dependent upon the existence and functioning of our nervous system, particularly the brain.

Whether or not we know anything about the functioning of a nervous system, or even that we have a nervous system, our mental life seems, for a knowledgeable third-person observer, to be dependent upon it. Chemical imbalances of neurotransmitters, tumors, lesions, drugs, neurosurgery, and all sorts of other things can affect our conscious experience in temporary and permanent ways by affecting our nervous system. Abilities and potentialities of consciousness as well as conscious states and episodes are affected by such factors. It is not just perceptual experiences that seem (in a first-person way) to be dependent upon something else. All our cognitive and reasoning processes seem (in a third-person way) also to be dependent. If conscious experience is so dependent upon the proper functioning of a nervous system even when someone knows nothing about it, this nervous system must exist independently of conscious awareness of it.

One response to this argument might be to claim that the characteristics of a nervous system are described and understood in terms of conceptual systems and theories that are only our best current conceptions, not the final truth of the matter. While this response is unobjectionable, it does not affect the major claim that *something* exists independently of our awareness of it. What it does bear upon is the correct characterization of this "something."

These two arguments that support the metaphysical reality of something independent of consciousness also support the metaphysical reality of time. If one accepts either or both of these arguments (all the phenomenological theorists discussed in Part II accept some version of argument 1), then one should accept the reality of some type of time.

1. Perception is commonsensically understood to involve the detection not only of something that exists independently of consciousness but also of some real temporal features of that something. Whatever concepts are applied in recognizing types of entities perceived, almost everything that we perceive is temporally extended, and there are always some temporally extended entities that are perceived. Just as sensory information seems to be received "from outside," so does the *temporal order* of the sensory information seem to be received "from outside." Whenever we perceive anything, there seems to be an input into consciousness of sensory information in a temporal order; that is, some information is temporally before other information. We have as little control over the fact

that there is temporal order to the information as we do over the fact that there is information at all. We have as little control over the specific order of the information as we do over the specific content of the information. Hence, our lack of conscious control over the temporal order provides the same good grounds for believing it to be metaphysically real as it does for believing that the source of the information is metaphysically real.

This point could be made in another way by emphasizing that it is *patterns* of sensory information that are received, not totally isolated individual bits of sensory information. An essential parameter of the received pattern is the temporal order among the components of the pattern. We always receive some temporal order of sensory information in receiving a pattern of sensory information.

In Part II I examined several philosophical theories that claimed that experienced temporal features derive *exclusively* from consciousness. Accepting the fact that perception always perceives temporally extended entities, they denied that the temporal order of sensory information is received. Although admitting that something exists outside consciousness and contributes to perception, the theories claimed that the temporal order in perception is produced by consciousness, not received from independent things. However, none of these theories showed that there is a phenomenological difference between the apparent reception of sensory information and the apparent reception of the temporal order of that information. Furthermore, none of them had any convincing arguments *against* the reception of the temporal order of sensory information. They relied instead upon the positive claim that consciousness *could be* the sole source of experienced temporal features. I will examine this positive claim in the next section. Here I want to emphasize that even if the positive claim were to be successful, this would not detract from the above argument.

2. If the existence and functioning of consciousness is dependent upon the existence and functioning of some ontologically real entity (or entities), there is good reason to think that this entity must be temporal. The existence and functioning of consciousness takes place over time and includes transitions from one state to another. It is important for mental life that the states occur one after the other and in a specific temporal order. That upon which consciousness is dependent must provide the necessary conditions for each of these states and for the *transitions between them*. It is hard to understand

how a non-temporal entity or a non-temporally ordered series of entities could be the necessary condition for the temporal order of mental life.

One response to this argument would be to emphasize that we do not know the intrinsic characteristics of real entities. Accepting the notion that real entities provide the necessary conditions for the temporal order of mental life, it might be claimed that we do not now understand *how* they do this, specifically whether they do so by themselves having temporal features. However, the plausibility of this response depends upon covering over the distinction between Kantian "things in themselves" and the real entities that scientific theories investigate. It is plausible that our current conceptions and theories are not the final truth of the matter only because we know that earlier conceptions and theories were able to be improved and that there are some things that we do not yet understand. With this conception of real entities, namely, as that to which improving conceptions and theories approximate, it would be very hard to deny that real entities have temporal features. While it is certainly true that our understanding of that which we now conceptualize in terms of the current neurophysiology may be improved, it is highly unlikely that any future theory would portray these real entities in totally non-temporal terms.

The alternative conception of real entities as unknowable "things in themselves" would block the argument to real temporal features, but it would also prevent *any* knowledge of real entities. We could not know that real entities were necessary conditions for mental life. Such a complete barrier to knowledge would require exceptionally strong justification. However, there do not seem to be any good reasons to think that real entities are completely unknowable.

Another possible response to this argument would be to deny that mental life is really temporal. Although mental life certainly seems to us to have temporal features, a two-level theorist such as Kant would claim that this is only an appearance and that consciousness is really non-temporal but usually understands itself to be temporal. In section 9.2 I will examine the two-level theory that claims that a two-level consciousness *could* experience all the temporal features that phenomenological reflection discloses in ordinary experience yet still be non-temporal. However, I want to emphasize that even if a two-level theory were capable of this, this would not show that mental life does not have temporal features, and so would not defeat the above argument.

9.2   Could Consciousness Be the Sole Source of Experienced Time?

One major component of the denial of temporal realism has been the contention that an ontologically real time is not necessary to explain our experience of temporal features. Kant, Heidegger, Sartre, and on some interpretations Husserl thought that consciousness itself was the sole source of experienced time, so that an ontologically real time was unnecessary. While each of their specific theories had some serious weaknesses, as demonstrated in previous chapters, these flaws might be attributed to other doctrines that they espoused, rather than to the claim that consciousness could be the sole source of experienced time. In this section I will consider whether consciousness *could be* the sole source of experienced time given the most favorable assumption, namely, that "things in themselves" form an ordered series, though not a temporal one.[3] This assumption would allow the reception of an order to sensory information. Only the specifically temporal features of what is perceived would have to be provided by consciousness itself.

9.2A   Single-Level Theories of Consciousness

A one-level non-temporal consciousness can immediately be rejected as a possible source of all experienced temporal features. As I argued in section 1.2, a consciousness that perceives the past-present-future features of worldly entities must itself have temporal features. What remains to be considered is whether a *temporalizing* consciousness as in Heidegger and Sartre could be the sole source. Such a consciousness would itself be temporal, and its temporality would *ex hypothesi* be the basic way in which time exists.

The provision that time be most basically an integral structure of consciousness effectively rules out the possibility of a temporalizing earlier-later consciousness. Earlier-later (B-series) time has always been identified with physical time. Although on a relational interpretation of physical time, the notion "at time t" is dependent upon the state of matter that exists (at time t), all contemporary interpretations of earlier-later time take temporal location and the order of temporal locations to be independent of consciousness. Hence, although it would be possible to try to defend a temporalizing earlier-later consciousness, there is no motivation to do so. Since we do experience past-present-future features, and earlier-later time is defended as a theory of material reality, if one is going to argue that temporalizing consciousness is the basic form of time, one should defend a temporalizing past-present-future consciousness.

Furthermore, there is an immediate objection to the notion that a temporalizing earlier-later consciousness is the source of all experienced temporal features. Without a set of independently specified dates at which phases of mental life exist, there would be serious problems in accounting for the *experience* of temporal passage. Each phase of mental life would be equally operative, each phase would take a different phase of the world to be present, yet there cannot be multiple phases of the world that are present. Ordinarily this issue is resolved by appealing to the fact that each phase of mental life occurs at a different time, but if these different times were dependent upon the different mental life-phases, this resolution would not work.

There are many different specific forms that a temporalizing past-present-future consciousness could have, depending upon the specific conceptions of the basic activities of consciousness and of how the temporal parts of consciousness influence each other. However, there are three basic features that any of these specific forms must share in order to be a temporalizing past-present-future consciousness. First, temporal extension must exist most basically as the temporal extension of consciousness. It must be the way in which phases of consciousness are both separated from and connected with each other. Second, pastness, presentness, and futurity must exist most basically as essentially connected features of consciousness. Consciousness must have a past dimension, a present dimension, and a future dimension, and these must operate together.[4] It is this "operating together" (being operative-as-past, operative-as-present, and operative-as-future) that makes possible the experience of temporal features in worldly entities (see theories 4 and 5 in section 1.3). Third, temporal passage must exist most basically as a transition in consciousness that has some explanation or reason within consciousness for its occurrence.[5] There must be something about temporal passage that ties it to temporalizing consciousness, and the nature of temporalizing past-present-future consciousness must require that future consciousness-phases become present and present ones become past. If there were no internal reason for the passage in consciousness, but it just happened, there would be no reason that it could not also "just happen" in real entities. This would make temporal passage independent of consciousness and contradict the claim that temporal passage exists most basically as a transition in consciousness.

Heidegger and Sartre portray temporalizing past-present-future consciousness as a free and acting consciousness. Temporal passage exists because consciousness essentially acts upon the world in order to make its freely projected future self (with the correlative state of the world) present. This notion of a free and mundanely acting temporalizing past-present-future consciousness contains a good deal more than the three features discussed above. In principle it would seem to be possible for a temporalizing past-present-future consciousness to have the above three features without either being free or being a practical agent. However, I have never come across a detailed theory of this sort.

Of the eight basic experienced temporal features that I discussed in Chapter 8, seven probably could derive from a temporalizing past-present-future consciousness that encountered a non-temporally ordered series of real entities.[6] The consciousness would only have to convert the non-temporal order of the real entities into a temporal order.[7] However, there are serious problems with a temporalizing past-present-future consciousness being the sole source of the experienced past-present-future features, particularly with the future dimension and with the passage of the future to the present. The basic problem is a conflict between experiencing the future-as-future and experiencing the present, given that the future is supposed to become present. What we portray as the future condition of the world may be very different from what eventually appears as present. This presents a problem because both conditions of the world are supposed to be the intentional correlates of one identical phase of consciousness that is operative-as-future and (later) operative-as-present.

In a temporalizing past-present-future consciousness, future phases of consciousness are supposed to operate together with present phases in the experiencing of temporal extension and temporal passage. Future phases, by being operative-as-future, are supposed to contribute the future horizon to the perception of worldly entities that is centered on the present. These identical phases are supposed to become operative-as-present through consciousness' internal dynamic. The passage in consciousness is a change in the forms of being operative of the phases of consciousness. When they are operative-as-present, the phases of consciousness portray their intentional correlates as present. As mentioned above, there does not seem to be any way that this theory can account for the actual differences between our immediate anticipations of what the future will be and our perceptions of what becomes present. How could the identical phase of consciousness have an intentional correlate when it is operative-as-present that is different from its intentional correlate when it is operative-as-future?

One attempt to respond to this problem would be to claim that in being operative-as-future a phase of consciousness intends a set of alternatives while in being operative-as-present it intends only one out of that set. The idea would be that the state of the world that actually becomes present need be only one of the alternatives that is intended by a consciousness-phase that is operative-as-future. Thus, there would not be a complete change in the intentional correlate of the identical phase of consciousness. The intentional correlate would just change from being a set of alternatives to being one single member of that set.

There are two reasons to reject this response. First, there is no experiential evidence that we always portray future states of the world as sets of alternatives. Our immediate anticipation of the just-future states of the world is normally of single and fairly definite states-of-affairs. Thus, this response involves postulating features of experience for which there is no phenomenological evidence. Second, even if it were accepted that we always portray future states of the world as sets of alternatives, there is no reason to think that these sets always contain what eventually appears as present. Events that are complete surprises to us do happen. It is hard to understand how this could be the case if we always portrayed the event as one of a set of possibilities.

These same reasons argue against another possible response: that any future moment of consciousness consists of a set of alternative consciousness-phases that are operative-as-future *as a set* but that only one member of the set becomes present (operative-as-present). This conception of the future of consciousness as containing various alternatives and not determining which of them becomes present is a central ingredient in the theories of *free* temporalizing past-present-future consciousness. However, such a theory does not resolve the two problems discussed above, and it has the additional problem that all future phases of consciousness are not experienced as sets of alternatives. When engaged in an action, we consider the immediately following steps of that action to be what we will do. We do not consider the immediately following steps to be one of a set of alternatives.

If the temporalizing past-present-future consciousness is supposed to be essentially an agent acting on the world (an acting consciousness), there is an additional problem for the thesis that consciousness is the sole source of experienced temporal features. A temporalizing past-present-future acting consciousness is supposed to make its future phases (with their intentional correlates) become present by acting on the world. Temporal passage is supposed to exist most basically as this motivated process of bringing its future into the present through action. Action portrays the future of the world as containing a determined range of possibilities. There are certain alternative (later) states of the world that at a given time can be brought about by action. We may misunderstand what specific range of possibilities is available, but we always understand that there is at a given time some specific determined range.

There is good reason to think that this determined range of possibilities is grounded in real entities because at that time it is outside our conscious control in the same way that what is perceived is (see section 9.1). The world, not consciousness, dictates what later states of the world might be brought about through action. Of course, our action in the world may be able to change things such that at a later time there is a different range of possibilities available, but if this possibility exists, it is itself one of the current range of possibilities.

Of the alternative states of the world in the range of possibilities, only one becomes present through action. The problem is how this can be consistent with the notions that consciousness receives (in perception) a non-temporally ordered series of information and that consciousness is the sole source of experienced temporal features. The difference between (a) an earlier determined range of alternative (later) states of the world and (b) a later single determinate state of the world (what becomes present) that is perceived would seem to require that real entities have temporal features. Since both are apparently grounded in real entities, at one time real entities must determine the range of alternative (later) states of the world, and at another time they must determine the actual state of the world that is perceived. Since a non-temporally ordered series of real entities could not change and any set of alternatives that it contained would unchangingly be a set of alternatives, a non-temporally ordered series of real entities could not be the source of both the determined range of alternative (later) states of the world and the single perceived state of the world.

There is another possible type of temporalizing past-present-future consciousness that I have not yet discussed. In light of my discussion in Chapter 8 of the need for an analysis of our awareness of the future that is different from the analysis of our awareness of the past, a temporalizing past-present-future consciousness might be proposed along the following lines. First, the temporal extension of this consciousness includes only the present and the past but not the future. The future of consciousness is *only* represented by some feature of the present of consciousness, so that the future has no real existence at all. Second, only presentness and pastness exist most basically as essentially connected features of consciousness. Phases of consciousness are operative-as-present and operative-as-past, but nothing is operative-as-future. We conceive there to be a future by means of present representations that project patterns and changes discerned in the past into the future. Third, temporal passage exists most basically as a transition in consciousness from being operative-as-present to being operative-as-past. This transition has some reason in consciousness for its occurrence. Since the future of consciousness is only conceived to exist, there is no passage from future to present.

Although this hybrid version of a temporalizing past-present-future consciousness does not succumb to the problems about the future becoming present, it has equally serious problems. First, since the non-temporal order of real entities is supposed to be the source of the received non-temporal order of sensory information, there is no satisfactory explanation of why non-temporally later members of the non-temporal series are not received along with the other members. This hybrid theory expressly rules out perception of the future, so that non-temporally later sensory information cannot be received along with what is understood to be present and past sensory information. However, the obvious way to explain this, namely, that reception of sensory information occurs only in the present, would attribute real temporal features to the real entities that are the source of the information. Whatever specific account is given of reception of sensory information, reception involves some type of relationship between real entities and consciousness. That the consciousness-side of this relationship occurs in the present does not explain why non-temporally later members of the non-temporal series are not "in contact with" the present phase of consciousness. If, on the other hand, some feature of the series of real entities explains this, this would seem to require that the series of real entities have some real temporal features.

The second problem is that there is no explanation within consciousness for why passage from being operative-as-present to being operative-as-past occurs. All the detailed theories of temporalizing past-present-future consciousness explain temporal passage in terms of making the future of consciousness become present, which displaces what was present into the past. This hybrid theory would require that there be an independent reason within consciousness for the present to become past. While it is not impossible that there be such a reason, I can think of no remotely plausible candidate.

9.2B   Two-Level Theories of Consciousness

In section 2.4 and in Chapter 5 on Kant, I discussed the possibility that a non-temporal consciousness might conceive an earlier-later temporal framework to be occupied by an intermediary consciousness all of whose phases themselves had a past-present-future temporal framework. (See Diagram 9.1). Each phase of the (conceived) intermediary level of consciousness would have a "favored point" in its framework that it regarded as present. By "looking through" the temporal frameworks of the phases of the intermediary level of consciousness, a non-temporal consciousness might be able to experience past-present-future temporal features in entities even though the real entities had no real temporal features.

In such a two-level consciousness, our ordinary experience is at

Diagram 9.1

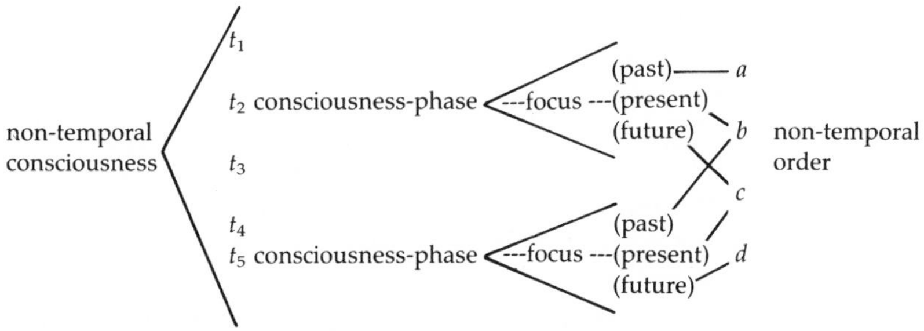

the level of the intermediary consciousness. We take our mental life to occur in time, and we perceive past, present, and future dimensions of the world. The ultimate non-temporal level of consciousness is supposed to underlie ordinary experience in that ordinary mental life *exists only as conceptualized* by the ultimate non-temporal consciousness. To accommodate our action and interested perception, the intermediary level of consciousness could be conceived to have motivations and powers to act and to be engaged in courses of action. Could such a two-level arrangement explain our perception of the eight basic experienced temporal features of worldly entities and our experience of our own mental life as temporal?

There are four major problems with this theory that a non-temporal two-level consciousness is the sole source of experienced time.

First, it is hard to make sense of the ultimate non-temporal level of consciousness. Its supposed experiences do not seem to be equivalent to the ordinary experiences for which it is supposed to provide an analysis. Because it would grasp together all the different phases of the intermediary consciousness, each of which portrays a different phase of the world as present, the non-temporal consciousness would grasp together multiple "present moments." Although each of these present moments would be understood to exist at a different earlier-later date, the ultimate consciousness would be equally aware of each of them (each of them would be equally before or "present" to consciousness). No earlier-later date would be emphasized over any other date, and no present moment would be emphasized over any other present moment. It is hard to understand what this would be like. It certainly is not intuitively recognizable as an analysis of our ordinary experience of temporal passage.

Second, even if the ultimate non-temporal consciousness could experience temporal passage in worldly entities and the temporal features of our mental life, *we* seem to occupy the position of the intermediary consciousness. It should be the intermediary consciousness that perceives temporal passage in worldly entities and experiences its own mental life as temporal. The consciousness that perceives temporal passage seems to be the same consciousness that perceives the past, present, and future features of worldly entities. This consciousness considers itself to be immersed in time and experiences its own thoughts and actions to be in time. The theory as developed does not allow the intermediary consciousness to experience the temporal features of its own mental life or to perceive temporal passage, because its phases are not unified in the right way.

Since the intermediary consciousness is *only* conceived to exist, there would be problems in revising the theory so that the intermediary consciousness could experience these features.[8]

Third, intentional action is not real according to the theory. Ordinary intentional action is a characteristic of the intermediary consciousness and so is *only* conceived to exist. Temporally extended intentional action, like temporally extended mental life, does not exist on its own. Although the non-reality of action does not generate any contradictions in the theory, it does highlight the theory's implausibility.

Fourth, the reception of the non-temporal order of sensory information and its conversion into an experienced temporal order is problematic for a two-level consciousness. Since only the non-temporal level of consciousness exists on its own, it would have to be related to real entities in the reception of the non-temporally ordered sensory information. The intermediary consciousness, which exists only *as conceived*, cannot receive non-temporally ordered sensory information. However, the order of sensory information is experienced in the action-oriented, past-present-future temporal framework of the intermediary consciousness, not the earlier-later temporal framework of the ultimate level of consciousness. There has to be some account of how the non-temporal consciousness could receive this ordered information and, instead of locating it in its earlier-later temporal framework, conceive the information to be received by the intermediary consciousness in an action-oriented past-present-future framework. Although this is not inherently contradictory, it is not clear how the ultimate non-temporal consciousness could do this.

Both the one- and the two-level theories have significant problems. There is no theory that succeeds in explaining how consciousness could be the sole source of experienced temporal features. There is also no positive evidence to think that consciousness is the sole source of experienced time. The only arguments that could support this thesis, the ontological arguments against a real time (see section 9.3) and the phenomenological claim that experienced time can be shown to be completely derived from the temporality of consciousness and the non-temporality of real entities (see Chapter 7), do not succeed. Furthermore, argument 2 from section 9.1 indicates that any *temporalizing* consciousness would depend upon an ontologically real entity that was temporal in nature. In light of this evidence, there is no reason to think that experienced temporal features are completely derived from consciousness.

9.3   *Responses to the Ontological Arguments Against a Real Time*

As I indicated in section 2.3, several ontological arguments have been offered to prove that time cannot be real so that it must exist only for consciousness.

1. Kant argues in the First Antinomy that time is essentially contradictory; time is such that the world must be thought both to have a beginning and not to have a beginning in time.[9] Since what is inherently contradictory cannot exist on its own, time cannot be real. However, we can have contradictory thoughts, so that time can exist as something conceived or intuited by consciousness.

As I explained in section 4.4, the Antinomy argument relies upon a past-present-future conception of time. The thesis argument assumes that time intrinsically passes so that "if we assume that the world has no beginning in time, then up to every given moment an eternity has elapsed, and there has passed away in the world an infinite series of successive states of things."[10] Hence, if successful, the argument would not prove that *any type* of time could not be real. Furthermore, as I demonstrated in section 4.4, the supposed contradiction does not stand up to critical scrutiny. Hence, it does not cast any doubt upon the ontological reality of time.

2. McTaggart also argues that time is essentially contradictory and so cannot be real. There are two stages to his argument: the first attempts to prove that the A-series (past-present-future) is essential to time, and the second attempts to show that A-series time is essentially contradictory. The argument of the first stage is that A-series determinations are necessary for change that is necessary for time. Whether this argument is successful or not, McTaggart's argument against the reality of time (or against the reality of just past-present-future time) requires that A-series time be essentially contradictory. It is this second stage that I will examine. However, I should note that even if the second-stage argument succeeded, a B-series (earlier-later) time could still be real if the first-stage argument failed.

McTaggart claims that A-series time is contradictory because: (*a*) "Past, present, and future are incompatible determinations. Every event must be one or the other, but no event can be more than one."[11] (*b*) "But every event has them all. If M is past, it has been present and future. If it is future, it will be present and past. If it is present, it has been future and will be past."[12] McTaggart conceives an event to be "the contents of a position in time."[13] As such, it is non-temporally extended; an event is an instantaneous entity. He wants to discuss the temporal passage of an entity, not its temporal extension. Obviously a temporally extended entity can have phases that are past and future with respect to a phase that is present.

This argument depends upon particular interpretations of "incompatible determination" and of "an event having these A-series determinations." Starting with the second, an instantaneous event can "have determinations" in two possible ways: in a tensed way and in a tenseless way. Thus, premise (b) could be interpreted as either:

   (b_1)   Every event has (at present) them all.

or

   (b_2)   Every event has (tenselessly) them all.

Given that an event is an instantaneous entity, b_1 is clearly false. No instantaneous event is at one time (at present) past and present and future. Rather, as the quotation in (b) indicates, it is these at different times. An instantaneous event has (at present) each of the different temporal determinations at different times. Thus, only the tenseless form $(b)_2$ is a true statement. Note that the tenseless form does not mention that the A-series determinations are had at different times because these are only had *in the tensed sense* at different times. B_2 could be rephrased as the essential claim: "If x is an event in time (A-series), then x has (tenselessly) pastness, presentness, and futurity."

The notion of "incompatible determination" can also be interpreted in a tensed and a tenseless way. Thus, premise (a) could be interpreted as either:

   (a_1)   No event can be (at present) more than one.

or

   (a_2)   No event can be (tenselessly) more than one.

Given that an event is an instantaneous entity, a_1 is clearly true. However, when joined together with b_2 it does not generate any contradiction because of the difference between the tensed and tenseless verbs. To generate a contradiction, a_2 would be necessary. However, a_2 is not obviously true. In fact, it seems to me to be obviously false, since b_2 is obviously true. In any case the plausibility of McTaggart's argument relies upon mixing tensed and tenseless statements. If the tenses of the premises are made explicit, there is no initial contradiction.[14]

This is not to claim that McTaggart's argument is merely sophistic. His argument does point to a puzzle about the "changing present" that I discuss in section 9.4. However, I am not convinced that there is any essential contradiction to the notion of a "changing present."

3. Heidegger, Sartre, and any other proponent of a temporalizing consciousness claim that time is most basically an essential structure of consciousness, that is, that time exists most basically as the essentially temporal existence of consciousness. The being of time is claimed to be identical to the being of acting consciousness. As such, time cannot exist on its own independently of consciousness. In this sense it is not real, although it is not merely a conception of consciousness, but rather the essential ontological structure of consciousness.

A major defense of the conception that time is most basically an essential structure of consciousness appeals to ontological classifications of ways of existing that seem to be known *a priori*. The ontological nature of time is first abstracted from time as experienced. Then the ontological nature of acting consciousness is revealed by a more complex process that mixes phenomenology with transcendental philosophy. Through a comparison of these two ontological natures, it is claimed that the identity between the being of time and the being of acting consciousness can be revealed.

There is good reason to be suspicious of any such ontological argument because of uncertainty about the ultimate classifications of ways of existing. However, there is a more serious problem with the claimed identity. To establish that "being temporal" is identical with "being actingly conscious," it has to be shown not just that they share all the relevant ontological features but also that *nothing else* shares these ontological features. If an entity that was clearly different from either time or acting consciousness did share these ontological features, it would demonstrate that these ontological features were not all the relevant ones (the ones necessary to establish identity). The dependence of time on acting consciousness would be refuted if entities that were not acting consciousnesses also shared with time the same set of ontological features.

It would be very hard to establish that no other entities could share the way of existing of time or of acting consciousness. This would require insight into the way of existing of any other possible entity. In fact Sartre does claim that any other entity would have to exist as Being-in-itself, but this is a mere ontological postulation. Neither Sartre nor anyone else has shown that no other entities could exist in the way that time exists. Without this premise, there is no argument against the ontological reality of time.

All the above arguments against the independent existence of time fail. There are probably other arguments with which I am not familiar, but in light of the positive evidence for the reality of time, I am confident that they also must be flawed. The case for the reality of time is just too strong.

9.4   Real Temporal Features and Mental Life

As the preceding investigations have shown, there is good reason to think that time is real, and there is no reason to think that time is not real. However, time can be real only by consisting of real temporal features, and I have so far said little about which specific temporal features should be taken to be real. I will consider real temporal features only with respect to real entities that do exist or might exist in time. Although a *de facto* empty time may be comprehensible, a time that *could not* be occupied by real entities is not comprehensible and is impossible. Hence, the temporal features of entities that do or might exist in time should exhaust the real features of any region of time. I will not consider those features concerning the whole of time, such as whether time is infinite or not.[15]

I do not want to make overly strong claims about which specific temporal features are real because I think that our understanding of real time can always be improved. Starting from the temporal features that we ordinarily experience, we might develop theories of real entities and of our perceptual and conceptual processes that attribute to real entities somewhat different temporal features (as in relativity physics) from those that we ordinarily experience. Any *revision* in the temporal features that we attribute to real entities, however, presupposes that we have some accepted temporal features from which to start. These are a necessary part of any data that could serve as evidence for a revised conception of real entities.

As a first approximation, it is reasonable to think that real entities possess all eight basic temporal features that we ordinarily experience worldly entities to have. Real entities have temporal locations, durations, lengths of duration, temporal divisibility, earlier-later relations, and past-present-future features, plus the special forms of length of duration and temporal divisibility. As I indicated in section 8.1, we perceive a temporal dividedness that indicates other possible divisions. However, perceived entities can only be temporally divided for perception within certain limits. Hence, the complete temporal divisibility of real entities can only be inferred because it cannot be perceived.

The reality of past-present-future features has been challenged by many philosophers on the grounds that a "changing present" is an incoherent notion.[16] Ordinary spatial motion requires that a displacement in one series (spatial location) be correlated with a displacement in another series (temporal location). If there is to be a purely "temporal motion" in which the Present changes its position in a series of earlier-later dates ($t_1, t_2, \ldots t_n$), a second temporal series ($T_1, T_2, \ldots T_n$) seems to be necessary. The Present must be at one date (t_1) at one time (T_1) and at another date (t_2) at another time (T_2). Alternatively, if the "changing present" is conceived on the model of qualitative change so that "presentness" is instantiated by different dates, a second temporal series still seems to be necessary to account for the fact that all dates do not simultaneously have "presentness." One date (t_1) has "presentness" at one time (T_1), while another date, (t_2) has "presentness" at another time (T_2).

The past-present-future notion of a "changing present" has not yet received a fully adequate analysis, but it also has not been shown to be incoherent. As George Schlesinger argues in *Aspects of Time*,[17] the notion that two temporal series are involved in the "changing present" does not necessarily lead to an infinite regress or to any other conceptual incoherence. In the absence of convincing arguments against the reality of past-present-future time, I think that we should take at face value our experience of worldly entities as having past-present-future features. The elimination of past-present-future time in favor of a time that has only earlier-later features would radically transform ordinary experience and everyday life.

That real entities possess the two special temporal features presupposes that there are real systems with functional parts. Only an entity with an inherent function or purpose has these special temporal features (see section 8.1), but it seems likely that such systems (for example, non-conscious organisms) do exist. The special forms of length of duration and of temporal divisibility would have to belong to real entities that did not possess the standard form of temporal divisibility, since these forms are incompatible.[18] In this respect such a system with functional parts would not exist *completely* within the same time as more standard real entities.

Given that there is a real time, does consciousness have real temporal relations with real worldly entities? Our commonsense conceptions of perception and of our own existence claim that there are such relations, but is there any reason to think that these are correct? Real temporal relations would exist whether or not they are conceived or represented in consciousness. Is there any evidence that phases of mental life are simultaneous with, earlier than, and later than real states of the world?

Argument 2 from section 9.1 provides the strongest case for real temporal relations between consciousness and real entities. The existence and proper functioning of our nervous system is a necessary condition for the existence and functioning of our consciousness. This "dependence relation" exists at any moment of mental life and throughout its entirety. Any phase of mental life is simultaneous with or later than states of real entities upon which it is dependent.

Perception is another case of real temporal relations. I argued in section 1.2 that a consciousness that perceives the past-present-future features of worldly entities must itself have temporal features. Temporally ordered phases of consciousness each portray a different temporally ordered phase of the world to be present. As I argued in section 9.1, in perception each phase of consciousness interacts with that temporal phase of real entities that is the source of the sensory information that it portrays as present.[19] Conjoining these two theses, temporally ordered phases of perceptual consciousness should interact with the temporally ordered phases of the real world that are the sources of the sensory information that the consciousness-phases portray as present. Whether consciousness contacts real entities or real entities contact consciousness, the connection of these two temporal entities should be a real temporal relation. Since the perceptual consciousness-phase is actual at a time and has earlier-later relations with other consciousness-phases, and the real entities (or phases of real entities) that interact with it exist at a time and have earlier-later relations with other real entities (phases), their relationship should be temporal. They should be temporally located vis-à-vis each other, and one must be either earlier than, simultaneous with, or later than the other.

Commonsense conceptions portray the perceptual act as occurring (*a*) at the same time and (*b*) for the same duration as the spatially separate object that is (supposedly) perceived. If the scientific account of the time of transmission of signals from their source to our sensory receptors is correct (*a*) is not true. Stellar events may be perceived millions of years after they occurred. Nevertheless, transmission times still involve real temporal relations. Instead of being simultaneous, the real spatially distant entity is earlier than the phase of mental life that it affects. Whether any difference could occur between the lengths of duration of the perceptual act and of the spatially distant entity that is (supposedly) perceived is less clear. If the length of duration of the complex signal from some real event were either compressed or expanded in time by its transmission, would we still be perceiving the distant event throughout the entire duration of the perceptual act? I tend to think not, but it may be that our concept of perception is not definite about such cases.

Action is another case of real temporal relations between consciousness and real entities. Bodily action is bodily movement that is governed throughout by an intention. However it is analyzed, this "governing relation" is a real relation between mental life and real entities (our bodies and perhaps other things). It should also be a temporal relation because both the intention and the bodily movements have temporal locations and earlier-later relations with other similar entities. Thus, they should have temporal locations vis-à-vis each other, and the intention must be either earlier than or simultaneous with the bodily movement that it governs.

In having these real earlier-later relations with real entities, mental life exists *at least partially* within the same time. Although consciousness has a special form of temporal location, which will be examined in the next chapter, it can always be temporally located (through the earlier-later relations) with respect to other real entities, and its duration can be compared with that of other real entities. This is what is true about the claim that mental life exists in the real time that is defined with respect to other entities.

10

The Special Temporality of Human Being

The temporal idealist tradition had an important insight: that human consciousness is temporally different from the non-conscious worldly entities of which it is aware. Humans exist through time in a way different from that of non-conscious worldly entities. Most of these have only the standard temporal features, but human temporal existence is different even from the temporal existence of systems with functional parts, which have some special temporal features. Having discussed in the last chapter the extent to which human consciousness exists within standard time by having real temporal relations with other real entities, I will examine in this chapter the ways in which it does not exist within standard time. In virtue of its special forms of temporal location, duration, and divisibility, human consciousness does not exist completely within the same time as real entities (even those with some special temporal features).

10.1   Time-Perception, Temporal Location, and Spatial Location

In section 3.2 I claimed that all the major theories of time-perception attribute special temporal features to perceptual consciousness. Of these special temporal features, temporal location is the most basic. A special form of temporal location is necessary for time-perception. External time-perception requires that phases of perceptual consciousness "reach across" to other temporal locations. To be aware of a temporally extended occurrence, a phase of perceptual consciousness must not be completely restricted to what would ordinarily be considered the date at which it exists. In perceptually contacting temporally extended entities, a phase of perceptual consciousness is not limited in its existence to one moment in time. It is not completely contained within one temporal location as standardly conceived. Rather, its existence spans standard temporal locations. This special temporal feature of spanning standard temporal locations is necessary for time-perception.

Only one of the theories of time-perception that I discussed in Chapter 1 did not *obviously* attribute a special form of temporal location to consciousness. The present representation theory at first glance seems to require only the standard form of temporal location. Assuming that a present phase of perception can be in contact only with entities that are simultaneous with it, the present representation theory introduces into consciousness an intermediate entity to be the object of direct contact. These intermediate entities, representations, are supposed to be simultaneous with the phases of perception and are supposed to represent earlier and later states of the world (and of the perceiving consciousness). Thus, phases of perceptual consciousness do not have to "reach across" to other temporal locations and appear not to require any special form of temporal location.

However, the present representation theory just *relocates* the special form of temporal location. Assuming for the sake of the argument that there are present representations, these would themselves have to "reach across" to other temporal locations. Each representation is supposed to *refer intrinsically* to some temporal location other than the one at which it exists and to portray some entity or entities (or their absence) that occur at that date.[1] It is the essential successful reference of these representations that requires a special form of temporal location.

The intrinsic referring of such representations makes them different from all other things that we ordinarily call "representations." Pictures, maps, diagrams, sentences, and other things that represent individual portions of reality do so *only because* of how they are used by conscious beings. The reference of pictures, maps, diagrams, sentences, and so on to other parts of reality is not intrinsic, but rather dependent upon the mind's reference. In the case of a present representation that·is supposed to be the basis of time-perception (in a first-person theory), however, this is not true. It is part of the representation's essential nature to represent some other temporal location and to do so by itself. If an entity is intrinsically a representation of a temporal location, rather than something that is just functioning as a representation in a certain system, its existence (as a representation-token) is not distinguishable from its representing of another temporal location.

Representations of other temporal locations successfully contact other temporal locations. This is necessary for their existence as entities *at* a time that refer to other times. Representations *at* a time are supposed to be different from non-temporally located representations. If it were not their nature to contact other times (but just "to portray" there to be other times), then perceptual consciousness would provide no basis for knowing that there was a real time. If there were no basis for knowing that there was a real time, there would be no basis for locating the representations *at* a time rather than outside time. Since it is part of the theory that the representations exist at a time, it should be part of the theory that the representations successfully contact other times.

It is also part of the theory that representations can misportray what occurs at some date; that is, they may get the facts at that date wrong. However, this presupposes that they do successfully refer to that other temporal location. Even if it were possible for a non-temporally ordered series of representations each to refer to some temporal location whose temporal order they mix up, this would still require that each representation successfully refer to some other temporal location, even though the relative location of that date was not portrayed accurately. If it is essential to the representations that they refer successfully to other temporal locations, their existence is tied to these other temporal locations. They could not exist as representations if they were wholly enclosed within one temporal location. If their being was totally limited to one temporal location, they would lose the character of representing other temporal locations. Thus, the representations themselves must have the special temporal feature of spanning standard temporal locations.

In response to the claim that time-perception according to any theory requires special temporal features, it might be argued that the same considerations should apply to space-perception, yet consciousness does not have a special form of spatial location that spans standard spatial locations. Since consciousness of a spatially extended entity involves awareness of many different spatial locations, should not perceptual consciousness have to "reach across" from its "here" to other spatial locations? If so, should not perceptual consciousness have to have a corresponding special form of spatial location? Yet the notion that consciousness "reaches across" to other spatial locations may sound implausible when it is applied to perceiving very distant objects, such as seeing heavenly bodies.

There are at least two features of the worldly entities that consciousness experiences that may lead to claims about special forms of temporality or spatiality for consciousness. One of these is the extension (spatial or temporal) of worldly entities, and the other is the distance (spatial or temporal) from us of the worldly entities. The traditional issues of time-perception concern our experience of the temporal extension and temporal passage of entities. It is these upon which I have focused because they provide a stronger argument for consciousness' special temporal nature. However, another argument based on the perception of temporally distant entities is possible, although this argument is far less convincing.

The reason that consciousness' "reaching across" may initially seem implausible when it is applied to the perception of spatially distant entities is that scientific accounts of the mechanics of perception describe how signals are transmitted from their sources and travel across space to our sensory apparatus. Since the signals travel right to where we are (the lens of the eye, the eardrum, etc.), it might appear that consciousness can just exist at the standard spatial location (or area) where its body is. This would probably be true if all that we ever perceived were signals that were contiguous with our bodies. However, we do perceive entities at a distance from us *as spatially distant*. It is not the signal at its final location with which perception is concerned. It is entities located elsewhere in space that perception detects by means of the signal. Hence, *assuming* that we do *irreducibly* perceive spatial distance from us, perceptual consciousness does "reach across" spatial locations and does require a special "standard spatial location spanning" form of spatial location.

Since signals take time to travel from their sources to our sensory receptors, the same issues arise for time-perception. If all that we ever perceive is signals that are simultaneous with the phases of perceptual consciousness, this would provide no basis for a special form of temporal location for consciousness. However, we perceive entities at a *spatial* distance from us, rather than the signals themselves. Since these entities are also at a temporal distance from us in real time, it is not implausible to claim that we perceive entities that are temporally distant from us, for example, that we "see into the past" when we see a stellar event that occurred many years ago.[2] The complications are twofold. First, commonsense perception does not portray the entities as temporally distant from us. We understand that the entities are temporally distant, but we do not perceive this temporal distance in the way that we perceive spatial distance. Second, in the case of very distant occurrences, such as stellar events, we would "see into" a past before our own births. These complications makes it more likely that the perception of temporally distant entities might somehow be analyzed in terms of simultaneous appearances. I am not going to offer any such analysis of perception or argue any position on the issue of reducibility. *Assuming* that the perception of temporally distant entities is irreducible, perceptual consciousness does "reach across" temporal locations and so must have a special form of temporal location.

There is a very significant difference between space and time with respect to the perception of spatially extended entities and the perception of temporally extended entities. Time-perception always occurs from some point in time.[3] One traditional problem of time-perception is how it is possible to perceive the temporal extension of worldly entities given the commonsense notion that perception itself occurs in time. Since we perceive past-present-future features while perceiving temporal extension, *at any given time* there is a distinct perceptual act-phase that portrays a distinct phase of the world to be present or temporally focal. It is this fact that there is *at any given time* a perception of temporal extension that generates the problem: how can consciousness at one time perceive the temporal extension of worldly entities that extend beyond that time?

The exact same problem does not arise for space-perception because, insofar as consciousness is spatial at all,[4] it seems to occupy a region of space that is itself extended in three dimensions. The spatial perspective for our perception does not originate from a point in space but from the extensive region of space that our sensory receptors occupy. After all, our sense of touch extends practically around the entire surface of our body, and even the retina is at least a two-dimensional surface. Thus, there is not the same mystery concerning how a spatially extended consciousness can perceive spatially extended entities *at all*. We can perceive by touch the entire surface of a smallish object simply by enclosing it in our hands, and some objects can be squeezed to reveal a third dimension. While there are significant puzzles about the integration of information from our different sensory modalities in the perception of three-dimensional entities, the perception of spatial extension at all does not require that consciousness "reach across" from one spatial location to another.

10.2   Special Temporality in My Theory of Time-Consciousness

Any theory of time-perception will have to attribute special temporal features to consciousness. In Chapter 8 I developed and defended a theory of time-consciousness. In this section I will examine the temporal features that this theory ascribes to consciousness with particular attention to the special temporal features.

There are strong theoretical reasons to think that phases of consciousness endure unchanged through brief periods of real time. As I noted in section 8.4, infinitesimal phases of mental life would have to have an infinite retentional capacity in order to retain even one second of our past mental life. However, that mental life is continuous in real time, as opposed to being experienced as continuous, is only an empirical fact. It seems to be the case that temporally extended mental life-phases occur "end-to-end" with no gaps in between, but it would be possible for such gaps to occur. It would also be possible for real time gaps to occur *within* a mental life-phase, as I am portraying them. Since a mental life-phase is extended in real time, it could be considered to consist of even smaller parts, all of which have the exact same now-consciousness feature and all of which retain the just-previous (larger) mental life-phase.[5] If some of these smaller parts were missing so that the (larger) mental life-phase was discontinuous in real time, this would have no effect on conscious experience. We could oscillate quickly into and out of actuality without there being any noticeable effect,[6] but there is no good reason to think that consciousness does. In the absence of empirical evidence, it is simpler to assume that consciousness is continuous in real time.

Although phases of consciousness are actual at standard temporal locations, they nevertheless have a special form of temporal location because they directly contact the phase just-previous to them and mediatedly contact a series of earlier phases. Each phase of consciousness (except the first phase) essentially has such a retentional feature that "reaches across" from its temporal location as standardly conceived to an earlier temporal location. Since retention "looks through" the just-previous phase to its intentional correlates and the just-previous mental life-phase itself has a retentional feature, a phase of consciousness also mediatedly contacts a series of earlier phases. This mediated contact is limited in that more removed phases of mental life "fade out." As a greater number of mental life-phases intervene between a retained phase and the retaining phase, the retained mental life-phase becomes less clear and distinct for the retaining phase.[7]

Given that it directly and mediatedly contacts other phases, a phase of mental life does not exist *completely within* the brief period of real time during which it is actual. Rather, its existence includes those moments or periods of time that it contacts and those through which it "reaches."[8] The temporal location of a phase of consciousness has this special form that spans standard temporal locations. If there were any real time gaps in the actuality of consciousness, they would be "spanned" by this retentional feature, and consciousness would have a type of existence during the gap.

As I explained in section 8.4, the protentional feature of a phase of mental life does not contact later phases of mental life. Nevertheless, protention does depict what it expects later phases and their intentional correlates to be like. I am not certain exactly how this projection into the future of patterns discerned in the past should be analyzed. It may involve some type of present representations of future occurrences. Whether such present representations would themselves have a special form of temporal location is not totally clear. Since we do have some direct perception of both earlier-later and past-present-future features by means of retention and its "looking through," it is possible that the reference of representations to the future is derivative in some way. It is possible that we represent the futurity of mental life and of other occurrences by representing the earlier-later relations between phases of mental life (with their intentional correlates). Futurity would be whatever is later than the present (current) phase. We would generate the idea of a future through recognizing that now past phases have later phases succeeding them. We would then imagine phases later than the present that succeed it. These would be the future. However, I want to emphasize that my theory does not *require* either that representations of the future do not intrinsically refer to later moments in time or that protention does not itself involve a special form of temporal location.

That phases of consciousness "reach across" to other temporal locations means that consciousness must also have a special form of temporal extension. The temporal extension of an entity is the set of *connected* temporal locations that it occupies. Since each phase of consciousness has a special form of temporal location in that it does not exist completely at the date at which it is actual, there is a sense in which each phase of consciousness itself has a temporal extension. Thus, the temporal extension of consciousness does not consist simply of the contiguous dates at which consciousness is actual. The temporal extension of consciousness is more complex in that it includes the moments of time that any phase contacts and those moments through which any phase "reaches."

Since retention contacts only earlier phases of one mental life, the special form of temporal extension will be indistinguishable from the standard form of temporal extension for any "complete stretch" of mental life whenever the actual existence of mental life is continuous through time.[9] Considered as a complete period, a period of one mental life can be considered to have a standard form of temporal extension so long as two other conditions are satisfied: (1) there are no gaps in the period, and (2) moments of the period contact *only* other moments in the period. The special form of temporal location of phases of consciousness will make a difference to the temporal extension of mental life if either of these conditions is not satisfied. Thus, if we black out or fall asleep for a short period of time but retain experiences on the other side of the gap, the temporal extension of consciousness will include these earlier experiences plus the period during the gap. Furthermore, the temporal extension of an (incomplete) stretch of consciousness that is actual from t_1 to t_2 will probably include some moments earlier than t_1 because these are ordinarily retained. Thus, an arbitrarily selected period of mental life will not ordinarily satisfy condition (2) because it normally contains retentions that "reach across" to earlier phases of mental life that are not actual during the period.

Phases of consciousness are actual at standard temporal locations, but their (retentional) intentionality "reaches across" to other temporal locations. The temporal extension of the *actuality* of mental life is comparable to the temporal extension of any other entity. The temporal extension of a "complete stretch" of mental life is also comparable to the temporal extension of other entities. Thus, the length of temporal extension of a "complete stretch" of mental life and the length of temporal extension of the actuality of *any* period of mental life are standard. How long either of these lasts can be determined by comparing them "end to end" with any other temporally extended entity or by the use of a repeating measure. However, the length of temporal extension of an incomplete stretch of mental life is not standard. Its duration cannot be determined by the usual comparisons because this duration consists both of moments of actuality and moments retentionally contacted and "spanned."

Any period of mental life cannot be divided into equally real temporal parts unless these parts are themselves "complete stretches"; that is, they include retentions only of other moments within the part. Normally, this is not the case; a subdivided period of mental life ordinarily includes retentions of earlier moments of mental life that were not actual during the period. For this reason, consciousness or mental life is not temporally divisible in the standard way. Mental life does not consist of self-contained units that are contiguous in time with each other. Rather, the temporal parts of mental life are specially related to each other in virtue of the "reaching across" of retention.

If allowances are made for the special form of temporal location of phases of mental life, these phases can be considered to have the standard earlier-later relations with each other. The dates at which phases of mental life are actual are earlier or later than each other, and although an individual phase may be considered itself to have a type of temporal extension, these extensions begin and end either earlier or later than each other. Thus, even as extended, the phases are related to each other as earlier-later.

Finally, mental life *may* have past-present-future features in addition to earlier-later features, although my theory of time-consciousness does not depend upon this. In section 9.4 I claimed that it is reasonable, as a first approximation, to think that real entities have past-present-future features because we experience worldly entities to have past-present-future features. Mental life is similarly experienced as passing from being future to being present to being past. In the absence of convincing arguments against the reality of past-present-future time, it is reasonable to accept mental life as it appears. However, if the notion of a "changing present" should ultimately prove to be incoherent or if our understanding of real time should ultimately abandon past-present-future features, a purely earlier-later mental life could still be conscious of time in all the ways that I have described.

10.3   Other Grounds for Human Special Temporality

Time-consciousness is a central and essential structure of human existence, but it is not the whole story. In sections 3.3 and 3.4 I outlined some further grounds that have been thought to support the special temporality of human existence. I will consider in this section whether there are any convincing arguments for the special temporality of human being other than that it is necessary for time-consciousness.

The theory of time-consciousness that I have defended does not claim *to exhaust* all the forms of time-consciousness. The recollection of earlier experiences and the expectation of later experiences, for example, are also types of consciousness that essentially concern time. It is possible that such other forms of time-consciousness may include special temporal features. I am taking no position on this issue. However, in this section I am looking for grounds for a special temporality of human being that do not reduce to *any* form of time-consciousness.

1. The denial of temporal realism cannot provide any convincing argument for the special temporality of human existence because some form of temporal realism is true, as I argued in Chapter 9.

2. A more promising line is the notion that human being is "ahead of itself" in being defined by its future that it is to be. At any given time humans are defined by their projects, that is, features of a future self that they are in the process of making themselves be. If the having of projects is not reducible to any psychological factors that exist solely at one time, as Heidegger and Sartre maintain, then the having of projects would involve a special form of temporal location.

Heidegger and Sartre interpret projects in terms of an ontology of time that I have rejected with respect to time-consciousness[10] and temporal realism.[11] However, the basic meaning of the notion of "project" is not ontological but phenomenological. "Project" is descriptive of certain structures of ordinary experience, specifically the ways in which our entire mental life seems to be actively moving toward the future. In having projects our consciousness has some of the characteristics of action. Working from the notion of *acting* consciousness, I will analyze having projects into two major features: having generalized intentions to make ourselves be certain types of persons, and the exercise of powers that is governed by these intentions. Do either of these features involve special temporal relationships with the future?

In regard to the first, in section 8.3 I claimed that my theory of time-consciousness could explain the experienced unity through time of intentions. For the purposes of time-consciousness, temporally extended intentions are unified in the same way that any temporally extended mental act is unified. A phase of an intention retentionally contacts earlier phases but does not protentionally contact later phases of the intention.

My theory of time-consciousness claims *only* that special forward relations between earlier phases of mental life and later phases are *not necessary for* time-consciousness.[12] My theory claims that protention does not ontologically unify phases of mental life, but it *does not claim* that other special forward relations could not exist. Since intentions seem to involve some "thrust into the future," there is a question whether some other special features besides those necessary for time-consciousness are involved. Is there any evidence that an earlier phase of an intention is *already* (at its date or at present) defined by its forward relation to later phases?

Abstracting from issues about the governing of the exercise of powers, the feature of intentions that might be taken to require such a special forward relation between earlier and later phases is "commitment." Intentions to do temporally extended actions include something like a commitment to continue to bring about the overall objective. Since all projects and almost all actions take some length of time to accomplish, and the intention is to accomplish the entire project or action, any phase of an intention prior to the accomplishment of the objective will concern objectives that are at least partially future. We intend to do not only those parts of the action that we are now doing, but also the later parts. This requires that the intention continue into the future. For an action *xyz* that extends from t_1 to t_3, there must be an intention to do *xyz* that extends (approximately) from t_1 to t_3.[13] Within any earlier phase of the intention to do *xyz*, there is the sense that the intention *will* continue until the accomplishment of the objective. We can intend to do a temporally extended action only if we have this commitment to continue to intend and to continue to do. In contrast with mental acts such as desiring and wanting that may just cease without requiring any further explanation, intentions are supposed to persist through adverse conditions (strength of will). One should not have an intention to perform a temporally extended action unless one is going to do one's best to carry it out.

In virtue of commitment, intentions might be thought to include a special forward relation. However, commitment does not *require* that an earlier phase of an intention be *already* (at its date or at present) defined by its relation to later phases of the intention. First of all, we can "change our minds" about any temporally extended action. Although a person could not abandon *all* her intentions before completion and still remain an intender, she can abandon any specific one. Secondly, and I think decisively, it is possible for any and all intentions just to cease before their fulfillment, such as when a person suddenly dies or is rendered unconscious. Since intentions can end at any moment because of their dependence upon neurophysiological structures, an earlier phase cannot *already* include an essential relation to later phases that may never exist (if the person dies or has her nervous system disrupted). Of course, someone might claim that it is only those intentions that are not cut off that have this special forward relation, but this response would be simply *ad hoc* because there are no other obvious pre-existent differences in the two cases. We consider an intention that is cut off by neurophysiological disruption to be just as much an intention as one that continues.

In Chapters 1, 8, and 9, I noted that the most plausible past-present-future ontology of time conceives the future to be a set of alternatives only one of which becomes present. In such a past-present-future time, what is future *as future* is defined by its relationship with what is present. According to this ontology, an earlier (present) phase of an intention might be already forward (futurally) related to a *set of alternatives* that includes a later phase of the intention, as well as the neurophysiological disruptions that would end the intention. Thus, although future mental life is dependent on future neurophysiological functioning, there could be some type of forward relation to later phases of an intention, but only to these phases as constituents of sets of alternatives.

This seems to me to be too weak a connection on which to base a claim for a special temporal feature of being already defined by a forward relation. The forward relation in this case is *with* the set of alternatives as a set, but the relevant forward relation should be with later phases of the intention (with only some of the members of the set).

Although the commitment feature of intentions does not prove the existence of special forward relations, it nevertheless does indicate something about the endurance through time of intentions. To account for the intending of action-phases that are not yet being brought about and governed, a theory of the nature of intentions would have to provide some other account of the *endurance* of intentions, that is, of the relation of earlier phases of the intention to later phases. The most obvious candidate is some type of causal account.

Perhaps earlier phases are among the causes of later phases, or perhaps the same factors that produce the earlier phases continue to produce the later phases. There is no particular theory of the endurance of intentions (or of other mental entities) for which I wish to argue. Any adequate theory of intentions would have to address the way in which an earlier phase includes some legitimate expectation or confidence that the later phases will come about. While such an analysis of the endurance of intentions will require that earlier phases depict the future, there is no reason that the analysis would need to invoke any special temporal relations of earlier phases with the future, unless the depicting itself requires this.

In regard to the second feature—the exercise of powers that is governed by our generalized intentions—the intentional exercise of powers seems to involve a special relation with the future because the earlier exercise of a power is defined by its relation to the later result that it produces. In general a power to produce a result is defined by the later result. Something is a power only in virtue of its control over what happens later. A consciously exercised power is conscious of this control over what happens later. One is conscious of being able to produce alternative results.

In intentional action a person consciously exercises powers in order to bring about intended results. Drawing upon the person's powers, an intention *initiates* either bodily or mental movement, such as moving one's hand or mentally adding numbers. Although the intention continues in order to monitor the bodily or mental movement, the initial causation is a relationship between an earlier phase of the intention and a later bodily or mental movement. There is an intentional exercise of powers *only if* the right movement results. If one's hand does not move or one's thoughts do not engage in adding, the relevant powers are not exercised, even though one initially thought that they were. The appropriate intentional action occurs only if the intended movement occurs. In virtue of this dependence upon what happens later, the intentional exercise of a power to act does require that acting consciousness have a special temporal relationship with what is later.

The continuation of intentions and of the movements that they govern can be undercut by disruptions of our neurophysiology, as I noted in discussing the first feature. Our conscious control over our future movements is also dependent upon the proper functioning of our neurophysiology and physiology. We may intend to move our hand, but our hand may not move. For this reason the exercise of powers in action cannot be considered to be a special futural relation, that is, a forward-directed relation between a present exercise and a future result. *In the present* conscious control over the future is not (yet) definite, because disruptions may always occur. It is only when the result occurs that the conscious exercise of a power is real. The conscious exercise of a power involves a special forward relation between an earlier phase of an intention and a later movement, but this does not exist until the movement has become present.

That something earlier is *defined* by its control over what happens later is why the conscious exercise of powers involves a special forward relation. In principle non-conscious entities might also be defined by their control over what happens later. As Heidegger and Sartre indicated, a piece of equipment is frequently defined in terms of what it does. In their theories equipment was dependent upon human purposes, so that they did not attribute this special temporal feature to independently existing entities. However, as I noted in section 9.4, there is good reason to think that there are independently real, functionally defined entities, such as non-conscious organisms. Some parts of such functionally defined entities would probably be defined by their control over what happens later.

3. That humans are "towards death" has also been thought to involve a special ontological relationship with the future. As I explained in Chapter 6, Heidegger maintains that being-toward-death is a particular way of being *at any given time* and that it differs from the ways of existing of worldly entities (being-ready-to-hand and being-present-at-hand).

Heidegger conceives human being essentially to include an implicit self-understanding of one's own finite lifespan. Accordingly, he conjoins two notions in the conception of being-toward-death: (*a*) that human life is essentially temporally finite in that it cannot continue infinitely through time, and (*b*) that humans at least implicitly take themselves to have finite lifespans and that this self-understanding *should have* certain effects on how they think about their own projects.

By itself, (*b*) does not require a special ontological relationship with its future. Even if, in accord with notion (*b*), humans do think differently about their own projects because they take themselves to have finite lifespans, this does not establish anything further about the *ontological* relationship of human existence with its future.

If (*a*), that human life *essentially* has a limited timespan, is correct, then it is plausible that human existence at any time would have to have a special temporal nature. Human existence at any time would have *to guarantee* that the person did not just live on and on (infinitely). This would seem to require some type of special relationship with its future so that the future lifespan was essentially, rather than contingently, limited. Just as an *essentially* immortal lifespan would require a special relationship between its present and future portions that did not exist in ordinary temporally extended entities, so an essentially finite lifespan would require a special relationship between its present and future portions.

The problem with the above basis for a human special temporal nature is that it is not clear that the timespan of human life is essentially limited. Many science fiction and fantasy stories have provided conceptually coherent accounts of what it would be like to be impervious to ordinary injuries and not to suffer the degenerative effects of aging. Such "immortals" seem just to continue to live on and on. There is no *obvious* reason why their lives could not continue infinitely.

The Heideggerean response to this challenge would probably appeal to notion (*b*). If it could be shown that understanding oneself to have a finite lifespan is a necessary condition of valuing one's own activities and that valuing one's own activities is an essential feature of human life, then a good case could be made for human life not being capable of continuing infinitely because a human would eventually realize that he was immortal. This realization would lead to no longer valuing one's own activities and to the cessation of human life (*qua* human). According to this line of argument, an immortal human who realized that he was immortal could no longer have projects for himself.

The supposed dependence of having projects on considering oneself to have a finite lifespan is an intriguing idea, but it seems to me to be a contingent cultural-psychological fact about certain people, rather than an essential feature of valuing, human valuing, or what it is for humans to have projects.[14] Just as some people cannot imagine how anything can be taken to be valuable if one does not believe in God, many people cannot imagine how anything can be taken to be valuable if one does not believe that one's own life has a finite timespan. Although this might establish that there is *some* (contingent) connection between the belief and valuing as psychological characteristics, it does not reveal any essential relationship. It does not establish that it would be irrational or impossible to continue to value one's own activities even though one took himself to be immortal. Unless such an essential relationship can be established, there is no good argument for human life having an essentially finite timespan and thus no good argument for a special relationship with its future.

4. That humans are at any given time defined by their pasts has been thought to involve a special backward-directed ontological relationship with the past. There are many ways in which humans are affected by their pasts. The current features of a person that might be thought to involve a special unity with the past (and thereby involve special temporal features) are acquired skills and abilities that a person realizes that she has, acquired psychological entities (wants, emotions, preferences, beliefs, etc.) that are not specifically about the past, acquired psychological entities that are in some way about her own past, and the obligation or responsibility *to appropriate* her past, that is, the obligation to take toward her own past some stance that affects her actions and outlook on the world.

First, acquired skills and abilities that a person realizes that she has might be thought to involve a special backward connection with her own past in two ways: insofar as these skills were acquired through earlier practice or previous experience, the currently existing skill is still based upon these earlier episodes, and to have (in the relevant sense) a skill or ability includes being confident that one can call upon the skill in performing actions. To be able to "count on" the skill in performing actions, a person must recognize its rootedness in earlier practice or execution.

Although the development of a skill through practice normally is an intentional bringing about of the skill, the first factor does not require any special backward connection with one's own past. Once a skill or ability exists, its existence is not defined by any connection with that which produced it. The skill or ability is distinct from that which produced it, even if this is a course of training or practice. Thus, the same skill might be produced by earlier practice and previous experience, or it might be produced by some entirely different means (taking a pill, having a neural implant, magic, etc.).

However, the basic meaning of "having a skill" does include a certain type of confidence in one's being able to do something. This confidence is usually based either on retaining or remembering one's former success in making use of the skill and how one acquired the skill. Thus, there may be a special connection with one's own past included within having a skill. However, since this connection is not something distinct from time-consciousness, it does not provide any additional grounds for the special temporality of human being.

Second, most of a person's acquired emotions, wants, preferences, and beliefs are grounded in his personal and cultural past. These psychological entities are most frequently a "natural outgrowth" from the person's origins; for example, what a person currently likes and wants should be understood in terms of what he formerly liked and wanted, what his friends and family liked and wanted, and what is liked and wanted within the larger society. Nevertheless, this influence of the person's past does not require any special connection with it. Once such psychological entities exist, their existence seems to be distinct from that which produced them. Whether or not any satisfactory theory of antecedent causation should ever be established, the psychological entities do not require the specific origin that they in fact had. This shows that they are not ontologically tied to the person's past in any special way.

Third, acquired psychological entities that are in some way about one's own past do, *prima facie*, involve more of a connection with the past via the "being about" feature. For example, if Mary is angry at John because John failed to invite her to a party, the current state of being angry, whether dispositional or occurrent, depends upon portraying past episodes in a certain way. Since there are a large number of different types of psychological entities that are in some way about one's own past, there are significant differences in the *types* of the "being about one's own past." Without attempting to catalogue all these types, I want to claim that insofar as "being about one's own past" does involve a special ontological relationship to the past, it does so as a form of time-consciousness, though not necessarily time-perception (for example, recollective memory of previous experiences might involve some special type of "contact" with the past). The reason for this is straightforward: any portraying of one's own past *as* past that was connected in some special way with the past experiences portrayed as past would be a case of time-consciousness, and *ex hypothesi* would be specially connected with the past through this time-consciousness feature.

Fourth, the obligation or responsibility to take toward one's own past some stance that affects one's actions and outlook on the world is based on the notion that past experiences can be a part of a person's past history without that person adequately acknowledging them. In such cases some philosophers have claimed that the person has an obligation to incorporate "having done and experienced" these earlier episodes into her current thinking in the form of evaluative stances, such as being ashamed of, being proud of, or considering oneself entitled to something because of the earlier episodes. In Sartre's notion of "having to be one's past,"[15] the thought is that a person should in some way consider herself responsible for all her past actions and experiences. Although there may be good grounds for being indifferent toward some past experiences, none can legitimately be ignored. This same conception occurs in some theories of personal identity, where personal identity is supposed to include this obligation.[16]

Such an obligation or responsibility could be thought to be a component of a special connection between the present stage of a person and past stages. The person *now* might be defined by past experiences and actions because of the obligation to take some evaluative stance toward them. If there is an obligation to take responsibility for past experiences and actions themselves (rather than the thought of the past experiences and actions), then a strong case could be made that the present person-stage is essentially connected with past person-stages, that is, that the present person-stage is what it is (obligated) only through its relation to these past person-stages.

Within our current conceptions and social practices concerning personal identity over time, there is some type of obligation to take responsibility for one's own previous experiences and actions. A person is generally not allowed to ignore relevant past experiences and actions in thinking about what he should now do and what his emotions and attitudes should be. However, the relevant question for the ontology of human being is whether this obligation is a feature of a special relationship with one's own past or merely a matter of socially shared conceptions of how a person should think and act. Is the person obligated by the past experiences and actions themselves (in relation to the present of the person) or is he obligated by the socially shared conventions concerning how a person should "take into account" his own past experiences and actions?

To resolve this issue definitively would require an extensive exploration of personal identity. It is plausible that there is some connection between this "obligation to take responsibility" and the ontology of persons, but a very strong connection (plus other ontological conclusions) would be necessary to support the claim that there is a special temporality involved. The connection that does exist is this. Personal identity in humans is such a complicated issue because normal humans are self-conscious in important ways. Being a person requires both that a consciousness apply "person concepts" to other people and to herself and that a consciousness evaluate her own characteristics as portrayed in these "person concepts."[17] Thus, since thinking about oneself in certain specific ways is an essential part of being a person at all, it is necessary that the present stage of a person conceptualize and evaluate her own characteristics, including the past instances and components of these characteristics. However, it is common that real people are sometimes deficient in conceptualizing and evaluating their own characteristics. Since this is a deficiency, there is something like a "built-in" requirement to correct these deficiencies when they occur. Perhaps this "built-in" requirement or some other "built-in" requirement is the basis for the "obligation to take responsibility." If "taking one's own actions and experiences into account" were part of the self-consciousness that is necessary for being a person at all, then the "obligation to take certain (neglected) actions and experiences into account" might be a "built-in" requirement grounded in the essential nature of a person.

However, even if the obligation to appropriate one's own past is grounded in the essential nature of a person, this alone would not prove that there is a special ontological relationship with the past. The ontological relationship would still depend upon the ontological standing of the essential nature of a person. If the category "person" was only a cultural conception and not a natural kind, one could deny that there was an independently real ontological connection with the past, even though a connection with the past was grounded in the essence of a person as conceived by our culture. There are some very interesting issues here that I cannot now explore. Hence, I will conclude this discussion inconclusively. There may or may not be a special ontological relationship with the past included within the obligation to appropriate one's own past.

5. The unity of diverse mental acts and other psychological factors into one consciousness *at any given time* depends upon how these entities interact *over time*. In discussing time-consciousness, I have said nothing about how the many mental acts that compose one mental life are unified with each other. Because it is not relevant to the time-consciousness issues, I provided no analysis in Chapter 8 of how multiple mental act-phases compose one mental life-phase. However, since simultaneous mental acts (and mental act-phases) can belong to different people and compose distinct mental lives,

some account of what makes a mental act part of one mental life is necessary.

In discussions of personal identity, this unity has frequently been assumed to be provided by all the psychological factors being possessed by or occurring in one human body.[18] In ordinary cases of normal humans, one human body will at any given time have one and only one mental life-phase connected with it. However, the non-ordinary cases of multiple personalities, commissurotomies ("split brains"), mental illness, brain injury, and extreme retardation show that the one human body–one mental life principle is not adequate. The unity of mental acts into one mental life requires a more sophisticated theory.

In "Person-Stages and Unity of Consciousness"[19] I developed and defended a complex theory concerning how multiple mental acts and other psychological factors are unified into one mental life (one unitary consciousness). Without repeating that entire analysis, I will rely upon some of its conclusions. A skeptical reader should consult the original article to see how well these conclusions are defended.

There are three conditions for a psychological factor (including mental acts and their intentional objects) to be part of a unitary consciousness: (a) that there be a system of well-integrated psychological factors that has a coherent worldview and a coherent program of action; (b) that the psychological factor be at least partially integrated into this system; and (c) that a partially integrated psychological factor be subject to a goal-directed process of increasing its degree of integration. One psychological factor is integrated with another when they are so interrelated that they interact normally with each other in the generation of features of consciousness. For example, two beliefs are integrated with each other when "what is believed" in each belief both serves as part of the context of meaning for the other and stands in evidential relations with the other. What is believed in the two beliefs is *joined together* and *operates together* in the ways that are normal in one first-person conscious experience.

However, people do have some mental acts and other psychological factors that are not well-integrated with most of their other ones. For example, what is believed in one belief may not be adequately conjoined and compared with what the person (psychological system) generally believes. Condition (c) is meant to capture the commonsense notion that such imperfectly integrated psychological factors are nevertheless parts of one conscious experience. In com-

monsense thinking, one consciousness may temporarily fail to conjoin and to compare what it believes, but it does not do so perma-
nently and it is deficient in doing so at all.

Both the integration of psychological factors and the process of
increasing integration of partially integrated psychological factors involve specifications of how the psychological factors will behave and
be changed *over time*. Since integration and increasing integration
define whether a psychological factor is or is not part of a unitary
consciousness *at one time* (a consciousness-phase or mental life-
phase), the defining conditions of a mental life-phase depend upon
its relations with earlier and later mental life-phases.

Through the above defining conditions, a mental-life phase has
special relations with earlier and later phases of the same one mental
life. Whether a unitary mental life exists at any given moment depends upon how what is actual at that time is related to what preceded it and what follows it. The unity of a mental life that encompasses many diverse psychological factors exists only *over a period of
time*. This unity cannot exist completely within any given moment of
time.

The unity of mental life requires special temporal relations of
one mental life-phase with earlier and later phases. However, I do
not want to require that in a past-present-future time the future be
already completely determinate, because the most plausible ontology of past-present-future time conceives the future to be a set of
alternatives, only one of which becomes present. This means that
for a mental life-phase in a past-present-future time, it may not be
settled at its date what is and what is not part of that mental life-
phase. Insofar as the mental life-phase is defined by forward relations with what is later, but what is later is indeterminate, the mental life-phase is indeterminate. Only when the indeterminate future
becomes a determinate present does the (now past) mental life-
phase become fully definite.

10.4 Implications of Human Special Temporality

That humans exist through time in a special way has important
implications for a large number of other traditional philosophical
questions. I will examine some of these implications in this section;
however, the complexity of the issues that are engaged does not
allow an exhaustive treatment.

1. Through retention a phase of mental life contacts a period of mental life that normally extends back some distance in time. This defeats skepticism about the just-past existence of anything. For as far back as retention reaches, there is conclusive evidence of the existence of mental life and strong evidence for the existence of the worldly entities perceived in that mental life. Russell's creationist worry "that the world sprang into being five minutes ago, exactly as it then was, with a population that 'remembered' a wholly unreal past"[20] can be answered. The retention that is necessary for any non-instantaneous mental act, including recollective memory acts, guarantees the reality of at least some previous period of mental life.

2. The special temporal nature of consciousness makes it non-reducible to the functioning nervous system upon which it is dependent. Even though a neurophysiological system as a system may have some special temporal features, as simply *neurophysiological* the system does not have that special form of temporal location that is necessary for time-perception. As I argued in section 10.1, *any* plausible model of time-perception will require that consciousness have a special form of temporal location whereby, at any given time, a phase of perceptual consciousness "reaches across" to other temporal locations. This special form of temporal location, which is apparently an emergent feature of complex neurophysiological systems, makes the temporal parts of consciousness "non-congruent" with the temporal parts of our nervous system as described in neurophysiology and biochemistry. Given that phases of consciousness do not have the same spatial-temporal locations as neurophysiological structures and events, an exhaustive reductive explanation of the former in terms of the latter seems to be impossible.

3. The special temporality of human being does not require or provide any support for human free will. This is a major negative conclusion of my investigations. Starting with Kant (or earlier with Leibniz), one of the main objectives of temporal idealism has been to make free will possible. Following a temporal idealist strategy, both Sartre and Heidegger thought that the special temporal nature of human consciousness (which temporalized time) included some form of free will. Having rejected their accounts of time-consciousness and temporal idealism, my investigations have revealed that the special temporality of human being is distinct from and independent of free will. Neither the special temporality necessary for time-consciousness, nor the special temporality necessary for the conscious exercise of powers, nor the special temporality necessary for

the unity of consciousness provides any particular basis for human free will.

It is of course possible that there are other special temporal features of human being that tie into free will. Since it is likely that if free will exists, it would include special temporal features, the search for such features is well directed. However, I have not located any special (futural) relations of consciousness with its future that provide support for free will, and the initially most plausible candidates have proven to be disappointments. Hence, my provisional conclusion is that human free will cannot be defended by appeal to the special temporal features of human being.

4. The special temporality of human being does not establish either that humans are essentially self-determining or that there is any obligation to be self-determining. One of the objectives of Heidegger and Sartre was to establish that human being is a rational power, a "being able to be" a (chosen) type of self. Determining one's own objectives for oneself, such as what values to hold and what sort of person to intend to be, was supposed to be a defining feature of human being. The intrinsic freedom that was supposed to be grounded in human existing through time was supposed to require or to obligate humans explicitly to determine themselves. The temporal ontology of human existence was to be the basis for the claim that refusing to be explicitly self-determining is a form of self-deceptive inauthenticity or bad faith.

Since metaphysical free will is so difficult even to characterize, let alone to prove, many philosophers would be satisfied with a demonstration that self-determination is an intrinsic part of human life. Whether or not humans are metaphysically free, if they essentially determine their own objectives, this might still support claims about the obligation to be explicitly self-determining and the inauthenticity of refusing to be self-determining.

Special forward and futural relations would probably be required for human being to be essentially self-determining. Hence, it is reasonable for a proponent of self-determination to search for such special temporal features. They may indeed exist, although no one has yet succeeded in specifying the relevant special temporal features and their connection with human self-determination. The special temporality necessary for time-consciousness does not provide any particular support for self-determination. The conscious exercise of powers presupposes that one already has objectives that govern the exercise, so that the special temporality necessary for the exercise does not help. My suspicion is that the special temporality necessary for the unity of consciousness in conjunction with various claims about how humans conceive themselves[21] might eventually provide some support for self-determination as an essential characteristic of persons. However, this suspicion has yet to be worked out in detail.

5. The unification of mental life-phases through retention has implications for theories of personal identity because retention involves direct links between phases of mental life at different times. Through retention, each phase of consciousness directly contacts the just-previous phase and mediatedly contacts a series of earlier phases. This retentional unification has not been utilized in mentalistic accounts of personal identity. Discussions of personal identity have treated recollective memory as the primary (and sometimes as the sole) "mental connection" between a present person-stage and previous person-stages. However, retention is a more basic mental connection in that it is presupposed by recollective memory and not vice-versa. Retention might resolve some of the classic problems of personal identity.

Retention provides a direct metaphysical and experiential link between later and earlier phases of mental life. The chain of retentions (phase$_4$ retains phase$_3$, which retains phase$_2$) is an important way in which an uninterrupted stream of consciousness is unified. The unity of consciousness through a normal waking day can be explained by means of a chain of retentions. If retention does "reach across" dreamless sleep and other extended periods of unconsciousness, there would be an unbroken chain of retentions leading back from any later stage of a person to any earlier stage of that person. The entire mental lifetime of a person might have the same type of unity that a normal waking day has.

6. The special forward relation that is necessary for the conscious exercise of powers has implications for theories of personal identity. The earlier exercise is defined by its control over the later bodily and mental movements that are the result of the exercise of the power. Such control over what comes later is an important constituent of personal identity, particularly in a past-present-future time. The varieties of such control have not yet been fully explored in theories of personal identity.

7. That the unity of mental life requires special temporal relations of one mental life-phase with earlier and later phases has important implications for theories of personal identity. Personal

identity is not reducible to a series of independently defined person-stages, because the defining conditions of one person-stage depend upon its relations with earlier and later stages.[22]

8. Points 5, 6, and 7 should have important implications for how the temporal parts of humans are conceived in ethical questions and social theory. They should affect the way in which the temporal parts of a person's life are conceived in utility calculations and in the application of deontological principles. The part of human life that is actual at one time can be more tightly connected with earlier and later parts that are closer in time. The exact nature of these connections can make an important difference to a large number of issues. For example, a person may now be less responsible for some past action than he was previously, because he is now less connected with the agent that performed the action. Similarly, it may be rational for a person to give his more distant future less weight in calculating the balance of burdens and benefits that would result from a course of action.

Conclusion

That humans are temporal in the ways that I have discussed in Chapters 8–10 is an important feature of human life. Being in time is part of human finiteness. In virtue of our finite temporal extensions, we have to confront our own inevitable deaths. In virtue of temporal passage, we are changed by living through time. We are transformed by our choices, actions, and experiences so that we can never simply repeat anything or retrieve a choice. Whatever else may be the same, we will be different.

Appendix, Notes, and Index

Appendix

Diagram A.1 depicts a present representation account of the hearing of the chord C-E-G. Representations are in brackets. At time t_1 the note C is heard. At time t_2 the note E is heard and it is accompanied by a representation of the earlier C. At time t_3 the note G is heard, and it is accompanied by representations of an earlier E and an even earlier C.

Diagram A.2 depicts the more complex representations necessary for a present representation account of the hearing of the chord passing through time.

Diagram A.3 (of theory 2) depicts the three features of each act-phase and what each feature is directly aware of. Note that at time t_2 there is an immediate memory that contacts time t_1 and an immediate anticipation that contacts time t_3. To hear the whole chord, there would have to be at time t_3 another immediate memory contacting time t_1. This is not included in the diagram for the sake of simplicity.

Diagram A.1

t_1 perceptual act-phase ⟶ object-phase   C

t_2 perceptual act-phase ⟶ $\begin{pmatrix} \text{representation} & \text{[C]} \\ \text{object-phase} & \text{E} \end{pmatrix}$

t_3 perceptual act-phase ⟶ $\begin{pmatrix} \text{representation} & \text{[C]} \\ \text{representation} & \text{[E]} \\ \text{object-phase} & \text{G} \end{pmatrix}$

Diagram A.2

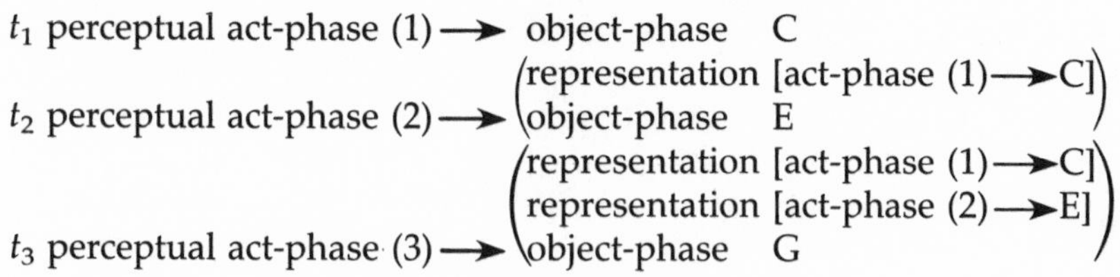

t_1 perceptual act-phase (1) ⟶ object-phase   C

t_2 perceptual act-phase (2) ⟶ (representation [act-phase (1)⟶C])
object-phase   E

t_3 perceptual act-phase (3) ⟶ (representation [act-phase (1)⟶C]
representation [act-phase (2)⟶E]
object-phase   G)

Diagram A.3

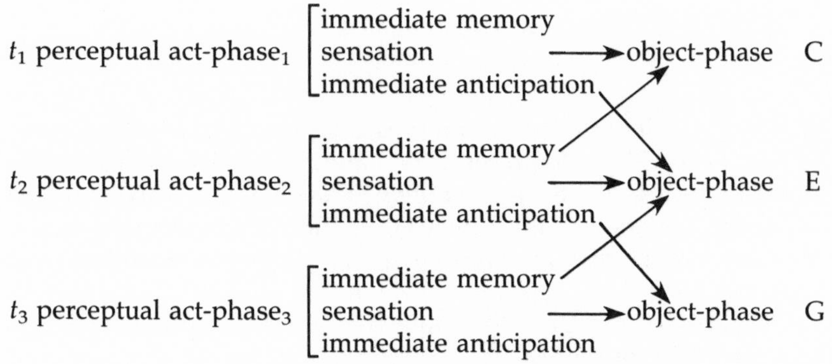

t_1 perceptual act-phase₁ ⎡immediate memory
sensation   ⟶object-phase   C
⎣immediate anticipation

t_2 perceptual act-phase₂ ⎡immediate memory
sensation   ⟶object-phase   E
⎣immediate anticipation

t_3 perceptual act-phase₃ ⎡immediate memory
sensation   ⟶object-phase   G
⎣immediate anticipation

Diagram A.4

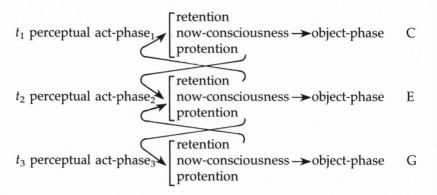

t_1 perceptual act-phase₁ ⎡retention
now-consciousness ⟶object-phase   C
⎣protention

t_2 perceptual act-phase₂ ⎡retention
now-consciousness ⟶object-phase   E
⎣protention

t_3 perceptual act-phase₃ ⎡retention
now-consciousness ⟶object-phase   G
⎣protention

Diagram A.4 (of theory 3) depicts the three features of each act-phase and what each feature is directly aware of.

Diagram A.5 (of theory 4) depicts the ways in which an act-phase at one time contributes to the perception that is centered at another time. At time t_2 perceptual act-phase$_2$ perceives the sounding of the note E. E is perceived in the context of an earlier C and a later G. This context is created by perceptual act-phase$_1$ (with its object C) being operative-as-just-past and perceptual act-phase$_3$ (with its object G) being operative-as-just-future. Each of these perceptual act-phases is also operative in other ways. For example, at time t_3 perceptual act-phase$_3$ is operative-as-present; the context for the sounding of G is created by perceptual act-phase$_2$ being-operative-as-just-past and perceptual act-phase$_1$ being operative-as-further-past.

Diagram A.6 (of theory 5) depicts both the ways in which phases of acting consciousness contribute to the perception and action that is centered at another time and the intrinsic change in which an acting consciousness is always engaged. Diagram A.6 spreads out what is portrayed in Diagram A.5 by separating off perceptual experiences that are centered at different times (different presents). The upper half (I) of Diagram A.6 portrays a past acting-consciousness-phase$_1$ and a future acting-consciousness-phase$_3$ contributing to the perception and action that is ongoing at time t_2. The

Diagram A.5

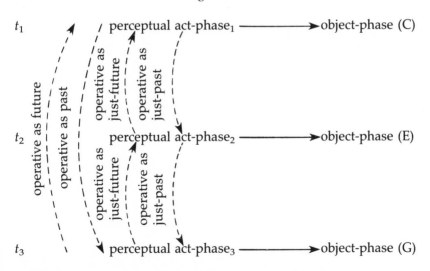

Diagram A.6

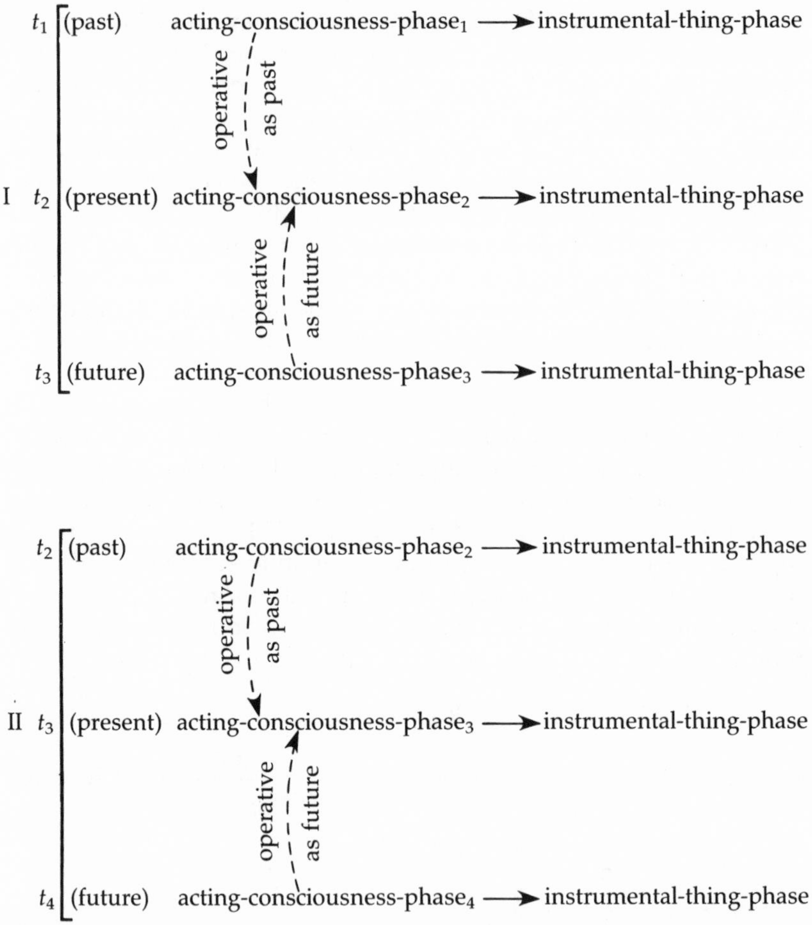

t_1 (past)   acting-consciousness-phase$_1$ ——▶ instrumental-thing-phase

operative / as past

I t_2 (present)   acting-consciousness-phase$_2$ ——▶ instrumental-thing-phase

operative / as future

t_3 (future)   acting-consciousness-phase$_3$ ——▶ instrumental-thing-phase

t_2 (past)   acting-consciousness-phase$_2$ ——▶ instrumental-thing-phase

operative / as past

II t_3 (present)   acting-consciousness-phase$_3$ ——▶ instrumental-thing-phase

operative / as future

t_4 (future)   acting-consciousness-phase$_4$ ——▶ instrumental-thing-phase

lower half (II) of the diagram portrays a past acting-consciousness-phase$_2$ and a future acting-consciousness-phase$_4$ contributing to the perception and action that is ongoing at time t_3. (If II were superimposed on I so that t_2 was directly over t_2 and t_3 directly over t_3, it would look very much like Diagram A.5.) Acting consciousness' intrinsic change of bringing its future into the present is portrayed by the transition from I to II.

Diagram A.7

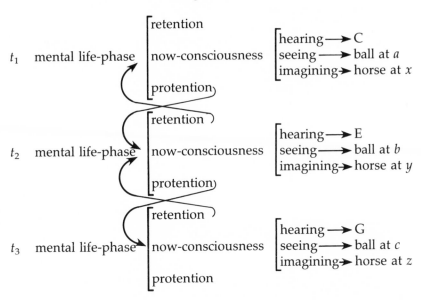

Diagram A.7 represents Husserl's three-feature structure as applied to hearing a melody, seeing a ball roll from place *a* to place *c*, and imagining a horse running from *x* to *z*.

Diagram A.9 represents the difference between the two types of retention.

Diagram A.10 represents my theory of time-consciousness.

Diagram A.8

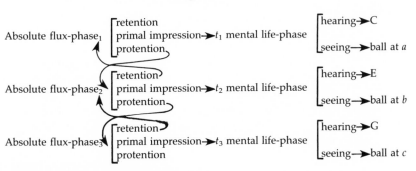

Diagram A.9

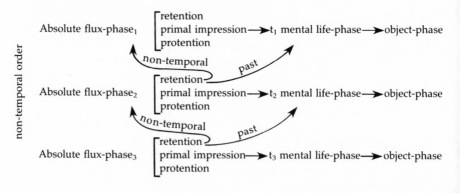

Diagram A.10

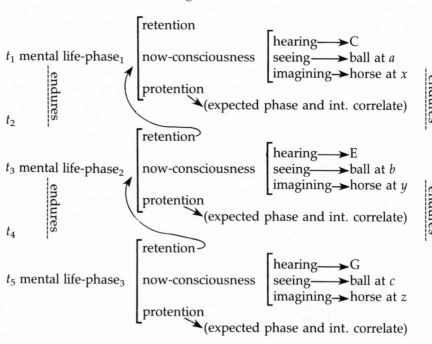

Notes

Introduction

1. In *From Folk Psychology to Cognitive Science* (Cambridge, Mass.: MIT Press, 1983), Stephen Stich provides a clear account of this debate.

Chapter 1

1. Time can be described either as past-present-future or as earlier and later temporal locations. The past-present-future description includes the passage of time, that is, the constant change in what is present. A description of time *solely* in terms of temporal positions that are earlier and later than each other portrays time as changeless. Many contemporary philosophers of time have adopted McTaggart's terminology of "A-series" for past-present-future and "B-series" for earlier and later temporal positions. See John McTaggart, "The Unreality of Time," *Mind*, no. 68 (Oct. 1908). Charles Sherover has convinced me that McTaggart's notion of an "A-series" itself contains important ontological assumptions and so should not just be substituted for time as past-present-future.

2. There are further issues concerning the "perceived background" versus the "understood background." I discuss many refinements in the notion of a horizon in section 8.4.

3. Emotions never concern *only* the past. Insofar as guilt is a way in which previous actions or experiences "color" our current experiences, guilt is not simply a focus on the past as past.

4. Augustine and James are concerned with the passage of time, but they do not discuss the perception of the passage of time. See Saint Augustine, *The Confessions of St. Augustine* (New York: New American Library

of World Literature, 1963), bk. 11, and William James, *The Principles of Psychology* (New York: Henry Holt, 1890), ch. 15. Examples of the contemporary analytic literature are Adolph Grunbaum's *Modern Science and Zeno's Paradoxes* (Middletown, Conn.: Wesleyan University Press, 1967), ch. 1, and George N. Schlesinger's *Aspects of Time* (Indianapolis: Hackett, 1980), ch. 2.

5. This argument would work even if one denies that there is any perceptual awareness of entity-phases as future.

6. This incompatibility depends upon the "logical subordination" of pieces of information in the focus-background arrangement. Hence, the same incompatibility applies to focusing upon spatial features and having as spatial background. One perceptual act-phase, such as seeing or smelling, cannot both focus upon some relevantly small entity (or entity part) and have it as background for what is focused upon.

7. Augustine, *Confessions*, bk. 11. Brentano's theory is in unpublished lectures described by Edmund Husserl in *Zur Phänomenologie des Inneren Zeitbewusstseins (1893–1917)*, ed. Rudolf Boehm (The Hague: Martinus Nijhoff, 1966). Among contemporary philosophers, D. H. Mellor in *Real Time* (Cambridge, Eng.: Cambridge University Press, 1981), ch. 9, presents a version of the representation theory: "For me to see *e* precede *e**, my seeing *e** must include something like a memory-trace of my seeing *e*. It need not be an explicit or a conscious memory, but some trace of the earlier perception must somehow be incorporated in the later one" (p. 144).

8. Bertrand Russell defends this model in "On the Experience of Time," *The Monist* 25, no. 2 (April 1915).

9. This is a one-level version of his theory. In *Zur Phänomenologie des Inneren Zeitbewusstseins*, Husserl moves from a one-level to a two-level theory. See the discussion in Chapter 5.

10. I have invented this theory as a bridge between theories 3 and 5. As described by Husserl in *Zur Phänomenologie des Inneren Zeitbewusstseins*, William Stern maintains a similar theory in "Psychische Präsenzzeit," *Zeitschrift für Psychologie und Physiologie der Sinnesorgane* 13 (1897).

11. Martin Heidegger, *Being and Time*, trans. John Macquarrie and Edward Robinson (New York: Harper & Row, 1962).

12. Jean-Paul Sartre, *Being and Nothingness*, trans. Hazel Barnes (New York: Washington Square Press, 1966).

13. I will later explore the type of temporal idealism that accompanies this account of time-perception. In this chapter I am abstracting from the issue of the reality of time.

14. Both D. H. Mellor in *Real Time* and George Schlesinger in *Aspects of Time* recognize that complete translations of A-series terms into B-series terms are not possible.

15. Given the notion that events exist tenselessly *only at* their temporal locations, real causal influences that operate across temporal locations are problematic. The Humean account of causation fits nicely with a B-series ontology of time.

16. Bertrand Russell, "On the Experience of Time."

Chapter 2

1. Aristotle, *Physics*, bk. ii, ch. 7.
2. G. W. F. Hegel, *Hegel's Philosophy of Nature*, trans. A. V. Miller (Oxford: Clarendon Press, 1970).
3. This position is very similar to the account of how a non-temporal, unchanging God could be aware of past-present-future features of the world. A non-temporal God could do this by being aware of finite consciousnesses that exist in an earlier-later time. If different phases of this intermediary consciousness exist (tenselessly) at different earlier-later dates, and each phase experiences other entities as past, present, and future, and the experienced past-present-future features can be defined in token-reflexive terms, then God can be timelessly conscious of "what time it is." See H. N. Castaneda, "Omniscience and Indexical Reference," *Journal of Philosophy* 64, no. 7 (April 1967).

Chapter 3

1. George N. Schlesinger, *Aspects of Time* (Indianapolis: Hackett, 1980), p. 3.
2. Most analyses of perceived time do portray it as basically the Newtonian time of commonsense conceptions. While there are limits to the smallest durations that can be perceived, as revealed by myriad experiments in perceptual psychology, this difference in "dividedness" is negligible for ordinary purposes. The *understood* divisibility is considered to be just an extension of the refinement in discriminations that can be made perceptually when different sensory modalities are employed or attention is devoted to the task.

Part II Introduction

1. Charles M. Sherover's *The Human Experience of Time* (New York: New York University Press, 1975) provides a good survey of this history.

Chapter 4

1. Immanuel Kant, *Kritik der reinen Vernunft* (Hamburg: Felix Meiner, 1956), A320/B377. All English quotations are from Norman Kemp Smith's translation, *Immanuel Kant's Critique of Pure Reason* (New York: St. Martin's, 1965).
2. See #5–6 in Kant's *Logic*, vol. 9 in *Kants gesammelte Schriften* (Berlin: Walter de Gruyter, 1923).
3. Kant, *Critique of Pure Reason*, B72.

4. *Ibid.*, A320/B377. On the generality, see #1 in Kant, *Logic*.

5. Kant, *Critique of Pure Reason*, A69/B94.

6. *Ibid.*, A68/B93.

7. *Ibid.*

8. These notions appear in *ibid.*, A198–199/B244.

9. All are in *ibid.*, A31–32/B47–48.

10. A few passages suggest that Kant entertained the idea that Arithmetic concerns the essential features of time, but these hints are never developed. See #10 of Kant, *Prolegomena to Any Future Metaphysics*, trans. James Ellington (Indianapolis: Hackett, 1977), and Kant, *Critique of Pure Reason*, A143/B182.

11. Just as there have been challenges to Kant's claims that the essential features of space are Euclidean, so there have been challenges to his claims about the essential features of time.

12. Kant, *Critique of Pure Reason*, B219, B225, B233, B257.

13. *Ibid.*, B225.

14. *Ibid.*, A41/B58.

15. *Ibid.*, A31/B47.

16. *Ibid.*, A35–36/B52.

17. "Space and time, together with the appearances in them, are nothing existing in themselves and outside of my representations, but are themselves only modes of representation" (Kant, *Prolegomena to Any Future Metaphysics*, #52c, p. 82 [Academy 341]).

18. This causal interpretation has been held by many interpreters, including P. F. Strawson in *The Bounds of Sense* (London: Methuen, 1966).

19. Among others, Martin Heidegger, in *Kant and the Problem of Metaphysics*, trans. James Churchill (Bloomington: Indiana University Press, 1962), has developed this interpretation.

20. Kant, *Critique of Pure Reason*, A192–193/B237–238, A211/B258.

21. We also intuit other features of ourselves as spread out in time, but these features, such as feelings and sensations of pain and pleasure, do not concern empirical knowledge.

22. Kant, *Critique of Pure Reason*, A33/B49–50. See also A22–23/B37.

23. *Ibid.*, A34/B50. See also A34/B51.

24. *Ibid.*, A77/B103.

25. See *ibid.*, A51/B75, A93/B126, B146, and A190–191/B235–236.

26. See *ibid.*, A191/B236 and A197/B242.

27. All that Kant says (in the Schematism) is that pure concepts have no image, but are rather rules for guiding pure synthesis. See *ibid.*, A142/B181.

28. See, for example, Robert P. Wolff's *Kant's Theory of Mental Activity* (Cambridge, Mass.: Harvard University Press, 1963) and Henry Allison's *Kant's Transcendental Idealism* (New Haven, Conn.: Yale University Press, 1983).

29. "*Imagination* is the faculty of representing in intuition an object that is *not itself present*" (Kant, *Critique of Pure Reason*, B151).

30. This synthesis is the necessary condition for the "association of

ideas" that is based on experiencing them together (in sequence). See *ibid.*, A100–102.

31. "The synthesis of apprehension is thus inseparably bound up with the synthesis of reproduction" (*ibid.*, A102).

32. *Ibid.*, A99.

33. *Ibid.*, A102.

34. As I am portraying the synthesis of apprehension, it is the "taking of intuitional data up into the activity of imaginative reproduction." See *ibid.*, A120.

35. *Ibid.*, A103.

36. *Ibid.*, A121; see also A106.

37. The application of this principle to different types of empirical objects (for example, fluids such as water versus solids such as a tree) produces complications that Kant does not discuss.

38. According to the resolution of the First Antinomy, we reason back to past states by applying the rules for ordered series of appearances.

39. Kant, *Critique of Pure Reason*, A103.

40. *Ibid.*, A103–104.

41. Passages that distinguish the synthesis of imagination from the understanding also support the Awareness of Reproductive Activity theory; see, for example, *ibid.*, A78–79/B103–104, A94, B233–234, A201/B246.

42. Kant usually maintains that we must be aware of this activity. For example: "Its synthesis, therefore, if the synthesis be viewed by itself alone, is nothing but the unity of the act, of which, as an act, it is conscious to itself" (*ibid.*, B153). However, he does sometimes suggest that we may fail to be aware of synthetic activity; for example: "For it is an act of spontaneity of the faculty of representation; and since this faculty, to distinguish it from sensibility, must be entitled understanding, all combination—be we conscious of it or not" (*ibid.*, B130).

43. See Kant, *Religion Within the Limits of Reason Alone*, trans. Theodore Greene and Hoyt Hudson (New York: Harper & Row, 1960), pp. 20–21 and 35.

44. Kant, *Critique of Pure Reason*, A539–540/B567–568; see also A541/B569.

45. *Ibid.*, B72. See also A19/B33, A251–252, and Kant, *Prolegomena to Any Future Metaphysics*, pp. 32–33 (Academy 288–289).

46. One reason that Kant conceives time and space to be frameworks of *intuition* is that he considers the basic propositions about their essential features to be synthetic propositions. As Kant develops the issue with respect to space and Geometry, a form of intuition can contain information that can be extracted out in terms of concepts (the "construction" of concepts; see A713/B741) but that is not most basically represented in the form of concepts. The form of intuition, which is presented in pure intuition, is a repository of information to which appeal can be made to ground the connection of two concepts in a synthetic proposition.

47. Kant, *Critique of Pure Reason*, A47/B64.

48. See *ibid.*, B41–42, A31/B47, and A32–36/B49–53.
49. *Ibid.*, A35/B51.
50. *Ibid.*, A35–36/B52. See also B54 and A42/B59.
51. *Ibid.*, A39/B56.
52. See *ibid.*, B71.
53. See *ibid.*, A320/B377.
54. *Ibid.*, A426/B454.
55. In *Kant's Transcendental Idealism*, pp. 40–45, Henry Allison defends Kant's notion of infinity against some of the more common objections.
56. Kant, *Critique of Pure Reason*, A427/B455.

Chapter 5

1. Edmund Husserl, *The Crisis of European Sciences and Transcendental Phenomenology*, trans. David Carr (Evanston, Ill.: Northwestern University Press, 1970); see pp. 185–187.
2. Edmund Husserl, *Cartesian Meditations*, trans. Dorion Cairns (The Hague: Martinus Nijhoff, 1960); see #21.
3. I have not made use of that portion of Husserl's working notes that are still unpublished, except for those passages that are quoted in other works.
4. The dates for the different periods are derived from John Brough's article, "The Emergence of an Absolute Consciousness in Husserl's Early Writings on Time-Consciousness," *Man and World* 5, no. 3 (Aug. 1972): 298–326.
5. Edmund Husserl, *Ideas*, trans. W. R. Boyce Gibson (New York: Collier, 1962), see #78, p. 201.
6. In the very late work *Experience and Judgment*, trans. James Churchill and Karl Ameriks (Evanston, Ill.: Northwestern University Press, 1973), Husserl portrays perception as involving interest, but inner time-consciousness is still considered to be interestless. See #23b, p. 110.
7. Edmund Husserl, *Zur Phänomenologie des Inneren Zeitbewusstseins (1893–1917)*, ed. Rudolf Boehm (The Hague: Martinus Nijhoff, 1966), see #45, p. 98. *The Phenomenology of Internal Time-Consciousness*, ed. Martin Heidegger, trans. James Churchill (Bloomington: Indiana University Press, 1966), is a translation of some of the material in the German volume; in this chapter, references will be to this edition with page numbers from the German edition given in brackets.
8. See sections 3.2 and 5.3.
9. Husserl, *Phenomenology of Internal Time-Consciousness*, #12, pp. 53–54 [G 32].
10. "We call the *whole melody* one that is *perceived*, although only the now-point actually is. We follow this procedure because not only is the extension of the melody given point for point in an extension of the act of

perception but also the unity of retentional consciousness still 'holds' the expired tones themselves in consciousness and continuously establishes the unity of consciousness with reference to the homogeneous temporal Object, i.e., the melody," *ibid.*, #16, p. 60 [G 38].

11. *Ibid.*, #17, p. 64 [G 41].

12. *Ibid.*, #22, p. 72 [G 49]. See also Husserl, *Ideas*, #78, p. 203.

13. Husserl, *Phenomenology of Internal Time-Consciousness*, #9, p. 47 [G 26].

14. *Ibid.*, #11, p. 52 [G 30–31].

15. *Ideas*, #77, p. 198, and #81, p. 218; Husserl, *Crisis of European Sciences and Transcendental Phenomenology*, p. 160.

16. Husserl, *Experience and Judgment*, #23b, p. 111; Husserl, *Phenomenology of Internal Time-Consciousness*, #24, p. 76 [G 52], and #26, pp. 79–80 [G 56].

17. Husserl, *Phenomenology of Internal Time-Consciousness*, app. 3, p. 140 [G 106], and #24, p. 76 [G 53].

18. While Husserl clearly maintains that an enduring perceptual act perceives passage, it is not clear whether a perceptual act-phase *intuits the passing* of an object-phase. Is there any direct grasping of the *being in transition* of an object-phase? Some texts suggest that there is an intuition of passing, of object-phases *becoming* further past, such as text 53, *Zur Phänomenologie des Inneren Zeitbewusstseins*, pp. 367–368. However, it is also possible to interpret Husserl as providing a reductive analysis of the perception of temporal passage. On such an analysis, a perceptual act's perception of the temporal passage of an object-phase reduces to the fact that each of the temporally ordered phases of this perceptual act has a different temporal perspective on any given object-phase. The object-phase seems to move through time because earlier perceptual act-phases protend it, a middle perceptual act-phase intuits it as "now" (while retaining the earlier perceptual act-phases that protend it), and later perceptual act-phases retain it. Izchak Miller in *Husserl, Perception, and Temporal Awareness* (Cambridge, Mass.: MIT Press, 1984) present such a reductive analysis.

19. Husserl, *Zur Phänomenologie des Inneren Zeitbewusstseins*, #34, #35, #36, app. 6, and text 54.

20. John Brough, "Husserl's Phenomenology of Time Consciousness," in *Husserl's Phenomenology*, ed. J. N. Mohanty and William McKenna (Lanham, Md.: University Press of America, 1989).

21. *Ibid.*, p. 49 of the typescript version.

22. For the above argument, see Husserl, *Phenomenology of Internal Time-Consciousness*, #35, #36, and app. 6.

23. John McTaggart, "The Unreality of Time," *Mind*, no. 68 (Oct. 1908).

24. Husserl, *Ideas*, #77, #78, and #82.

25. Husserl, *Cartesian Meditations*, #18, p. 43.

26. See Husserl, *Formal and Transcendental Logic*, trans. Dorion Cairns (The Hague: Martinus Nijhoff, 1969), #107b, p. 284, and app. 2, #2c, p. 318,

and *Experience and Judgment*, #64a, p. 254, and #42, p. 175. The three-feature structure seems to be ascribed to mental acts in #23b, p. 111, of *Experience and Judgment*.

27. See Husserl, *Cartesian Meditations*, #31, p. 66.

28. See Husserl, *Phenomenology of Internal Time-Consciousness*, #33, and *Experience and Judgment*, #23a, p. 107.

29. On attention to what is "still held in grasp," see Husserl, *Experience and Judgment*, #23. On recollective memory not being mediated by an image, see Husserl, *Phenomenology of Internal Time-Consciousness*, #28, p. 83 [G 59].

30. See Husserl, *Cartesian Meditations*, #31–#33.

31. Husserl, *Phenomenology of Internal Time-Consciousness*, #36, p. 100 [G 75].

32. Some of the texts in Husserl, *Analysen zur Passiven Synthesis, Husserliana XI*, ed. M. Fleischer (The Hague: Martinus Nijhoff, 1966), and in the unpublished "C" manuscripts suggest this.

33. See Husserl, *Phenomenology of Internal Time-Consciousness*, #28, and *Experience and Judgment*, #23.

34. Brough's article, "Husserl's Phenomenology of Time-Consciousness," discusses this.

35. See Husserl, *Erste Philosophie, Husserliana VIII*, ed. Rudolph Boehm (The Hague: Martinus Nijhoff, 1959), pp. 67–68.

36. Husserl, *Ideas*, #49, p. 137.

37. For a very detailed discussion of the issue of "transcendental illusion," see William McKenna, *Husserl's "Introductions to Phenomenology"* (Boston: Martinus Nijhoff, 1982).

38. See Husserl, *Cartesian Meditations*, #41.

39. "We can divide every interval *ad infinitum* and with every division we can envision the later points of division produced mediately through the earlier, and thus any given point you choose is finally produced by one of infinitely many augmentations (of which each is the same infinitely small augmentation). It is also thus with regard to temporal modifications—or, rather, whereas with other continua the talk of generation was only figurative, what we have here is a real description" (Husserl, *Phenomenology of Internal Time-Consciousness*, pt. 2, app. 1, p. 130 [G 100]). See also #16, pp. 60–63 [G 38–40].

Chapter 6

1. There is another reason for Heidegger's procedure, his thought that Being might be ontologically dependent upon human existence.

2. Heidegger, *Being and Time*, trans. John Macquarrie & Edward Robinson (New York: Harper & Row, 1962), p. 58, hereafter cited as *B&T*. Refer-

ences to the seventh German edition, *Sein und Zeit* (Tübingen: Max Nie-meyer, 1979), will appear as *SZ*.

3. "Dasein's *kind of Being* thus *demands* that any ontological Interpreta-tion which sets itself the goal of exhibiting the phenomena in their primor-diality, *should capture the Being of this entity, in spite of this entity's own tendency to cover things up*" (*B&T*, p. 359).

4. Heidegger, *The Essence of Reasons*, trans. T. Malick (Evanston, Ill.: Northwestern University Press, 1969), p. 85.

5. Heidegger, *The Basic Problems of Phenomenology*, trans. Albert Hofstadter (Bloomington: Indiana University Press, 1982), p. 175, hereafter cited as *BPP*.

6. See Heidegger, *The Essence of Reasons*, pp. 59–79, and *The Metaphysi-cal Foundations of Logic*, trans. Michael Heim (Bloomington: Indiana Univer-sity Press, 1984), pp. 174–180, hereafter cited as *Logic*.

7. "In Being-with, as the existential 'for the sake of' of Others, these have already been disclosed in their Dasein. With their Being-with, their disclosedness has been constituted beforehand; accordingly, this disclosed-ness also goes to make up significance—that is to say, worldhood" (*B&T*, p. 160).

8. "We designated by the term 'significance' this totality of relations of the in-order-to, for-the-sake-of, for-that-purpose, to-that-end" (*BPP*, p. 262).

9. *B&T*, pp. 471–472.

10. *BPP*, p. 261.

11. *BPP*, pp. 261–264; *B&T*, pp. 459–464.

12. *BPP*, p. 262.

13. This notion of the publicness of world-time seems to be somewhat different from the account in *Being and Time*, where publicness is connected with dating time in terms of the natural day-night cycles that are the same for everyone. See *B&T*, pp. 465–467.

14. *BPP*, p. 264.

15. *B&T*, pp. 458–459.

16. *BPP*, pp. 303–312.

17. *B&T*, p. 474.

18. See Isaac Newton, *Mathematical Principles of Natural Philosophy*, trans. Andrew Motte and Florian Cajori (Berkeley: University of California Press, 1934).

19. *B&T*, pp. 475–479.

20. *B&T*, p. 469.

21. *B&T*, p. 470.

22. *B&T*, p. 467.

23. *B&T*, pp. 470, 474; *BPP*, p. 257.

24. *B&T*, pp. 95–102.

25. *B&T*, p. 435.

26. *B&T*, pp. 351–352.

27. *B&T*, p. 237.

28. See *B&T*, p. 376.

29. This interpretation of the Care structure and the Temporality structure differs in some ways from the impression given in the discussion of Befindlichkeit in div. 1, ch. 5, sec. 29 of *B&T*. Befindlichkeit is there characterized as revealing facticity: Dasein's "that it is" that is "veiled in its 'whence' and 'whither'" (p. 174). Thrown facticity is frequently interpreted to be the brute existential facts (1) that I exist and thus *have to be* an issue for myself, (2) that I have to exist in a certain specific environment, and (3) that I have to exist with certain specific personal characteristics. While I do not object to this interpretation of thrown facticity, it does not bring out anything that is specifically *past* in nature. These existential facts concern the present and future; it is only the heritage of our "world-view" that is specifically past in nature.

30. See *B&T*, p. 178, on this submission to one's world.

31. *B&T*, pp. 343–348.

32. *SZ*, p. 328: "Die Zeitlichkeit 'ist' uberhaupt kein *Seiendes*. Sie ist nicht, sondern *zeitigt* sich" (*B&T*, p. 377).

33. *Logic*, p. 206.

34. Heidegger makes this claim in many places (see my section 6.4). One example is: "We call the temporal attribute of entities within-the-world 'die Innerzeitigkeit.' . . . But time, as Innerzeitigkeit, arises from an essential kind of temporalizing of primordial temporality" (*B&T*, p. 382; *SZ*, p. 333).

35. This is the origin of the "mathematical projection" of Being-present-at-hand. The temporalizing of the understanding of presence-at-hand is discussed in *B&T*, pp. 408–415.

36. *B&T*, p. 379 and p. 399.

37. *B&T*, pp. 375–376.

38. *B&T*, p. 183.

39. *B&T*, pp. 246–252.

40. *B&T*, pp. 269–270.

41. *B&T*, p. 228.

42. *B&T*, p. 255.

43. *Logic*, p. 153.

44. *BPP*, p. 169.

45. In *Heidegger and the Problem of Knowledge* (Indianapolis: Hackett, 1983), pp. 197–206, Charles Guignon recognizes this inconsistency in Heidegger's thought, but defends his claim that the metaphysical notion of "independent existence" is meaningless.

46. For example, *BPP*, p. 271; *Logic*, p. 203; *B&T*, p. 382.

47. In *Heidegger and the Philosophy of Mind* (New Haven, Conn.: Yale University Press, 1987), ch. 4, Frederick Olafson discusses some of the problems that these passages present. Olafson favors the view that Heidegger *could* accept a real earlier-later time, but he does not address the important

issue of the relationship of Dasein's existence to a real time (does Dasein really occur in an earlier-later time?).

48. *BPP*, p. 262.

49. *B&T*, p. 472.

Chapter 7

1. Jean-Paul Sartre, *Being and Nothingness*, trans. Hazel Barnes (New York: Washington Square Press, 1966), hereafter cited as E. The French edition, *L'Etre et le Néant* (Saint Amand, France: Gallimard, 1979), is hereafter cited as F.

2. E 219–221, F 195–197.

3. E 217, F 194.

4. E 217, F 194.

5. E 226–231, F 201–205.

6. E 281, F 246–247.

7. E 200–201, F 180; E 268–269, F 236.

8. E 170, F 154.

9. E 176–179, F 159–162.

10. E 422, F 368; E 424–425, F 370.

11. E 290–291, F 254–255.

12. E 183–184, F 165–166; E 265–266, F 233–234.

13. E 269–271, F 237–238.

14. E 273–274, F 240–241.

15. E 285, F 249–250.

16. E 281, F 246; E 436–437, F 380.

17. E 273–275, F 240–241.

18. I develop this notion of a "simple action" in considerably more detail in "Sartre's Nihilations," *Southern Journal of Philosophy* 20 (Spring 1982): esp. 101–102.

19. E 285–292, F 250–255.

20. In many respects Sartre's analysis is very similar to that of defenders of a B-series time. They and Sartre both claim that the A-series features of worldly entities are not real but rather derive from consciousness. However, unlike Sartre, these philosophers accept the reality of the B-series and conceive consciousness to exist within it.

21. E 230, F 204.

22. E 170, F 154–155; E 207, F 185–186.

23. E 173–174, F 157–158; E 277, F 243.

24. E 172, F 156–157; E 638–639, F 554.

25. E 176–179, F 159–162.

26. E 422, F 368; E 424–425, F 370.

27. E 182–184, F 165–166; E 578–579, F 503–504.

28. E 185–186, F 167–168; E 598, F 520.

29. E 279, F 245; E 292, F 256.

30. E 209–210, F 187–188; E 272–273, F 239–240.

31. E 175, F 158–159; E 206–208, F 185–186.

32. E 207, F 186.

33. E 269, F 236.

34. E 168–169, F 153.

35. I explore these interconnections in more detail in "Sartre's Nihilations," esp. secs. 1 and 2.

36. E 185, F 167.

37. E 165, F 150.

38. While Sartre denies that there is a real time, he does claim that *if there were* a real past and a real future, they would be inaccessible to consciousness unless consciousness itself is (ecstatically) its past and its future. See E 162–163, F 148; E 180, F 162.

39. E 28–29, F 33.

40. E 122, F 113.

41. E 190, F 171.

42. E 195, F 175.

43. See also E 253, F 223–224.

44. E 281, F 246.

45. E 293, F 257.

46. Under point A2c in section 7.1A, I discussed Sartre's notion that motion defines the present of the instrumental-thing. Since "being in motion" is supposed to involve an "exteriority to self," "being in motion" itself reveals its origin from the For-itself. If we accept Sartre's claim that the motion of an enduring thing defines its presentness, then he can argue that presentness reveals its origin from the For-itself because motion does. However, I earlier pointed out why it is phenomenologically dubious that motion defines the present of instrumental-things.

47. This corresponds to another way in which the past of acting consciousness defines its present, through having been present to —————— (C1a).

48. See E 282, F 248.

49. "Each *this* is revealed with a law of being which determines its threshold, its level of change where it will cease to be what it is in order simply not to be. This law of being, which expresses 'permanence' is an immediately revealed structure of the essence of the 'this'" (E 282, F 248).

50. "These potentialities or probabilities, which are the meaning of being beyond being, are *in-itselfs beyond being*, and precisely for this reason they are *nothings*. The essence of the inkwell is *made-to-be* as a correlate of the possible negation of the for-itself" (E 271, F 238).

Chapter 8

1. I think that reflection and introspection are basically the same thing and that both of them are different from our ordinary awareness of our conscious life. Psychological critiques of "introspective reports" frequently classify together *all* reports about the subject's conscious life. They fail to distinguish reports based on reflection from those that are not. There are cases of reports that are clearly based on reflection and cases that clearly are not, but many cases are hard to classify. There are several different sources for reports that are not based on reflection. Some are based on our non-reflective awareness of our own mental life. Some are really speculations about ourselves. Some critics of introspection think that all cases of supposed introspection are really inferences, based on socially accepted theories about how people work, about what is going on in us.

2. See Richard Nisbett and Timothy Wilson, "Telling More than We Can Know: Verbal Reports on Mental Processes," *Psychological Review* 84 (1977); Norman Dixon, *Preconscious Processing* (New York: John Wiley, 1981); and William Lyons, *The Disappearance of Introspection* (Cambridge, Mass.: MIT Press, 1986), ch. 5. Daniel Holender's "Semantic Activation Without Conscious Identification in Dichotic Listening, Parafoveal Vision, and Visual Masking," *Behavioral and Brain Sciences* 9, no. 1 (1986), provides a useful critique of some of the claims about "subliminal perception."

3. See Nisbett and Wilson, "Telling More Than We Can Know." That there is a special brain mechanism that underlies explicit conscious awareness of information, as contrasted with "knowledge that is expressed in performance without subjects' phenomenal awareness that they possess it," is one of the conclusions of a survey of the psychological effects of certain types of brain damage. See D. Schacter, M. McAndrews, and M. Moscovitch, "Access to Consciousness: Dissociations Between Implicit and Explicit Knowledge in Neuropsychological Syndromes," in *Thought Without Language*, ed. Lawrence Weiskrantz (Oxford, Eng.: Oxford University Press, 1988).

4. It is possible that a set of categories is meaningful only insofar as it ultimately is action-guiding. If this complicated thesis were true and action implicitly affirmed the independent reality of some entities, then it would be impossible to suspend completely all reality claims.

5. Since equipment is usable by other people, it might be thought that an interestless or non-acting consciousness could encounter equipment by perceiving that it is used by consciousnesses other than her or himself. However, it is highly unlikely and perhaps impossible that an interestless and non-acting consciousness could develop and understand the concepts necessary for understanding action in others.

6. See Paul Fraisse, *The Psychology of Time* (New York: Harper & Row, 1963), ch. 3; Francoise Macar, "Time Psychophysics and Related Models,"

and John Michon, "The Compleat Time Experiencer," in *Time, Mind, and Behavior*, ed. John Michon and Janet Jackson (Heidelberg: Springer, 1985).

7. In "The Making of the Present: A Tutorial Review," *Attention and Performance*, ed. J. Requin (Hillsdale, N.J.: Erlbaum, 1978), John Michon explains the "specious present" in terms of these larger patterns, as does Fraisse in *Psychology of Time*.

8. There is a further feature, "being in transition" at any given time, that may or may not be included in temporal passage. I discuss this issue in section 8.4, point 7.

9. Furthermore, these smaller phases might not *by themselves* retain (or protend) at all. Retention (and protention) might require the participation of many of these smaller phases.

10. My view differs from that of Izchak Miller, who claims in *Husserl, Perception, and Temporal Awareness* (Cambridge, Mass.: MIT Press, 1984), pp. 139–142, that we do experience infinitesimal phases in the sense that we intend worldly entities as "spread out" continuously through time. However, he claims that we do not perceive infinitesimal phases because we do not individuate them.

11. There are also differences among the different varieties of mental act in the *specifics* of this "fading out."

12. There are other types of unity of mental life-phases, but these are not connected with the three-feature structure or time-consciousness. I discuss some of the "forward-directed" forms of unity in section 10.3.

13. A. N. Prior takes this approach in "Thank Goodness That's Over," *Philosophy* 34 (1959): 12–17.

Chapter 9

1. If the notion of a non-temporal absolute flux is taken seriously, Husserl's theory has to deny the ontological reality of time. See section 5.4.

2. The presumption that specific sensory information comes from outside consciousness can be defeated (in such cases as hallucinations and dreams) by noting inconsistencies over time in the patterns of information. However, that these cases might be taken as revelations of another realm of reality indicates the importance of the lack of control criterion.

3. There would be serious problems in accounting for how we can know that real things form such a non-temporally ordered series, but I am ignoring these for the sake of the argument.

4. This "operating together" is necessary to provide for the *coordinated change* in consciousness that is the basic form of temporal passage. All the phases of consciousness must *change together*. The mutual dependence of "operating together" explains why, if there is change, it is a coordinated change.

5. Temporal passage requires some explanation or reason because, in contrast with the first two features, it is not *just* a permanent way in which

consciousness exists, but also a constant occurrence. Why it continues to happen calls for some explanation.

6. There might be problems with the special temporal features of equipmental entities because these can be encountered only by an acting consciousness.

7. There are questions that would have to be answered about *how* this works—for example, why the non-temporal order is converted into one specific temporal order rather than into its inverse.

8. The experience of temporal passage requires that there be multiple phases that are unified in one consciousness that changes its temporal focus over time. The intermediary consciousness would have to have some unity of its multiple phases that yielded the experience of temporal passage (at the intermediary level). To experience the temporal extension of its own mental life, a phase of the intermediary consciousness would also need to be connected with other phases. However, since these intermediary consciousness-phases do not exist on their own, it is not clear how they could either "contact" or "operate together with" each other. The theory would have to claim that each phase was *conceived* to be connected in the appropriate ways with the other phases. It is not clear, however, whether the non-temporal consciousness could conceive this coherently without itself undergoing change.

9. Immanuel Kant, *Critique of Pure Reason*, trans. Norman K. Smith (New York: St. Martin's, 1965).

10. *Ibid.*, A426/B454.

11. John McTaggart, "The Unreality of Time," *Mind*, no. 68 (Oct. 1908), p. 468.

12. *Ibid.*, p. 468.

13. *Ibid.*, p. 458.

14. There have been many attempts to reconstruct McTaggart's basic argument. I cannot here examine all these reconstructions, but I think that they all fail.

15. Such cosmical features are not experienced and require a fairly complete theory of time.

16. Among others, J. J. C. Smart in "Time," *The Encyclopedia of Philosophy* (New York: Macmillan, 1967), and Donald C. Williams in "The Myth of Passage," *Journal of Philosophy* 48 (1951).

17. George N. Schlesinger, *Aspects of Time* (Indianapolis: Hackett, 1980), pp. 30–34.

18. These entities with special temporal features are emergent upon entities with standard temporal features; for example, an organism is emergent upon its chemical components.

19. In light of the scientific notion that signals travel from distant events and objects to our sensory receptors, the real entities that are the sources of our sensory information might be considered to be either the proximate signals or the more distant sources of the signals. See section 10.1.

Chapter 10

1. It is important to keep in mind that these are representations in a first-person theory of experience. In the Introduction I explained how third-person theories of experience would encounter no particular problem with time-consciousness. Any one-dimensional matrix that exists fully at one time could be used in a causal system to record and to store information about occurrences in time.

2. In *A Theory of Perception* (Princeton, N.J.: Princeton University Press, 1971), pp. 48–49, George Pitcher makes this argument that we do perceive past entities. In *An Introduction to Contemporary Epistemology* (Oxford, Eng.: Basil Blackwell, 1985), Jonathan Dancy likewise claims "that an object such as a distant star can have ceased to exist by the moment at which we are directly aware of it" (p. 147).

3. Phases of consciousness are not experienced to be extended, even though they are extended in real time, as I argued in 8.4.

4. The Cartesian tradition claims that consciousness is essentially non-spatial.

5. These smaller parts might not *by themselves* retain or protend at all. Retention and protention might require the participation of many of these smaller parts.

6. Because mental life-phases "reach across" to earlier phases, mental life would not go totally out of existence during such a gap. The "reaching across" would always span a gap during which mental life was not actual.

7. This "fading out" is discussed in sections 8.3 and 5.2.

8. This is one reason for being dubious about "perceiving past events" in the cases where the signals from the past events take a long time to reach us. It is implausible to think that a consciousness had some type of existence for years before its birth simply because we can see stellar events that occurred hundreds of years ago.

9. A complete stretch of mental life is one whose phases are in contact *only* with other phases of the stretch.

10. See sections 8.2 and 8.3.

11. See section 9.1.

12. A "forward" relation is a non-symmetrical relation from something temporally earlier to something temporally later. A "futural" relation is a forward relation between something present and something future.

13. I consider intentional action to be action that is not only *initiated* by an intention but also *governed continuously* by it. Even in the cases of causal sequences that, once initiated, unfold without further intervention, there has to be some monitoring of the unfolding sequence to ensure that nothing goes wrong. Without this minimal "being governed by the intention," the continuing causal sequence would not be an intentional action because it would no longer be intended. Thus, temporally extended intentional actions must be governed by temporally extended intentions.

14. Sartre makes a similar argument against Heidegger's notion of Being-toward-death in pt. 4, ch. 1, sec. I, subsec. E of *Being and Nothingness*.

15. See section 7.2.

16. See Terence Penelhum, "The Importance of Self-Identity," *Journal of Philosophy* 68, no. 20 (Oct. 1971).

17. There is an extensive discussion of how these factors affect personal identity in my "Person-Stages and Unity of Consciousness," *American Philosophical Quarterly* 22, no. 3 (July 1985).

18. See, for example, John Perry, "The Importance of Being Identical," in *The Identities of Persons*, ed. Amelie Rorty (Berkeley: University of California Press, 1976), p. 71.

19. McInerney, "Person-Stages."

20. Bertrand Russell, *The Analysis of Mind* (New York: Macmillan, 1921).

21. See McInerney, "Person-Stages," pt. 3.

22. This point is argued extensively in *ibid*.

Index